Introduction

This updated version of *The Times Style Guide* aims to provide writers and sub-editors with a quick reference to contentious points of grammar and spelling, and to guide them through areas where confusions have arisen in the past. It is a guide, not a straitjacket. Consistency is a virtue, but it should not be pursued at the expense of clarity, elegance or common sense.

By the standards of its predecessors this is a permissive volume. It avoids unnecessary prescription and prohibition. It tries to distinguish linguistic superstitions from grammatical rules. It hesitates to condemn common usage that neither baffles nor offends. English is not a language fixed for all time. Speech changes and its written form should change too. *The Times* must use the language of its readers, but that language at its best, clearest and most concise.

The guide sets out the paper's detailed preferences in such fields as capitalisation, hyphenation and variant spelling. More general entries are intended to encourage reflection about words and the way we use them. While all *Times* journalists should follow house style, they should not do so unthinkingly. Considered exceptions can (and often must) be made, especially in direct quotes, in features, diaries and other less formal kinds of writing, and with columnists whose individual voices should be heard and whose flow of argument should be preserved.

Where extra guidance is needed, and for all spellings, hyphenations etc not covered by the guide, staff are expected to use as their first point of reference *Collins English Dictionary*. Other helpful resources are the *New Oxford Dictionary for Writers and Editors* (Odwe), the *Concise Oxford* or *Chambers*. For place names *The Times Comprehensive Atlas of the World* should be consulted.

Further advice on style and on good writing may be found in the familiar authorities: Fowler (*Modern English Usage*), Partridge (*Usage and Abusage*), Gowers (*The Complete Plain Words*) and their admirably brisk US counterpart Strunk & White (*The Elements of Style*). The compendious *Chicago Manual of Style* contains sensible (American) guidance on almost everything. Kingsley Amis's *The King's English* takes a more idiosyncratic approach. All are valuable works of informed and considered opinion; none should be regarded as a repository of unbreakable rules.

There are thoughtful books on the particular challenges of journalistic writing by Harold Evans (*Essential English for Journalists, Editors and Writers*) and Keith Waterhouse (*On Newspaper Style*).

Acknowledgments

Special thanks to Isabella Bengoechea, Magnus Cohen, Fiona Gorman, Alan Kay, Matthew Lyons and Siobhan Murphy, who worked on production of the book at *The Times*, and to Gerry Breslin, Jethro Lennox, Kevin Robbins and Sarah Woods at HarperCollins.

Thanks also to Nic Andrews, Chris Broadhurst, Josie Eve, Hannah Fletcher, Jeremy Griffin, Robert Hands, Oliver Kamm, Nick Mays, Robbie Millen, John Price, Chris Roberts, Fay Schlesinger, Mark Shillam, Craig Tregurtha, Emma Tucker, Roland Watson, Rose Wild and John Witherow at *The Times*; and to Tim Austin, Richard Dixon, Sir Simon Jenkins and the late Philip Howard, who were responsible for earlier editions of this guide.

Aa

a, an use *a* before all words beginning with a vowel or diphthong with the sound of u (as in unit) — a eulogy, a European etc; but use *an* before unaspirated h — an heir, an honest woman, an honour. Whether or not to use *an* before an aspirated h when the first syllable of a word is unaccented — hotel, historian, heroic — is a matter of preference; *The Times* prefers *a*. With abbreviations, acronyms, initials, be guided by pronunciation: an LSE student, an RAF officer, an NGO

abbreviated negatives (can't, don't, shan't etc, and similar abbreviations/contractions such as I'll, you're) should be discouraged except in direct quotes, although in more informal pieces such as diaries, sketches and some features they are fine when the full form would sound pedantic

Abdication cap with specific reference to Edward VIII's; in general sense use lower case

Aboriginal (singular, noun and adjective) and *Aborigines* (plural), for native Australian(s); *aboriginal* (lower case) for the wider adjectival use

absorption is the noun from absorb; absorbtion is a non-word that has found its way more than once into *The Times*

abstraction often an escape from precise meaning and a sign of lazy writing. Beware words such as situation, crisis, problem, resolution, question, issue, condition. A newspaper is about what happens and what people do; it should use concrete words. A headline, especially, may be killed by an abstract noun or phrase

abu means "father of" so must not be separated from the name that follows, ie Abu Qatada at first mention remains Abu Qatada ("father of Qatada"), not simply Qatada, and certainly not Mr Qatada

accents give French and German words their proper accents and diacritical marks, unless they have passed into common English usage. Use accents as appropriate also on capital letters and in headlines. With anglicised foreign words, no need for accents (*hotel, depot, debacle, elite, regime* etc), unless it makes a crucial difference to pronunciation or understanding, eg *cliché, façade, café, exposé.* NB *matinee, puree* etc.

In Spanish give accents only on the names of people, if they can be checked. In other Spanish words and place names, ignore accents and diacritical marks except for n with the tilde (*Ñ or* ñ, as in El Niño); this is considered a distinct letter of the alphabet in its own right and is also familiar to (and easily pronounceable by) most English-speaking readers

Achilles' heel a small but deadly area of weakness in someone seemingly invulnerable (like the Greek hero of the Trojan war, hence cap and apostrophe); but *achilles tendon* (lower case, no apostrophe, as the connection with the myth is more remote)

acknowledgment as with most (but not quite all) such words, no middle e

acronym a word formed from the initial letters or groups of letters of words in a set phrase or series of words, eg *Opec*, from the Organisation of Petroleum Exporting Countries, or *Ukip* for the United Kingdom Independence Party. If the acronym is easily pronounced and usually spoken as a word, write with an initial cap and then lower case: *Opec, Nato, Ukip, Rada, Bafta, Nice, Acas, Asbo* etc; follow this house style whatever the organisation itself may choose to do. Acronyms do not normally take the definite article.

Non-acronym abbreviations based on initials that are spelt out separately in speech (ie not pronounced as a word) remain in caps, and normally retain a definite article: *the BBC, the RAF, the CBI, the LSO, the UN, the EU* etc. A few, by convention, take an unpleasant mixture of upper and lower case: *MoT, the MoD, the DfE, the IoD.* All but the most familiar organisations, bodies, concepts and things should be named in full at first mention with the initials in brackets. However, a lot of initials in text will produce an unappetising alphabet soup, so use as sparingly as possible; after first mention try to vary with a suitable word: the ministry, the corporation, the department, the institute etc

Act theatre, ballet, opera etc, use cap and use roman numerals when naming, specifying or giving references: *Macbeth*, Act I, Act II etc; for more general refs use lower case, eg "in the second act of the play", "in the third scene of Act II"

Act and *Bill* (parliamentary) cap when giving full name (the Data Protection Act, the Assisted Dying for the Terminally Ill Bill etc) but otherwise lower case: "a bill intended to decriminalise assisted suicide"; "the act covers the gathering, storing and processing of personal information" etc

action as a transitive verb meaning undertake ("The marketing department will action this") is corporate jargon of the most irritating kind; avoid

active verbs generally better (and shorter) than passive

actor, actress for women use the feminine designation

AD, BC note that AD comes before the date, eg AD35; BC comes after, 350BC. Both have no spaces. With century, both are used after, eg 3rd century BC/AD. The terms BCE and CE (Common Era) are not to be used by *Times* writers but may exceptionally be allowed to a guest columnist/letter writer if context/courtesy seems to demand it (eg Lord Sacks, as chief rabbi, preferred CE in his Credo columns)

addresses no commas in 1 Pennington Street, 3 Thomas More Square, 1 London Bridge Street etc; and do not abbreviate.

No commas either between county names and postcodes, eg West Sussex BN6 9GS

adjectives do not overuse, especially in news reporting. Ask if the adjective is necessary and what it adds. Try to use adjectives to add precision, not merely for colour or emphasis. Beware especially those adjectives that come unbidden to mind with particular nouns: serious danger, devout Catholic, staunch Protestant, blithering idiot

administration (US) now lower case (cf government) even when specific, eg the Trump administration; generic always lower case, eg a lame-duck administration; also lower case adjectival, eg an administration official

Admiral do not abbreviate to Adm Jones etc except in lists; upper case when used as a title (Admiral Jones), at subsequent mentions "the admiral"

ad nauseam not ad nauseum

adrenaline with the final e

advance notice is faintly tautologous, but probably defensible; "advanced notice" is just wrong

adverbs as with adjectives (only more so), do not overuse, and never use without thought. Ask what, if anything, is being added or changed. Consider if there might be a better way of achieving the same effect, eg by using a more vivid or dramatic verb: to rush or race, say, rather than to run fast.

Adverbs are rarely a good way of beginning a sentence. "Interestingly", "ironically", "oddly" all clumsily flag something that ought to become obvious to the reader soon enough.

When adverbs are used to qualify adjectives the joining hyphen is rarely needed, eg heavily pregnant, classically carved, colourfully decorated. In some cases, however, such as "well founded", "ill educated", when used before the noun, eg a well-founded rumour, write the compound with the hyphen. The best guidance is to use the hyphen in these phrases as little as possible or when the phrase would otherwise be ambiguous. Thus, "the island is well regulated", but "it is a well-regulated island"

advertisement prefer to advert or ad, especially at first mention; but the shorter forms are perfectly acceptable (and often preferable at second mention and in headings etc)

adviser never advisor

-aemia not -emia, for blood conditions such as *anaemia, leukaemia*; thus *anaemic, leukaemic*

affect, effect as a verb, to affect means to produce an effect on, to touch the feelings of, or to pretend to have or feel (as in affectation); to effect is to bring about, to accomplish. If in doubt, always consult the dictionary. Affect as a noun should be used only by psychologists, among themselves

affidavit a written declaration on oath. Such phrases as "sworn affidavit" and "he swore an affidavit" are, strictly speaking, tautologous

Afghan noun or adjective; an *afghani* (lower case) is a unit of currency, not a person

Africa note north Africa, east Africa, west Africa, southern Africa, all lower case: these are locators, not place names (unlike South Africa)

African-American hyphenate

Afrikaans the language; *Afrikaners* the people. *Afrikanders* a breed of cattle

after almost invariably to be used rather than "following" and always preferable to such ponderous constructions as "in the wake of". Remember that *after* is a useful way of indicating a clear and particular temporal relationship; do not say *after* if what you mean is *when*. Also beware of lazily using *after* to convey a cause relationship. "The British player won a place in the final after beating the seeded German" is journalese for "... *by* beating the seeded German"

afterlife one word

ageing takes the middle e

ages are helpful to readers; they add context and human interest, particularly in stories involving unfamiliar people. Use common sense. Information should be useful or interesting, not distracting; there is no need to give an age for every minor figure mentioned in passing in a news report, or to tell *Times* readers how old the prime minister is whenever she crops up.

Normal style is "Joe Brown, 33, a porter," but occasional variations such as "Andrew Hunt, who is 74," are fine. For children's ages, except in headlines, write out numerals up to and including ten: "Emma Watson, seven, who ...", "Emma Watson, who is seven", "Emma Watson, aged seven", "the seven-year-old Emma Watson" etc. For consistency, however, use figures for both numerals if one is lower than ten and one higher so, eg "children aged 5 to 14" (not "five to 14"). In headlines, numerals save space and may often be clearer: "Children aged 7 are victims of school sexting epidemic." For more general ages use lower case decades, ie "I wish I was still in my thirties" etc.

Note caps in *Ice Age, Stone Age,* the *Dark Ages* etc

aggravate means to make (an evil or complaint) worse. It does not mean to annoy or irritate

AGM caps, but prefer *annual meeting* in text

ahead of do not use in the sense of timing to mean before/prior to/in advance of

aide-memoire roman, hyphen, no need for accent; plural *aides-memoire*. Traditionally minded French speakers might prefer the plural to be aide-mémoire; aide is a verb, not a noun, and there is still only one mémoire being aided, so the form is invariable; since the French spelling reform of 1990, however, the tendency has been to treat such composites as simple nouns and add an s at the end of all of them, so most younger

French people would probably write aide-mémoires. All this is academic; aide-memoire has been anglicised through common use (no accent, no italics, no attempt at French pronunciation); in the process it has acquired various more or less awkward English plurals, of which the most widely accepted seems to be aides-memoire; this may be poor French, but it is comprehensible English, and if it is good enough for Collins, the OED and the National Archives (where British government and diplomatic aides-memoire are catalogued and stored), it should be good enough for us

Aids (acquired immune deficiency syndrome) is not a disease, but a medical condition. Diseases that affect people who are HIV-positive may be called *Aids-related diseases*; but through custom and practice we can now afford to relax our rule about never saying "died of Aids". Write *HIV/Aids* when appropriate regarding the virus and the condition together

airbase, **airstrip**, **airspace** no hyphens

air conditioner, **air conditioning** no longer hyphenate as noun; but hyphenate adjectivally, eg an air-conditioning unit

aircraft prefer to planes wherever possible. Remember that not all aircraft are jets, some are still turbo-prop. Do not use the American airplanes

aircraftman, **aircraftwoman** not aircraftsman etc

aircraft names are italicised, like ship or locomotive names, on the rare occasions when they are needed, eg the *Enola Gay* (Hiroshima bomber)

aircraft types B-52, F-111 etc (roman, hyphens between letter and numbers just because it looks neater)

air fares two words, as *rail fares, bus fares* etc

air force cap Royal Air Force (thereafter the RAF), otherwise all lower case: the US air force (USAF, or in Second World War contexts USAAF), Brazilian air force; and lower case in adjectival use, eg an air force raid. No hyphen, even adjectivally

airplane ugly Americanism; do not use

airports as a general rule for British airports, use the name of the city or town followed by lower case airport, eg Manchester airport, Leeds/Bradford airport, East Midlands (formerly Nottingham) airport, Luton airport; but Heathrow, Gatwick, Stansted are fine on their own

air raid two words (unlike *airstrike*)

air show two words; lower case even when specific, eg the Paris air show, the Farnborough air show

airstrike one word in military sense, but *air raid* (two words)

AK47 no need to hyphenate the Kalashnikov assault rifle

akimbo use only with reference to arms (never legs). It means hands on the hips with elbows turned outwards

al- as the prefix to Arabic nouns (including names), prefer the al- to the el- form, except where the el- has become widely accepted. The prefix is dropped from names at second mention, so that Bashar al-Assad becomes Assad

Albert Hall, the prefer to give *Royal* at first formal mention (that is its name); subsequently (or informally) fine without

alcohol its strength is measured either by volume (a percentage) or by the more traditional proof system, of which there are British and American variants. Do not confuse the percentage and proof systems by writing, eg that a drink is 48 per cent proof. As an example, a spirit that is 40 per cent alcohol by volume (ABV) is 80 degrees proof on the American scale (which runs from 0 to 200, and the proof number being precisely double the ABV figure); on the old British scale, which runs from 0 to 175, 40 per cent ABV would be 70 degrees proof. On the British scale, 100 degrees proof spirit (57.1 per cent ABV) is the minimum strength of distilled alcohol that when mixed with gunpowder sustains its combustion, and this property was used to test the traditional rum ration in the British navy. Since 1980 Britain has used the ABV system. See **drink-drive**

A level no hyphen as a noun, but A-level results etc (hyphenate when adjectival). A levels now embrace AS levels and A2s, and can still be used as the generic phrase and in historical context. But use *O levels* (same hyphenation rules) now only in historical context

alfresco one word, roman

algebra take great care in writing and presenting algebraic expressions. Individual terms should be in italics. Be sure that superscripts, including squares of numbers, and subscripts are properly rendered, eg $E=mc^2$. As an example in narrative text: "Dr Edwards noted that the mass, m, is proportional to Ax where A is the area of the burger and x is its thickness. If all other parameters remain the same (heat of grill, absence of sudden downpour, mood of cook and so on), then t, the total cooking time, is proportional to x^2A." See **italics**

alibi not a general alternative to excuse; it means being elsewhere at the material time

Alistair always check the spelling of this name (Alastair, Alasdair, Alister etc)

all in phrases such as "all the president's men" there is no need to write "all of the president's men"

Allahu akbar (God is greatest); note also *alhamdulillah* ("praise God", approximately equivalent to the Judaeo-Christian alleluia/hallelujah)

allcomers one word

allege avoid the suggestion that the writer is making the allegation; somewhere in the story always specify the source. Do not assume that use of this verb will keep you out of legal trouble; if in doubt, ask a lawyer. Do not use *alleged* as a synonym of ostensible, apparent or reputed

All Hallows Eve not Allhallows

Allies cap the Allies in the Second World War context; generally, lower case *alliance*, as in the Atlantic alliance, Gulf War alliance etc

all right never alright, except in the television programme *It'll be Alright on the Night*

All Souls College Oxford (no apostrophe)

all-time avoid as in all-time high; use *highest* or *record high* instead

al-Qaeda thus, hyphen and ae

alsatian lower case, the German shepherd dog. See **dogs**

alternate (adj) as well as being English for "every other" or "every second" in a sequence, is also American for *alternative*. This latter use is to be resisted, firmly, although we may need to concede that *alternate history* has gained more or less universal currency to denote the "what if" school of fiction that imagines, eg life in a Britain occupied by victorious Nazis after the Second World War

alternative of two, *choice* of three or more, but there is no need to be obsessive about this

alternative vote (AV) system; note also *first-past-the-post* system

alumnus a (singular, male) graduate of a particular educational institution; *alumni* is the plural, including for mixed groups. The female equivalents are *alumna* and *alumnae*

ambassador lower case even when specific (see **capitalisation**); the French ambassador; "he was appointed ambassador to Japan"

ambience prefer to the French spelling ambiance

Amendment spell out and upper case for clarity in relation to the US constitution, eg the First Amendment, the Fifth Amendment etc

Americanisms generally to be resisted, unless they have clearly passed into standard English use

American spellings allow US spellings for proper names of institutions, well-known landmarks etc. So Lincoln Center, World Trade Center, Labor Day, Medal of Honor, Pearl Harbor etc; in practice this means US spellings may be retained in proper names used with initial caps, as it will be clear what is going on; job titles that in our style become lower case (ie almost all of them) should be anglicised (the secretary of defence etc, so that they do not just look like spelling mistakes); for all other words use English spellings.

Be aware that the differences are not all as obvious as writing *theater* for *theatre* or missing the u out of words such as *colour*; eg US usage does not double the final l of the root verb in forms such as *traveller, cancelled, fuelled, modelling* etc; *license* is both verb and noun in US English, and so, confusingly, is *practice*; avoid all of these and be ready to change them in agency copy or quotes

America(n)/US in general, try to use *American* as in "American cities", "American food" etc; but *US* in headlines and in the context of government institutions, such as US Congress, US navy, US military operation. Never use America when ambiguity could occur with Canada or Latin America

amid not amidst; similarly *among*, not amongst

amok not amock or amuck

ampersand use in a company name if the company uses it

amphitheatres in classical context are oval or circular (eg the Colosseum in Rome); do not confuse with *theatres*, which are semi-circular or horseshoe-shaped

Amsterdam treaty (lower case t), but the Treaty of Amsterdam

analogue in all contexts, noun and adjective

anathema meaning accursed, consigned to perdition; there is no need for an article, thus: "It is anathema to me." Although a noun, it is quasi-adjectival in usage

ancestor strictly means a person from whom another is directly descended, especially someone more distant than a grandparent. Do not use in the looser sense of predecessor; eg Queen Elizabeth I is not the ancestor of the present

Queen. An ancestor is not a descendant, so do not mix them up

ancient Briton/Britain ancient Greek/Greece, ancient Egyptian/Egypt, ancient Roman/Rome, the ancient world; seems fine to lower case the a on ancient but cap the national adjective or noun

and also do not use together

androgynous not androgenous in reference to having both male and female characteristics; *androgenic* refers to male hormones, eg testosterone

aneurysm not aneurism

angioplasty is a procedure carried out by cardiologists and is not surgery

Anglesey never Anglesea

anglicise, anglophile, anglophobe, anglophone all lower case

angst roman, lower case

animals cap proper nouns or adjectives derived from them when naming breeds of animals (or species of birds): *Indian elephant, Nile crocodile, Bengal tiger, Arctic tern, Dartford warbler, African grey parrot, Bewick's swan* etc; otherwise all lower case. When referring to individual animals in stories or captions, use "he" or "she" if the sex is definitely known or if the creature is called by a masculine or feminine name (eg Felix the cat had only himself to blame). But use "it" if sex is unspecified or irrelevant. On the racing pages, horses are always "he" or "she". See **anthropomorphism**

annexe noun, but *to annex* verb

anniversary by definition, is the date on which an event occurred in some previous year. So avoid such nonsense as the "nine-month anniversary" or the "300-day anniversary" of something

answerphone or answering machine

Antarctic around the South Pole, *Arctic* around the North: capitalise, spell correctly and do not mix up

antennae plural of antenna in zoological sense; *antennas* in radio or aerial sense

anthropomorphism the lazy option in captioning photographs of animals; try instead to convey some real information about the creatures or the photograph

anti in compounds, generally no hyphen (unless hideous or confusing without) but always hyphenate before a capital letter, eg anti-American

Antichrist initial cap, no hyphen

anticipate widely (and acceptably) used to mean *expect*; better, however, to preserve the senses of to foresee something and react (to anticipate a blow), or to do something before the due time (so that to anticipate marriage is quite different from expecting to marry)

anticlimax no hyphen

anticyclone no hyphen

antidepressant (noun or adjective), no hyphen

antihero no hyphen

Antipodes, Antipodean cap A when referring to Australia and New Zealand

antisemitic, antisemitism arguments have been advanced for using the unhyphenated form to mean specifically hatred of Jews, which is what is almost always intended, and anti-Semitism to denote hostility to a whole group of Semitic peoples; the distinction seems rather effortful but it reinforces our preference for avoiding hyphens where we can

antisocial

antisocial behaviour order *Asbo*; plural *Asbos*

anti-tank one that probably looks better with a hyphen

anti-terrorism another

antiviral one word

any more always two words

apart from prefer to the Americanism "aside from"

ape, aping, apish

aphelion the point in its orbit when a planet or comet is farthest from the sun. See **perihelion**

apostrophes with proper names/nouns ending in s that are singular, follow the rule of writing what is voiced, eg Keats's poetry, Sobers's batting, *The Times's* style (or *Times* style); and with names where the final s is soft, use the s apostrophe, eg Rabelais' writings, Delors' presidency; plurals follow normal form, as Lehman Brothers' loss etc.

Note that with Greek names of more than one syllable that end in s, generally do not use the apostrophe s, eg Aristophanes' plays, Achilles' heel, Socrates' life, Archimedes' principle; but note Jesus's (not Jesus') parables. Beware of organisations that have variations as their house style, eg St Thomas' Hospital, where we should respect their preference.

Take care with apostrophes with plural nouns, eg women's, not womens'; children's, not childrens'; people's, not (usually) peoples'. Also beware of moving the apostrophe when creating plurals: a lot of shepherd's pies, two rival builder's merchants, two private member's bills, etc.

Use the apostrophe in expressions such as two years' time, several hours' delay etc.

Some place names and many company names have lost their apostrophes: Earls Court, St Andrews, Barclays, Lloyds the bank (but Lloyd's the insurance market), Morrisons etc; others — Sainsbury's, Sotheby's, Christie's etc — have not; always check.

An apostrophe may for clarity be used to indicate the plural of single letters — p's and q's — if the alternative seems worse; a rare instance of a permissible greengrocer's apostrophe. See also **do's and don'ts**

apothegm maxim; prefer to apophthegm

apparatchik

appeal do not use the Americanism "appeal a verdict or decision"; English usage requires *appeal against*

appellations, titles, honorifics, names on News pages, although not on Features and Sport, almost every adult surname should be granted the courtesy of a title. Give the name in full at first mention, then refer to Mr, Mrs, Ms. There may be occasions when it is more appropriate at second mention to use just a first name (Bob, Sue etc). Such occasions will be rare; they require justification and careful thought.

The exceptions, who may be referred to by surname alone are: convicted offenders (or, rarely, offenders still on trial but who have clearly admitted guilt, see 6 below), the dead (but not the quite recently dead, except in obituaries; in news reports be particularly sensitive when writing about victims of crime); and, mostly in the Arts, Sport, Books and Diary sections, where common usage omits a title. On News pages, similarly, sportsmen, artists, authors, film stars, pop stars, actors etc should now normally not be referred to as Mr/Mrs/Ms, except in court cases or exceptional occasions where guilt would be implied by omitting the honorific. Where sportsmen, entertainers etc have been given honours, it will often seem more natural to refer to them by their full title once at first mention ("Sir Mick Jagger") and thereafter as "Jagger" (rather than "Sir Mick"). Minors may when appropriate be referred to by first name alone.

General rules:

1. First mention, Herbert Palfry, Juliette Worth, subsequently Mr Palfry, Mrs/Miss/Ms Worth; only children should be referred to by first names alone.

2. Put the name first, then the age (if relevant), then the description; eg Penélope Cruz, 34, the Spanish actress; avoid the journalese construction "actress Penélope Cruz" or the like.

3. Avoid initials and middle initials (as in eg American names) unless the person is best known thereby (eg WG Grace, PJ Harvey, JK Galbraith, Cecil B DeMille, AJP Taylor, all with no full points).

4. Ms should be used when a woman wants to be called thus, or when it is not known for certain if she is Mrs or Miss.

5. Dr need not be confined to medical doctors; if a public figure with an academic doctorate from a reputable university insists on being called Dr, we can allow them the title as a courtesy, although we should discourage this unless the doctorate (and the expertise it suggests) is of some interest or relevance to the story. Generally, as for Mr/Mrs/Miss/Ms, do not use Dr at first mention.

6. Court proceedings, professional body disciplinary hearings etc: accused people should be accorded the appropriate title (Mr, Miss etc), however guilty they may appear, after name and first name have been given at first mention; only convicted persons or those who have admitted guilt in recognised legal or disciplinary proceedings should be referred to by surname alone. But do be sensitive especially in murder cases, where the accused is given, for example, his "Mr"; the victim (despite the dead not usually being given a title) should here be accorded the courtesy of the title. Otherwise the stark contrast of, say, Mr X being accused of the murder of Dando, can appear gratuitously offensive

appendix plural *appendices,* but *appendixes* in anatomy

Apple Computer not Computers, for the Mac company

appraise means evaluate; *apprise* means inform. Never confuse

appurtenance

April Fool's Day, April fool, but **All Fools' Day**

aqueduct not aquaduct

Arabic refers to the language. Use *Arab* in such phrases as "the Arab world"

Arabic names there is no universally accepted system of transliteration. Arabic has 28 letters, many of which change shape, sometimes considerably, depending on whether they stand alone or on where they appear within a word: initial, medial, final. Vowels are largely ignored in most printed and handwritten text. There are ligatures and diacritical marks by the dozen. There are consonants with no direct counterparts in English, and sounds with no obvious equivalents at all.

Attempts to replicate these complexities (with elaborate spellings and much use of apostrophes) are confusing and look a mess. Clarity, simplicity and a degree of consistency should be our aims. Where there is a western consensus on a spelling, eg among reputable news agencies, big media outlets and/or diplomatic sources, we should follow it, except in the very few cases where a different preferred spelling is specified in this guide. For other cases these are some very basic guidelines:

prefer *al-* to el- or Al (and to variants such as as- ash- ad- or ul-) unless an individual or corporation is established in the West and has a preferred or familiar western style (eg Al Jazeera, the broadcaster, or Saudi royals who are Al; also Mohamed Al Fayed, who may or may not be entitled to style himself thus, but does). Drop al- when not giving the full name (eg Bashar al-Assad becomes Assad)

end names in i not y (*Ali*, not Aly etc)

do not use the apostrophe in eg Ba'ath

do not generally attempt to distinguish long and short vowels, but in common names with long vowels generally prefer ee to i (eg *Rasheed* rather than Rashid; *Fedayeen*, not Fedayin; *Mujahideen*); prefer *ou* to u or oo (eg *Yousef, Mansour* etc)

prefer q to k or kh (*Rafiq, qat*)

abu, abd, abdul, bin, bint: these are not self-contained names but words meaning "father of", "slave of" etc. Usually lower case, except as the first word of a name, they attach to the name that follows and must not be separated, eg Abu Qatada remains Abu Qatada, Osama bin Laden becomes bin Laden)

Arab Spring cap for the uprisings at the start of 2011 in north Africa and the Middle East

arbitrate, arbitration do not confuse with *mediate, mediation.* An arbitrator hears evidence from different parties then hands down a decision; a mediator listens to the different arguments then tries to bring the parties to agreement

archaeologist, archaeology

archbishops

1. Anglican archbishops and diocesan or suffragan bishops in the UK: at first mention, the Archbishop of Barchester, the Most Rev John Smith; or the Bishop of Barchester, the Right Rev John Smith, or (if a doctor) the Bishop of Barchester, Dr John Smith; subsequent references, the archbishop or bishop (lower case), or Dr Smith (if so entitled), never Mr Smith.

2. The Archbishop of Canterbury is primate of All England, the Archbishop of York is primate of England.

3. Anglican bishops are consecrated, Roman Catholic bishops ordained.

4. Roman Catholic archbishops, at first mention: the Roman Catholic Archbishop of Liverpool, the Most Rev John X, subsequent mentions Archbishop X or the archbishop; bishops, first mention the Roman Catholic Bishop of Plymouth, the Right Rev Christopher Y, thereafter Bishop Y or the bishop, unless he has a doctorate, when he is Dr Y; Anglican and Catholic archbishoprics carefully avoid overlap, but there is no reason readers should know this, so it may be helpful to spell out in this way at first mention which church is involved

arch-rival hyphenate in the sense of chief rival. For combinations using the prefix arch-, some will look better hyphenated while others can be a single word, eg archbishop

Argentine is the adjective; an *Argentinian* is a person from Argentina (never the Argentine)

Argyle for socks, jumpers and the Plymouth football club; *Argyll* for the Scottish county and its regiment, the Argyll and Sutherland Highlanders

armada cap in historical reference to Drake etc, otherwise lower case; try to avoid (or at least limit) imprecise use of this word: it means a fleet of *armed* ships, so strictly should not be applied to just any collection of boats or ships; *flotilla* might sometimes be a better word for what you want

Armageddon cap

armchair, deckchair no hyphens

armed forces, the lower case; also *the services*

Armistice Day is not the same as *Remembrance Sunday* (unless November 11 falls on a Sunday)

arm's length as in "he was kept at arm's length"; but hyphenate as a modifier, eg "the former partners now have an arm's-length relationship"

army cap the British Army, if naming in full (but otherwise and thereafter the army, eg "he joined the army"; "government efforts to reform the army"); otherwise all lower case: the Belgian army, the Swiss army, the US army; always lower case when used adjectivally, eg an army helicopter, a British army tank, a Swiss army knife

A-road, B-road etc hyphenated

around do not use as an alternative to *about*

Arran Isle of, in the Firth of Clyde; but the *Aran Islands* (note one r) off Co Galway in western Ireland, and *Aran Island* (singular) off Co Donegal; and an *Aran sweater* etc

arrest rarely necessary to add "by the police"; an arrest made by anyone else is worth explaining. If, unusually, there is a good reason for specifying a particular squad or unit, then do so: he was arrested by the anti-terrorist squad, by officers investigating phone-hacking, by detectives from South Yorkshire police who had travelled to Spain etc

art deco artistic style/movement (see below), lower case seems fine, but use caps if needed for clarity

artefact do not use artifact

artiste not a word to use seriously; prefer *entertainer, performer, singer, dancer* etc

artistic knights with these, use only surname in their artistic contexts (eg Rattle conducted the Berlin Philharmonic with panache), but full title in news stories with, for example, political or social contexts (eg Sir Simon Rattle visited No 10 yesterday). Similarly, McKellen played Lear, but Sir Ian McKellen led the gay rights march

artistic movements/styles generally lower case for all period or stylistic designations — *baroque, classical, neoclassical, rococo, modernist, minimalist, postmodern* — except in the context of quite specific art historical discussion (of, eg an exhibition of German Expressionist painting) or where clarity is helped by a capital: the romantic movement, for instance, can usually be lower case like the rest, but there may be times when it matters that Romantic verse, as written by Byron or Keats, is not necessarily romantic verse, in which case use a cap for clarity

Arts and Crafts movement seems to need caps for clarity

as beware of sloppy use in sentences such as "They were moved out as the blast tore open the building"; what is meant is "*after* the blast ...". The sport headline "Martis makes crucial mistake as Mowbray's men go down" wrongly suggests that the blunder by Shelton Martis, the West Bromwich Albion defender, was unconnected to his team's relegation from the Premier League in May 2009. In fact, it was his error that led to a first Liverpool goal. After that, his team lost and went down to the Championship. Avoid having lots of headlines using "as"; ensure here as well as in copy that its precise meaning of "when" is retained. It is not a synonym for "before" or "after"

Ascendancy for clarity cap when referring to the landowning Protestant minority in Irish historical context

ascendant, ascendancy prefer to ascendent, ascendency

Asian while this is obviously an adjective pertaining to Asia, or a person from that continent, note that in Britain it can have a narrower officially sanctioned, although in some quarters controversial, meaning of a person who comes from, or whose parents came from, India, Pakistan or elsewhere in south Asia; be aware that using it in this way (especially in eg crime stories) may annoy British Asians of other backgrounds. In North America *Asian* is more likely to refer to people from China, Japan or elsewhere in east Asia

aside from do not use this Americanism. Write *apart from*

as of (with dates) prefer *on, after* or *from* to make clear what is meant

assassin, assassinate, assassination to be used only in the murder of a statesman or politician from a political motive; not to be used for the killing of general celebrities or others

assizes like quarter sessions, no longer function, having been replaced by the Crown Court

assure you *assure* your life; *ensure* means to make certain; you *insure* against risk

as to avoid in the sense of the much preferred *about*

asylum seeker no hyphen

at the present time, at this time use *now*; but avoid the phrase "as of now"

Atlantic (Ocean) North Atlantic, South Atlantic, but *transatlantic*

attendee ghastly word that there was no need to coin; avoid

attorney-general, solicitor-general both are hyphenated; they are law officers, not legal officers

aubrieta prefer to aubrietia and aubretia (named after Claude Aubriet). The genus, as per standard botanical style, is *Aubrieta*

auditor general lower case, no hyphen

Auntie not aunty as antique colloquialism for the BBC

autumn statement delivered by the chancellor, lower case

awards such as Baftas, Oscars etc should be lower case, eg best actor, best director. Also, note Academy award. See **prize**

awayday one word

Awol absent without leave, not AWOL

axing no middle e; but try to avoid in sense of cutting jobs, dismissal etc

ay (yes), *aye* (ever), *Ayes* (debate)

Bb

b (abbreviation for born), no full point, eg b 1906. Likewise d for died: d 1997

baby boomer (no hyphen) a person born in the postwar demographic baby boom (roughly 1946-64)

baby-walker

baccalaureate use anglicised spelling with lower case for general use, but cap in specific context of the *International Baccalaureate*, taken in some British schools; and note the specifically French examination or degree from which this derives, the *Baccalauréat* (italic, cap, accent, no final e)

backache, **backbreaking** but *back pain*

back benches (parliamentary) two words; but *backbenchers*, *backbench* (adjectival, as in backbench revolt)

back burner no hyphen, but be sparing of the cliché "on the back burner", especially when context renders it idiotic ("Never put an explosive issue on the back burner")

backlash overworked word; try to avoid

backstreet(s) noun or adjective, no hyphen; similarly, *backyard*

back-up noun, hyphenate

bacteria is the plural of *bacterium*. Bacteria and viruses are different and the terms are not interchangeable. Make sure the terminology is correct. Note that antibiotics are used to treat bacterial but not viral infections

bail out as in to bail someone out of trouble; also bail water from a boat; but *bale out* of an aircraft by parachute, to escape. NB *bailout* (one word, as noun)

bait see **bated**

balk not baulk

Balkans prefer to Balkan states. This region includes the former Yugoslav republics of Slovenia, Croatia, Bosnia Herzegovina, Serbia, Montenegro and Macedonia, as well as Romania, Bulgaria, Albania, Greece and the European part of Turkey

ball plural in Court Page headlines is *dances*

ballgown one word

balloted like *benefited, budgeted* etc, has only one t

Baltic states (lower case states) from north to south, and coincidentally in alphabetical order, they are Estonia (capital Tallinn), Latvia (capital Riga) and Lithuania (Vilnius). Do not use the abbreviated Baltics

bandana prefer to bandanna

B&B with caps and closed up around ampersand as abbreviation for bed and breakfast

banister not bannister

bank holiday bank holiday Monday etc, lower case

Bank of England retain cap for clarity in subsequent refs to the Bank

Bank of Mum and Dad

bankruptcy in Britain people file a petition for bankruptcy; they do not file for bankruptcy

baptistry prefer to baptistery

Bar, the (legal); also cap for the *Bar* (but not the bars) *of the House of Commons* and cap in military honours sense, eg DFC and Bar

barbecue, barbecuing barbeques should be confined to pub menus

barcode one word

bar mitzvah lower case, roman; also *bat mitzvah* for girls

barony pertains to barons (who are Lord X, never Baron X, except in the formal announcement that a title has been gazetted). *Baronetcy* to baronets (hereditary titles carrying the prefix Sir, eg Sir Fred Y. *The Times* does not usually use the Bt suffix except with obituaries). Knighthoods, which also use the title Sir, are not hereditary

baroque lower case like similar terms

barter to exchange one thing (or service) for another; not a synonym for *bargain* or *haggle*

basically greatly overworked word that rarely adds anything to a sentence. Always try to avoid

basis "on a ... basis" is a cliché and to be avoided. For "employment on a part-time basis" say "part-time employment". Other usages are similarly redundant ("on a regular basis" — "regularly"; "on a daily basis" — "daily"; "on a voluntary basis" — "voluntarily", "willingly", or "without pay", depending on context; and so on)

Basle (Switzerland), not Basel or Bâle. But note, FC Basel, the football team, and Art Basel, the art fair

Basque country, the

bated/baited note the difference: *bated* breath; *baited* hook; *bait* as a verb is to persecute, tease or torment (as in bear baiting); *bate* is the verb to use of a tethered hawk beating its wings and trying to jump from its perch, should you have occasion to write about such a thing

battalion never batallion. Say the 1st Battalion, the 7th Battalion etc (not First, Seventh)

battle try to avoid using as a transitive verb as in "The students battled the police ..."; use "fought" or "battled against" instead; be wary of using at all (along with similar language) in relation to illness (battle against cancer etc)

battle cry

battleship a heavily armoured warship of the largest type, with many large-calibre guns. Beware. Battleship is not synonymous with warship: eg cruisers and destroyers are warships but they are not battleships. Historically, a battleship (line-of-battle ship) was any warship of sufficient size and armament to take her place in the line of battle; in other words, a ship of the line

BBC no need to spell out as British Broadcasting Corporation, although "the corporation" is a useful alternative in text. Avoid "the Beeb" except, on rare occasions, in columns or commentaries . The BBC is an organisation fond of capitals. Most are unnecessary. BBC job titles, like any others, are lower case: controller, chairman, director-general, governor. So are BBC television and BBC radio and the BBC charter. The BBC Trust may be capped when there is a risk of ambiguity, but is generally lower case. Caps for the historic radio stations: the Light Programme, the Home Service and the Third Programme

BC See **AD**

be-all and end-all note hyphens

beanbag one word

Beatles, the no need to cap *the* unless at the start of a sentence; similarly the Clash, the Killers, the Rolling Stones, the Smiths, the Who etc (now even the The, should there ever be any need to refer to them again)

becquerel lower case for the radioactive unit, symbol is Bq

bedizened archaic but lovely word meaning dressed or decorated gaudily or tastelessly

Bedouin prefer to Beduin for the nomadic peoples of Middle Eastern and north African deserts

beg the question refers in logic to an informal fallacy whereby an argument assumes its own conclusion: eg "this usage is unattractive because it is ugly"; that sense seems worth preserving. More commonly used as just another (less good) way of saying "raise (or ask) the question"; some readers are (logically) annoyed by this

beleaguered a cliché, especially in a political context, so best avoided

Belfast *north,* *south,* *east* and *west,* lower case

bellringer, bellringing, belltower no hyphens

bellwether not bellweather

benchmark no hyphen

bendy bus two words

benefited not benefitted

benzene is a substance obtained from coal-tar; *benzine* is a spirit obtained from petroleum

Beretta a type of pistol favoured by James Bond, not to be confused with a *biretta* (not berretta), a hat worn by Catholic clergy

Bermudian not Bermudan; but *Bermuda-rig* to describe the most common configuration of sails on modern cruising and racing boats (a fore and aft rig with a tall triangular mainsail and single headsail)

Berne use the anglicised version of the Swiss capital's name (not Bern)

berserk not beserk

Berwick-upon-Tweed the northernmost town in England. North Berwick is in Scotland

beseeched prefer to besought

best loved, best-loved etc ensure there is a hyphen if you mean a best-loved writer rather than a best loved writer

bestseller one word; likewise, *bestselling*

bête noire no longer italic; final e on noire; *bugbear* is a good English word that you might prefer

betting odds use a hyphen (16-1, 6-4 etc), not a slash (16/1). For odds-on, smaller figure comes first (1-2, 4-11 and so on). The higher the odds, the less likely something is; if the chances of something happening are raised, the odds are lowered. Not everyone understands odds as well as they think they do. If in doubt, consult the racing desk

bi- take care with this difficult prefix. Its correct use is in Latin compounds, where it has the force of two, not half, such as *bicentenary/bicentennial* (a two-hundredth anniversary), or *biennial* (recurring every two years). *Biannual* means twice a year; to avoid confusion, write out *twice a year*

biased

Bible cap and roman, not italic, in the religious context; but *biblical* (lower case); biblical references thus: II Corinthians ii, 2; Luke iv, 5. Write *bible* (lower case) in a metaphorical sense, eg "For many, *Vogue* is the fashion bible"

Bible belt

biceps, triceps same form for the singular and the plural of these muscles

bid prefer not to use in text as synonym of *effort, attempt* or *try*, although it may be used sparingly in headlines in this sense

big bang lower case for the event postulated by cosmological theory relating to the beginnings of the universe (lower case); note *big-bang theory* (hyphen as modifier). But *Big Bang* (caps) to distinguish the modernisation of the London Stock Exchange in October 1986

bight is a curve in a coastline or river; *bite* involves teeth; *bytes* are units of digital information in computing. Do not confuse

Big Society, the philosophy of community involvement once espoused by the Conservatives under David Cameron

Bill and *Act* caps only when fully identified or when clarity demands

billion one thousand million, not a million million. Write £5 billion, £15 billion (£5bn, £15bn in headlines), three billion, 15 billion etc

bin Laden, Osama note lower case "bin", except where it is the first word of a headline or sentence. Avoid the "Mr" designation, as with Saddam Hussein etc. The organisation founded by bin Laden is *al-Qaeda* (not al-Qaida). Bin Laden was killed in his compound in Abbottabad, Pakistan, in the early hours of Monday, May 2, 2011 (time differences mean it was still May 1 in Washington and London)

bin liner

biological terms with Latin terms, cap letter for first (genus) word, then lower case for the second (species); and italicise for all but the most common, eg *Turdus merula*, the blackbird

birds cap proper nouns or adjectives derived from them in names of species: Arctic skua, Montagu's harrier, Cetti's warbler, Slavonian grebe, etc

Biro is a trade name and misuse is aggressively policed, so cap; generic alternative is *ballpoint pen*

birthday people and animals have birthdays; everything else has anniversaries. Write 33rd birthday, 65th birthday etc (any number higher than *tenth*)

birthrate, **birthright**, **birthplace** no hyphens; but *birth control*, *birth certificate* etc

bisexual pronouns *he* and *his* can no longer refer to both sexes equally; *he or she* will sometimes do. Always be sensitive in this contentious area. It is often easier to use the plural *they*, for *he or she*, and sometimes even the ugly *their* for *his or her*. Do this only when necessary. Do not, for instance, write "one of the Chelsea players threw *their* shirt into the crowd", or "each nun has *their* own list of tasks" — the sex of those involved in both cases is quite clear and should be stated

bishops once consecrated they are bishops for life unless defrocked; retirement from a see does not make anyone "a former bishop"

bit abbreviate to b; thus *kilobit* (kb), *megabit* (Mb) etc

bite (as with teeth) must not be confused with the computing term *byte* or the geographical *bight*

blacklist one word as noun or verb

blackout noun, one word

black (people), lower case; do not use "non-white" or "coloured" — and never "immigrants" (which many are not). Unless you want to evoke South Africa under apartheid, prefer "black people" to "blacks". Be sensitive to local usage: African-American is now standard usage in the United States, for instance, while Afro-Caribbean (or African-Caribbean) and Black British are widely used in the UK. See also **coloureds, race**

blackspot (accident, unemployment etc), one word; similarly, *troublespot, hotspot*

blame take care with this word; blame is attached to causes, not effects. So say "Bad weather is blamed for my bronchitis", NOT "My bronchitis is blamed on bad weather"

bloc use in context such as the former *Soviet bloc*, a *power bloc* etc; but *block vote*

blond (noun and adjective) for men, *blonde* for women; but all should have blond hair

blood groups write, eg O negative (no hyphen)

bloodied but unbowed, a cliché best avoided, but written thus if used; but *red-blooded* etc

blood sports two words; similarly *field sports, motor sports*

bloody mary lower case for the cocktail of tomato juice and vodka

blowsy prefer to blowzy

blue lower case for an Oxbridge sportsman or woman and for the award itself

blue-chip hyphen as modifier, eg a blue-chip company

blue-collar workers as white-collar workers

blueprint avoid this greatly overworked word when all you mean is *plan, scheme* or *proposal*

bluetongue one word for the notifiable disease afflicting ruminants

bluffers be very cautious. *The Bluffer's Guide/Guides* are trademarks, rigorously protected by their publishers. So generic phrases such as "a bluffer's guide to ..." must be avoided

Blu-Tack proprietary so must cap

boat is generally used of a small vessel, including fishing boats up to the size of a trawler; a ship is a large seagoing vessel big enough to carry smaller boats. In the Royal Navy, submarines are called boats. All take the pronoun *she* and the possessive *her*

Boat Race caps for the annual Oxford-Cambridge race on the Thames

Bobcat should not be used in a generic sense as a description of skid-steer loaders or other equipment

Boche derogatory slang for Germans; *Bosch*, the household appliance or power tools manufacturer

bodyline one word, no quotes for the cricketing tactic; use lower case in general usage such as *bodyline bowling* but cap for the *Bodyline tour* (of the 1932-33 Ashes)

boffin avoid as a synonym of *scientist*, except ironically or in direct quotes

Bogart, Humphrey but **(Sir) Dirk Bogarde**

bogey (golf, plural *bogeys*); *bogie* (wheels); *bogy* (ghost); but note *bogeyman*

Bohemia, Bohemian cap only in specific reference to the geographical entity but lower case *bohemia, bohemian* metaphorically

Bolshevik

bolshie lower case for rebellious; cap in (derogatory) political context

bolt hole two words

bombs *car bomb, fire bomb, nail bomb, petrol bomb, suicide bomb* etc; but hyphenate verbal or adjectival use, eg to *fire-bomb*, a *nail-bomb* attack

bombshell in metaphorical use, as in "drop a bombshell", is a cliché. Avoid

bonanza another greatly overworked word that should be avoided wherever possible

Bonfire Night initial caps; see **Guy Fawkes Night**

Book of Common Prayer, the roman

bookshop

boom overused word

Boötes pronunciation requires a diaeresis on the name of the constellation, should you ever have to refer to it

border lower case, even the one between England and Scotland (north of the border); cap the (Scottish) Borders; remember that the border is not marked by Hadrian's Wall

bored with/by not of

-born normally prefer to use nationality, rather than country, eg English-born, but there are exceptions, eg Singapore-born; for counties, cities etc, normally use the noun, eg London-born, Manchester-born, Dorset-born, but again there are exceptions, eg Cornish-born

born/borne the second is what you want except when writing about birth. Something to be borne in mind; a theory borne out by the facts; an initiative (or a tree) that has borne fruit; shame borne in silence etc

borstals no longer exist; they are now young offender institutions

bortsch Russian or Polish soup

Bosphorus a strait, not a river

Botox trade name, so must cap

bow tie no hyphen

box office as noun, two words; but hyphenate when adjectival (eg box-office success)

box sets *boxed* sets may be more logical for the collections of CDs, DVDs etc, but no one says it; we must concede defeat

boy band two words. Note also *girl band*

boyfriend, girlfriend

boy's own as generic phrase, lower case and roman; but the old publication was called *The Boy's Own Paper*

braille lower case

brainchild try to avoid this cliché

branch in police context, eg special branch, anti-terrorist branch, lower case unless there is any risk of confusion

breakthrough avoid describing every bit of medical and scientific progress as a breakthrough — "a significant development or discovery, especially in science". It isn't

breakout, breakdown (as noun, each one word); but to *break out* etc, and *break-up* (hyphenate as noun)

breastfeed(ing) no longer use hyphen

breaststroke no longer hyphenate the swimming discipline

Breathalyser (cap, proprietary), but *to breathalyse* (lower case, generic)

breathtaking no hyphen

breech birth

brevity Verbosity clouds meaning. Brevity is a virtue, in phrases, sentences, whole passages of writing. Even in words. Use short rather than long ones if you can: "be" rather than "exist", "go" rather than "proceed", "know" rather than "comprehend", "do" rather than "perform", "execute" or "carry out". Whenever you write a long word, consider a short one instead. When you write a long sentence or paragraph, ask yourself why

Bric Brazil, Russia, India and China collectively, all relatively fast-growing developing economies; thus, eg the Bric countries. (The financial wizards who coined Bric are also responsible for Mint: Mexico, Indonesia, Nigeria and Turkey. Mercifully, perhaps, this has yet to gain quite the same currency in the wider world; if it has to be used at all, it should be explained)

bridges cap as in Severn Bridge, London Bridge, Southwark Bridge, Golden Gate Bridge

Britain is now widely used as another name for the United Kingdom or Great Britain, and pragmatically we accept this usage. Strictly, *Great Britain* = England, Wales, Scotland and islands governed from the mainland (ie not Isle of Man or Channel Islands); *United Kingdom* = Great Britain and

Northern Ireland; *British Isles* = United Kingdom and the Republic of Ireland, Isle of Man and Channel Islands

British Overseas Territory eg Anguilla; Bermuda; British Antarctic Territory; British Indian Ocean Territory; British Virgin Islands; Cayman Islands; Falkland Islands; Gibraltar; Montserrat; Pitcairn Islands; South Georgia and the South Sandwich Islands; St Helena, Ascension and Tristan da Cunha; Turks & Caicos Islands. Note that they may have a premier rather than a prime minister, so always check

Britpop not Brit Pop; and *Britart*

Broadmoor inmates are patients, not prisoners, as it is a hospital

broadsheet retains some currency as a way to describe the serious British press, even though most British newspapers are now of a smaller format (tabloid, or compact; Berliner etc). *Quality, serious* or (at a pinch) *upmarket* may be used as appropriate synonyms

Brobdingnagian cap. Huge, immense, unnaturally large; from Brobdingnag, the imagined land of giants in Swift's *Gulliver's Travels*; use sparingly, for colour and rhetorical force, eg "a politician with a truly Brobdingnagian ego"

brownfield, greenfield as in building sites. But note *green belt* (two words)

brownie points lower case

Brummie (not Brummy), *Geordie, Scouse* etc, people and dialect, all capped

Brylcreem

BSE bovine spongiform encephalopathy, or *mad cow* (no need for quotes) *disease*. See **mad cow disease**

buddleia thus. *Buddleja* (cap, note j) is the scientific spelling, after Linnaeus, for the genus of shrubs known commonly as butterfly bush, but despite that, Collins and Oxford dictionaries give *buddleia* (lower case, note i) as the common spelling, and that is what we must use. See **wisteria** (what is it with botanists?)

budget lower case; the budget, Philip Hammond's budget, budget day; also note *pre-budget report* and *autumn statement* (lower case)

buffalo plural *buffaloes*

Buggins's turn awkward, perhaps, but consistent with *Times* style of such possessives

buglers, trumpeters cavalry regiments have trumpeters, infantry regiments have buglers. They are not interchangeable

builder's merchant(s) as in *shepherd's pies*, the apostrophe does not move in the plural

bulletproof adjective or verb, one word

bullion is gold or silver in unminted form

bull-mastiff, bull-terrier

bullring, bullfight(er)

bullseye

bumf prefer to bumph

bunga-bunga lower case, hyphen, eg in the context of sexually charged déshabillé partying linked to Silvio Berlusconi, the former Italian prime minister. The derivation is uncertain and theories abound, including genuine African origins, a Fascist colonialist-racist construct or a word given to Mr Berlusconi via Colonel Muammar Gaddafi, the deceased Libyan leader

bungee jumping no hyphen

bureau plural *bureaux* or *bureaus* depending on context; eg bureaux de change, Citizens Advice Bureaux; but prefer *bureaus* for writing desks and distant newspaper offices

burka prefer to burqa for the long, enveloping garment worn by Muslim women in public. The *niqab* is the piece of cloth that they use to cover the face. The *hijab* is a covering for the hair and neck

Burma not Myanmar (except in direct quotes); the inhabitants are *Burmese*, while *Burmans* are a Burmese people

Burns Night (caps, no apostrophe) falls on January 25

burnt not burned

Burton upon Trent no hyphens; and note the colloquial *gone for a burton* (lower case)

bus, buses noun; but in verbal use, *busses, bussed, bussing*

Bush, George W do not use Jr. Refer to him subsequently as Mr Bush or the former president. Refer to his father as the first President Bush or George Bush Sr

"businesses that depend on water" beware this and similar phrases. All businesses depend on water to some extent; some businesses, eg farms, are especially dependent on water

But there is no grammatical rule to prevent it starting a sentence; even Fowler describes this as a superstition. Be aware, however, that there are readers (and editors) who dislike it, and that it is easily overdone. Be sure, in any case, that "but" is the word you want; it often seems to be used to add a note of spurious drama where all that is meant is "and"

buyout and *buyback* one word as nouns; but prefer *buy-in, take-off, shake-out, shake-up, sell-off, sell-out* etc with hyphens, wherever the composite noun looks hideous

buzzword one word

by-election

bylaw

bypass noun or verb

by-product

bystander

byte (abbreviate as B) is a computer term for a small collection of *bits* (binary digits), roughly equivalent to one character. Do not confuse with *bite* (as with teeth). But note *soundbite*

Byzantine cap in historical context (art, architecture, empire); lower case in general use (complexities etc)

Cc

cabbie (not cabby) as colloquialism for *taxi driver*

cabinet lower case in both British and foreign use, whether used as a noun or adjectivally, except (rarely) if a cap seems absolutely necessary to avoid confusion. Note *Cabinet Office*, but *cabinet secretary* (or *secretary of the cabinet*), *war cabinet*. All cabinet committees should be lower case, eg the cabinet committee on science and technology

Caernarfon (town and parliamentary constituency, no longer Caernarvon), but *Lord Carnarvon*

caesarean section lower case. Babies are *delivered*, not born, by this surgery

café with accent

caffeine prefer to caffein

cagoule but *kaftan*

call centre noun, two words; hyphen as adjective, eg call-centre manager

call-up (noun), but *to call up*

camaraderie not cameraderie

Cambridge, University of colleges and halls are: Christ's College; Churchill College; Clare College; Clare Hall; Corpus Christi College; Darwin College; Downing College; Emmanuel College; Fitzwilliam College; Girton College; Gonville and Caius College; Homerton College; Hughes Hall; Jesus College; King's College; Lucy Cavendish College; Magdalene

College; Murray Edwards College (formerly known as New Hall); Newnham College; Pembroke College; Peterhouse; Queens' College; Robinson College; St Catharine's College; St Edmund's College; St John's College; Selwyn College; Sidney Sussex College; Trinity College; Trinity Hall; Wolfson College

came as or *comes as* overused device that links, or tries to link, two loosely related bits of news within a single story ("The announcement of the rise in interest rates came as demonstrators took to the streets"); often smacks of desperation

camellia not camelia

camomile prefer to chamomile

Canada nationally there is a prime minister; in the provinces there are premiers

Canadians are rightly annoyed when they are designated as Americans. Beware. Among prominent Canadians are Paul Anka, kd lang, Joni Mitchell, Donald Sutherland, Neil Young etc etc

canal boats do not use the term "barge" indiscriminately; *barges* are towed, unpowered boats for transporting cargo. Use the term *narrow boats* for the boats on the narrow 7ft-wide canals, or *canal boats* for wider vessels on wider canals. If in doubt, use *canal boat* (never canal barge)

canapé accent

cancer take care not to describe cancer as "the biggest killer" in the UK. Heart disease is. Beware of writing about cancer in terms of battles, fights, brave struggles etc: such language can imply a lack of strength or effort or will on the part of others who succumb to the disease; this rightly upsets and offends

cannon (military) same form for singular and plural; but *canons* (ecclesiastical, both churchmen and church laws), and *canon* as a collection/list of an author

Canute prefer the traditional spelling to the more historically authentic Cnut, if only to mitigate the consequences of careless typing. Remember that his intention on the seashore was to demonstrate the worthlessness of temporal power; he knew he was going to get wet

canvas (as in painting); plural is *canvases*; *canvasses* with central ss is of the verb "to canvass" (ie polling)

CAP all caps for clarity; when spelt out is lower case *common agricultural policy*; similarly, *common fisheries policy* (CFP)

cap and trade noun; adjectivally hyphenate, eg a cap-and-trade system for carbon emissions

capitalisation too many capital letters are ugly and distracting. Capitals are often unnecessary. Try to avoid them unless to do so causes confusion or looks absurd. There will always be room for discretion and common sense, and clarity is more important than consistency, but if in doubt use lower case. Do not use capitals to indicate importance or (with some rare, specified exceptions) as a mark of respect. Avoid especially what the 1959 edition of this guide called the "local interest" capital: "the Canteen of the works journal, the Umpire of the laws of cricket, the Directors of the company prospectus, the Village Hall of the parish magazine".

The following guidance sets out some general principles. See also under individual alphabetical entries.

Job descriptions, titles and names

Almost all job descriptions should be lower case. This includes all company chairmen, vice-presidents, managing directors, chief executive officers, general secretaries, ambassadors, editors etc.

There are, however, some (not many) job descriptions that are also titles, ie that are commonly (and formally) used in conjunction with the proper name of the person holding the position in question. These take a capital when used as titles in front of the name but lower case at all other times. So, for instance, we would refer to President Trump but to Donald Trump's election as president of the United States. We would refer to President Putin but to the Russian president's influence on the world. We would refer to Professor Jones, but to the professor's latest book.

In British usage *political job descriptions* are not generally attached to names as titles in this way. We do not refer to Prime Minister May, or to Chancellor of the Exchequer Hammond or to Foreign Secretary Johnson. These should all, therefore, be lower case at all times. Theresa May, the prime minister; Philip Hammond, the chancellor of the exchequer; Boris Johnson, the foreign secretary. Similarly the secretary of state for defence, the permanent secretary, the shadow chancellor, the cabinet secretary, the leader of the opposition, the minister of state for policing, criminal justice and victims at the Home Office. This may seem unsettling at first, but it is clearer and more consistent than any of the other options. The Speaker is a rare exception, as clarity seems to demand a cap (a deputy speaker remains lower case, however, as there is no risk of comparable confusion); be prepared to consider similar exceptions as they arise; do not pursue consistency at the expense of clarity or common sense.

The *titles of ecclesiastical dignitaries* may be said to describe a position or job, but they also name an individual holder of that position (even when no surname is given), and they may be attached as titles in front of a name (as political or other job titles in British usage are not). As a courtesy, they take a capital letter when used as names (which in practice will generally be at first mention); subsequent references are lower case; in this they are treated in the same way as aristocratic titles (see below) rather than, eg political jobs. This may be slightly anomalous, but it is probably what most *Times* readers expect, even in a secular age. So, the Archbishop of Canterbury, or Archbishop Welby, but then the archbishop;

the Bishop of London, or Bishop Chartres, then the bishop; the Dean of St Paul's, or Dean Inge, subsequently the dean; the Archdeacon of Barchester, or Archdeacon Grantly, then the archdeacon. Lower case when referring not to the individual but generally to holders of the office: future archbishops of Canterbury, the role of dean of Westminster, the first woman bishop of Gloucester etc.

Royalty etc The Queen, exceptionally, and as a courtesy, remains the Queen (upper case) at subsequent mentions, whenever the individual monarch is intended (likewise in historical stories referring to the reigning monarch of the day). There is no need for other monarchs or for senior members of the royal family to have capitals at all times; so, treat in the same way as senior clergy: the King of Spain, then the king; the Duke of Edinburgh, then the duke; the Prince of Wales, or Prince Charles, then the prince; the Duke of Cambridge, then the duke; Prince Harry, then the prince. The courtesy of a capital at all times is also extended to the Pope, whenever the individual pontiff is intended. When referring to the position of queen or pope rather than the person, use lower case: "the Queen (or Queen Elizabeth II) has had an impressive reign, which any future queen will struggle to match"; "the Pope (or Pope Francis) is the first pope to come from Latin America".

Aristocrats The Duke of Wherever is thus at first mention; subsequently the duke; never Lord W. *Other aristocrats* take a capital when named in full: the Marquess of X; Viscount Y; the Earl of Z; at subsequent references all normally become Lord X, Y, Z (although the marquess, the viscount, the earl etc would be acceptable for occasional variety). Lower case when not naming individuals: an earlier marquess of Bath, future earls of Oxford, the seat of the dukes of Devonshire etc.

Similarly with *military ranks*, General Jackson would usually remain General Jackson at subsequent mentions, but the general might be used if variety seems necessary.

Police ranks are capped when attached to names: Chief Inspector Morse etc; subsequently the chief inspector or Mr Morse; chief constable, like prime minister, is not generally used with a name. We don't say Chief Constable Jones, it remains lower case: Mr Jones, the chief constable; the chief constable of Merseyside etc.

With few exceptions, such as those indicated, resist using capitals to indicate the dignity or supposed dignity of a position.

Government departments etc The names of specific government departments and other significant national or international bodies or organisations are upper case when the full name is used (the Ministry of Defence, the Department for Education, the European Commission, the Law Society, the Football Association, the Independent Press Standards Organisation) but otherwise (or subsequently) lower case: the ministry, the education department, the commission, the regulator etc. The Home Office, the Foreign Office, the Cabinet Office, the Treasury remain upper case. All committees, etc, are lower case. In local government, generally upper case only for the name of the place: Norwich city council, West Somerset rural district council planning department (if such a thing exists).

Political terms in general Government, parliament, administration and cabinet are always lower case except when used as part of an official title, such as Government House, Houses of Parliament, Her Majesty's Government or the Cabinet Office. The opposition is likewise lower case; there is some risk of ambiguity, but context will usually make quite clear what is meant. (Her Majesty's Opposition, like Her Majesty's Government, would be upper case if for some reason used.) Also lower case for all references to the state (except in naming, eg the US State Department): a state visit, the state opening of parliament, church and state. The word party is upper case where it it integral to the title: thus Labour Party, Conservative Party, Social and Democratic Labour Party

(SDLP) and United Kingdom Independence Party (Ukip). Similarly in the case of foreign parties where the equivalent word is integral to the title: Popular Party (Partido Popular of Spain), Workers' Party, Freedom Party etc.

Terms derived from proper names There are grey areas here and common sense is required.

As a general principle, with terms derived from the names of people (or peoples), the closer the connection with the proper name, the more likely it is to be upper case. Christian values, Thatcherite Tories, Homeric epithets and Marxist academics, for instance, all depend for their significance on the proper noun from which they derive; without knowing something of Christ, Margaret Thatcher, Homer or Karl Marx, we will not understand what is meant. When we talk of spartan conditions, herculean tasks, gargantuan appetites and quixotic acts, however, we are using words which have become common adjectives; they denote familiar attributes, and their meaning may be understood by people who know nothing of Greek history or myth, and who have never read Rabelais or Cervantes.

It will often be difficult to draw such a neat distinction, however. In such cases, rather than waste time worrying over how close the connection may be between a word and the person or place to which it refers, consider what is likely to seem more natural to the reader. This is an area in which our general preference for lower case may have to be qualified. Because we are so used to seeing them capped, the names of people and places (and the proper adjectives derived from them) tend often simply to look wrong when lower case.

For examples see the lists under *food and drink, animals and birds, dogs, cheeses, wines* etc. They are not exhaustive. They undoubtedly contain some expressions where the capital letter may seem otiose; the question to ask then is whether the needless capital in those phrases is more irritating than a missing capital would be in the rest.

God Cap when referring to the deity of monotheistic religions. No need for he, his, him to take cap unless there is a risk of confusion. Where there are many gods, use lower case, as in the Greek gods (or eg the Greek god of war).

When spelling out *capitalised abbreviations* such as CAP (common agricultural policy) use lower case.

Compass points and other terms indicating location except in proper place names, these are now generally lower case: east London, central London, west Africa, eastern Europe etc. See entries below

capsize is spelt thus. See **-ise, -isation**

captions are often read before the reports to which they relate. They need to make sense on their own, and to explain as much of the story as space allows. It is surprising how often this basic journalistic principle is overlooked. They should be clear, informative and, where appropriate, witty; they should make the reader want to go on to read the story. What they must not be is pointless or dull. Do not state the obvious. Readers can see the photograph for themselves; there is no need to describe what it quite clearly shows; say something useful or interesting about it instead. Dismal local-paper caption clichés — sharing a joke, in happier times etc — are banned.

Style in captions When a caption covers two or more images it should start with the main one. When space is tight, especially on single-column "mugshots", the name may be just the surname, even when the person is titled, eg Sir Marcus Fox would be simply Fox, as in headlines. Where women are photographed be sensitive: readers complain about our omitting the Christian name, especially in court cases where the woman is the victim. Where possible give the woman's full name, although this is not a hard-and-fast ruling.

When identifying faces with *left* and *right* etc, use commas rather than brackets (eg Fred Smith, left, and his wife, Jean, leaving the court); make the identification in the caption fit the sequence of faces (left to right) in the photograph. Words such as "pictured" and "inset" should be redundant. Note that, as in text, double quotation marks are used in captions, including narrow-measure captions next to narrow-measure illustrations. Don't tie yourself in knots trying to link lots of pictures in a single caption of continuous prose; if it can be done, and done elegantly, so much the better; if not, opt for clarity instead and link separate caption elements with semi-colons

carabiniere (lower case), an Italian police officer; plural *carabinieri*

carat a measure of purity in gold (24-carat is 100 per cent); in precious stones and pearls, a measure of weight. The international carat is standardised at 200mg (0.2g; about 7/1000th of an ounce)

car boot sale no hyphen

carcass

cardholder

cardiac arrest not synonymous with *heart attack*; check which is meant, and do not change one to the other

careen to sway or cause to sway dangerously over to one side; too often confused with *career*, to move swiftly along, rush in an uncontrolled way

care home company etc no need to hyphenate

cargo prefer *cargos* as the plural

carmaker one word

car park two words; *multistorey car park*

carpetbagger one word

case was "an overworked word" in the 1959 edition of this guide; it still is

cashcard in general sense; *cashflow, cashback*

cash for honours, cash for peerages no need for quotes for these two phrases; but they do need hyphens when adjectival, eg the cash-for-honours inquiry, the cash-for-peerages affair

Cashpoint is Lloyds Bank's trademarked cash machine system, so takes the cap and must not be used generically; in the general sense, use *cash dispenser* or *cash machine*, or less formally, *hole in the wall*

Castilian (*castellano*) is the standard spoken and literary Spanish of Spain; *Catalan* is the distinct language of Catalonia

casualties be cautious in use of early and unconfirmed estimates of casualties in instances of terrorism, militia gunfights or disasters. Give the estimate's source where possible, and be aware of politically inspired exaggeration

catapult not catapault

Catch-22 there is a hyphen in the title of Joseph Heller's 1961 satirical novel; avoid altogether the grossly overworked cliché Catch-22 situation

catchphrase one word

cathedrals cap when giving the full name, eg St Paul's Cathedral, Wells Cathedral; similarly the names of churches, eg St Mary's Church, Ely, unless we know that the church name specifically excludes it, eg St Stephen's, Ely

Catherine one of those names that should always be checked: Catharine, Katherine, Katharine, Kathryn etc are all possible. cf **Alistair**

Catholic in church context, say Roman Catholic at first mention if necessary to make clear that this is what is meant. Eg if there could be confusion with Eastern rite churches or with those Anglicans who call themselves Catholic. Otherwise, if context is clear, just say Catholic

CAT scan to avoid confusion, exceptionally keep caps in this acronym; not Cat scan

cat's eyes should preferably be called reflecting roadstuds. Catseye is a trademark

caviar no final e

CBI no need to spell out as Confederation of British Industry

ceasefire

ceilidh social gathering (Highland)

Cellophane is proprietary, so cap

celsius, centigrade use either term. In news stories use centigrade first then fahrenheit in brackets at first mention, eg "The temperature rose to 16C (61F)." Take great care with conversions, which often seem to go wrong

census lower case even in specific cases, such as the 1901 census, the 2001 census

centenarian also *septuagenarian, octogenarian, nonagenarian*

centenaries use *centenary, bicentenary, tercentenary*; after that, say *four-hundredth anniversary* or *five-hundredth anniversary*

central Europe with lower case c; also *central London* etc; likewise *northern Europe, southern Europe.* Use lower case also for *eastern* and *western Europe* except in historical context of the Cold War, but *Central America* needs cap for clarity

centre, the as with (the) left and (the) right, use lower case in political context unless clarity demands a cap. Similarly for compound nouns, the centre left, the centre right, and for adjectives, a centre-left politician with a rightwing policy

Centre Court at Wimbledon upper case; likewise No 1 Court, No 14 Court etc

centrepiece no hyphen

centring but *centering* of arches in bridge-building

centuries the style is the 3rd century BC, the 9th century, the 18th century etc; and adjectivally with the hyphen, eg 20th-century architecture

Ceylon the former name for Sri Lanka. The people are Sri Lankan, the majority group are the Sinhalese

cha-cha-cha not cha-cha

chainsaw one word

chair do not refer to anyone as a "the chair of" anything, unless in a direct quote. Neither must you use "chairperson". A man must be referred to as a *chairman* and a woman as a *chairwoman*. Even if a person's official title is "chair of ..." use chairman or chairwoman (lower case). This is not sexist, it is simply a preference for calling things (and people) by their names, and a reluctance to allow ugly and unnecessary jargon to replace perfectly good words. A professor may, however, be said to hold the chair of theoretical physics, or whatever; a person can chair (used as a verb) a committee; and questions can be put through the chair (which is the office held). Similarly, write *spokesman* or *spokeswoman*. If the gender of the person is not clear, write spokesman

chaise longue two words, no hyphen; plural *chaises longues* (s on both words)

chamber (lower case) of the House of Commons

champagne lower case, because we use it as an English common noun rather than a French proper name. Use only, however, for the product of the Champagne region of France, to which its proper application is restricted by law; otherwise write, eg Russian sparkling wine. The champagne producers protect their name rigorously. See **wines**

Champions League (European football), no apostrophe

chancellor of the exchequer lower case

changeable

Changing the Guard not ... of the Guard

Channel, the upper case. Generally, no need to write "the English Channel" for the body of water between England and France

Channel tunnel lower case tunnel, unless there is some possibility of confusion; also, *Channel tunnel rail link*

Chanukkah prefer this to variants such as Hanukkah etc, for the Jewish festival of lights

chaos overused, and often hyperbole; *confusion, disorder, upheaval, turmoil, disarray*: say what is meant

charge that an Americanism, never to be used as a synonym of *allege that*

charisma has become a boring cliché; try to find an alternative such as *presence, inspiration* etc

charters (as in John Major's now forgotten initiative) lower case

château plural *châteaux*

Chatham House rule, the strictly speaking just the one, so don't write Chatham House rules. It says that information disclosed at a meeting may be used or reported by those present on condition that neither the source nor anyone else attending is identified

chat room two words, but *chatline* one

chat show, **game show**, **quiz show**, **talk show** etc no hyphens when used as noun or when adjectival, eg chat show host; note also *chatline, sexline*

cheap goods are cheap, prices are low

check-in (noun) but *check in* (verb)

checklist, **checkout counter** note also *checkup* (noun); *check up* (verb)

cheerleader one word

cheeses we tried making these all lower case. It worked, but it always seemed a triumph of consistency over common sense. Readers are used in most contexts to seeing capital letters at the start of proper nouns and adjectives, especially place names. So that is what we should do. Wensleydale, Lancashire, Red Leicester, Cheshire and their foreign equivalents simply seem more natural than the lower case alternative. This will give us a few more capital letters in the paper than we might like, but for it to become a problem, we would have to write about cheeses a lot more often than we do. Exceptions are made for cheddar and brie, which are almost universally treated as common nouns (Canadian cheddar, Irish cheddar, Somerset brie). See **foodstuffs**

chequebook one word, either as noun or adjective (eg chequebook journalism)

chi prefer to qi for the vital energy in oriental medicine, martial arts etc believed to circulate around the body in currents

chickenpox no hyphen; similarly *smallpox*

chief constable lower case, the chief constable of Lancashire or the chief constable. Do not write, eg the chief constable of West Midlands police, but simply the chief constable of the West Midlands

chief inspector of prisons/schools also *chief medical officer*

chief of the defence staff is the professional head of the British armed forces and the principal military adviser to the defence secretary and the government; the *chief of the general staff* is the professional head of the British army

chief petty officer is an NCO (non-commissioned officer) in the Royal Navy, not an officer

Chief Rabbi cap at first mention when naming the individual, then the chief rabbi or refer to as Rabbi X or Lord Y (like the Archbishop of Canterbury). See **capitalisation** (*titles of ecclesiastical dignitaries*)

chief whip lower case

child access, child custody do not use these terms regarding divorce unless in direct quotes and from lay people. Under the Children Act 1989 children are given *residence* with one parent and the other in disputed cases has *contact*. Put more simply, children live with one parent and the other is allowed to see them

childcare as healthcare

childminder one word

child pornography/child porn never use these terms, except in direct quotes. Use instead *internet child sex abuse, sex abuse images*, or similar

children's names generally for under-18s, write eg John Jones at first mention and then simply John at second mention

child-sex abusers/offenders use hyphen

chilli (plural *chillies*) prefer to chili

chill out two words as verb; one word as noun or adjective

chimera prefer to chimaera

chimpanzees are apes, not monkeys

Chinese cap C in idioms such as Chinese whispers, Chinese walls

Chinese names use the Pinyin rather than the traditional Wade-Giles, so write *Beijing, Mao Zedong* (though *Chairman Mao* or just *Mao* are acceptable), *Zhou Enlai* etc. Normal style is to place family name first, then given name, so that the actress Zhang Zivi, for instance, becomes Zhang at second mention. For place names, follow *The Times Atlas of the World* except where older usage is well established, eg the special administrative regions *Hong Kong* (not Xianggang) and *Macau* (not Aomen); and the autonomous regions *Tibet* (not Xizang) and *Inner Mongolia* (not Neimengu)

chip and PIN no hyphen as a noun or adjectivally

chocoholic but *shopaholic* and *workaholic*

chopper, **copter** not to be used as substitutes for helicopter, even in headlines

Christ discourage use as a casual exclamation or expletive; it offends many readers

Christ Church (the Oxford college), two words, thus, and never Christ Church College

Christchurch in Dorset and New Zealand

christened Christians are christened; ships, trains and people not known to be Christians are named

Christian, **Christianity** *unchristian, non-Christian, antichristian, Antichrist*

Christian Democrat cap when referring to specific European parties for both noun and adjective, as in Christian Democrat MP

Christian names take care in context of non-Christians; in such cases use *forename* or *first name*

Christian terms mostly lower case when possible but cap eg *the Bible, the (Ten) Commandments, the Cross, the Crucifixion, the Resurrection, Mass, Holy Communion* (and simply *Communion*), *Eucharist, Blessed Sacrament, Advent, Nativity* (also cap adjectival *Advent calendar, Nativity play*), *the Scriptures*; also when naming the persons of the Trinity, *God* (*the Father*), *Jesus Christ* and the *Holy Spirit*; but then follow the Vatican and Lambeth Palace in using lower case for *he/his* except where clarity demands a cap ("Isaiah looks forward to God rescuing His people", ie God's, not Isaiah's). Cap the names of books of the Bible: *the Book of Revelation, Acts of the Apostles, the Gospel of (or According to) Matthew*; but generally lower case for *the apostles, the disciples, gospel, the gospels*. Use lower case for *evensong, matins*. There are columnists and feature writers who like to use eg God, Christ and Jesus as harmless exclamations or mild expletives; they should know that this offends many *Times* readers

Christmas Day, **Christmas Eve** seem to need caps

church cap in names — the Church of England, St James's Church, Piccadilly etc — but otherwise only if absolutely necessary to distinguish an institution from a building ("the Church is often said to be in terminal decline, but the church I attended on Sunday was absolutely packed"). Context will usually suffice to make clear which is meant, so lower case should be possible more often than not

Church in Wales not Church of Wales for the disestablished Anglican church once headed by Dr Rowan Williams

churchwarden one word

cinemagoer as *concertgoer, operagoer, theatregoer* etc

cipher not cypher

circa abbreviate simply as c (roman) followed by a space

City of London the City, City prices

civil list (lower case unless clarity demands caps) has been replaced by the *sovereign grant* (also lower case unless clarity demands caps)

civil partnership commonly referred to as gay marriage before gay marriage became legal. A suggested shorthand for headings is *civil union*

civil service, also *civil servants* lower case as a noun unless clarity demands a cap. Otherwise lower case in adjectival use, eg a civil service memorandum. Lower case for the administrative grade, ie *permanent secretary*, *deputy secretary* and *assistant secretary*, when used as part of the full title; thus, Sir Alfred Beach, permanent secretary to the Ministry of Defence

civil war generally lower case but by convention cap the *English Civil War* and the *American Civil War*

claim do not use when simply *said* or *declared* would do. The word carries a suspicion of incredulity. Also, avoid the loose construction in sentences such as "The firm launched a drink which is claimed to promote learning ability". This should read "... a drink which, it is claimed, promotes learning ability". Do not allow terrorists to "claim responsibility" for their crimes

claims and facts remember to distinguish between a claim and a fact, particularly in headlines/standfirsts. Witnesses to rioting telling amid confusion of up to 600 people dead did not justify an unequivocal standfirst death toll of 600; if claims are made, say who is making them

clamour, clamouring but *clamorous*

clampdown not banned, but use as little as possible

Clapham Junction is not Clapham. It is not even in Clapham. They are separate places and their names are not interchangeable.

Clapham is in the London Borough of Lambeth; Clapham Junction is in the Battersea part of Wandsworth. A reader helpfully noted, at the time of the London riots in August 2011: "The Victorians are responsible for the confusion that has persisted for generations. When they opened their large interchange station in 1863 they designated it Clapham Junction because that district was then much more genteel than working-class Battersea"

clarinettist

Class A, B or C drugs (cap C)

clichés and hype We are lucky to have intelligent and sophisticated readers. They buy *The Times* to avoid the hype and the stale words and phrases peddled by some other papers. Words such as shock, bombshell, crisis, scandal, sensational, controversial, desperate, dramatic, fury, panic, chaos etc are too often ways of telling the readers what to think. Let them decide for themselves.

Any list of proscribed formulas is soon out of date, as old clichés give way to new. There may be nothing inherently wrong with the words or phrases themselves. They gain currency in the first place because they seem vivid, amusing, fresh. Soon, however, they become fashionable, are overused, grow tired and stale, then finally cease to mean anything much at all. A good writer or editor will know when a word or phrase has outlived its usefulness

climate change levy lower case, no hyphen

clingfilm lower case, one word

cliquey

clock tower two words

closed-circuit television

Clostridium difficile is a bacterium, not a virus. Write *C. difficile* at second mention (and as a bonus do not pronounce it "DIF-ficil": it is not French but Latin. Try "dif-FI-chil-ay")

clothing say *menswear, women's wear, children's wear, sportswear*

cloud-cuckoo-land two hyphens

clouds no need to italicise the names. Four main types: nimbus produce rain; stratus resemble layers; cumulus resemble heaps; and cirrus resemble strands or filaments of hair. Prefixes denote altitude, ie strato (low-level), alto (mid-level) and cirro (high-level)

clubbable

co- the prefix does not normally require a hyphen even before an e or another o unless confusion or utter hideousness might result. Thus *co-operate* (but *uncooperative*), *co-opt, co-ordinate* (but *uncoordinated*), *coeducation, coexist*

CO_2 use subscript

coalface, coalfield, coalmine (each one word) similarly *coalminer* (but prefer miner)

coalition lower case noun or adjective, eg the coalition government

coastguard lower case and one word, in the British context; but note the *Maritime and Coastguard Agency* (caps for full name), although the *coastguard service* (generic) retains the lower case. The US *coast guard*

coasts lower case *south coast, east coast, west coast* and *north coast* in all contexts

coats of arms see **heraldry**

Coca-Cola (hyphen); note also the trademark Coke. Similarly Pepsi-Cola. If in doubt about the identity of a beverage, write the lower case generic cola

cock a snook not snoop, please

cockfight no hyphen, as *bullfight* and *dogfight*

cockney lower case for the person, the dialect and adjectival use

codebreaker, codebreaking one word

coeducation(al) but permissible to use *co-ed* in headlines as coed would look hideous

coexist

cognoscenti roman, not italic

Coldstream Guards may be called *the Coldstream* and the men *Coldstreamers* or *Coldstream Guards*; neither should be called Coldstreams

Cold War caps

collarbone one word

collectibles (not -ables) items sought by collectors

collective nouns usually use the singular verb, as with corporate bodies (the company, the government, the council etc). But this rule is not inviolable; the key is to stick to the singular or plural throughout the story: sentences such as "The committee, which was elected recently, presented their report" are unacceptable. Prefer plural use for the couple, family, music groups and bands, the public, sports teams

Colombia is the country; *Columbia* is the Hollywood studio, university, river and Washington district. Also, note *British Columbia* and *pre-Columbian*

colons throw meaning forward and introduce lists

Colosseum in Rome; *Coliseum* in London

Coloureds (in South Africa), cap; not to be used in any other context

comedienne avoid; use *comedian* (or, if you must, *comic*) for both sexes

comeuppance no hyphen

commander-in-chief, officer commanding lower case

Commandments cap in biblical context, as the *Ten Commandments*, the *Fourth Commandment*

commando plural *commandos* (not -oes)

commas Unnecessary commas interrupt the flow of a sentence; omit the comma before *if, unless, before, after, as, since, when* unless the rhythm or sense of the sentence demands it.

Keith Waterhouse, as so often, had sound advice: "It is not the function of the comma to help a wheezing sentence get its breath back. That, however, is how the comma earns much of its living in journalism." If your sentence needs a comma just to stop the reader collapsing in a heap before reaching the end, you might do better to recast it as two sentences anyway.

There is often no need for a comma after an adverbial formation at the beginning of a sentence: "Last week we were told etc", "Until now there has been no need etc", "In opposition the Lib Dems said etc", "Minutes later the announcement was made".

Avoid the so-called Oxford comma; write "he ate bread, butter and jam" rather than "he ate bread, butter, and jam", except where to do so might create nonsense or confusion: "For lunch they had lamb with roast potatoes, and chocolate mousse."

Commas with names and descriptions may help to indicate number. If "he was accompanied by his brother John" suggests that he has other brothers who did not accompany him, then "he was accompanied by his brother, John" makes clear that John is the only brother he has. With brothers the distinction may seem too subtle to bother about; it is worth bearing in mind when naming someone's wife.

There is no need to put a comma between adjectives that form a kind of unit or where the last adjective is in closer relation to the noun than the preceding one(s), eg fine dry evenings, a good little boy.

Keep commas where they should be logically in "broken" sentences. Thus, the comma goes outside in the following example: "The trouble is", he said, "that this is a contentious issue"

Commission when named: the *European Commission,* the *Competition Commission*; lower case in other refs

commissioner of the Metropolitan Police

commit do not use as an intransitive verb without a direct object, eg "he wants to commit to the reforms"; write "he wants to commit himself to the reforms" or "he wants to make a commitment to the reforms"

committee on standards in public life examines standards of conduct of all holders of public office. It is different from the *select committee on standards and privileges*, which deals with the conduct of MPs (subsequent mentions, the *privileges select committee* or lower case *the committee*)

committees are generally lower case but note 1922 *Committee* (cap) of Tory backbenchers, as it looks odd lower case. Cabinet and select committees should be lower case

common agricultural policy lower case, abbreviated as CAP for clarity; similarly, *common fisheries policy* (CFP)

common market usually use EU or EC (see **Europe**), although *common market* is acceptable in its historical context

common sense (noun), but *commonsense, commonsensical* (adjective)

common serjeant lower case. Note j spelling

Commons (keep cap) takes singular verb, eg "the Commons is debating ..."

Commons fees office lower case. At subsequent mention *the fees office* for the place where decisions are made about whether to reimburse members' expenses for moats and beams

Commonwealth heads of government meeting lower case after cap C

communiqué

communism, communist as with socialism and socialist, the best rule of thumb is to cap only when in specific party context, eg a Communist candidate, a Communist rally, the Communist mayor of Lille; but communist ideology, communist countries etc. Likewise *fascist*. It will help to think of a parallel with *conservative/conservatism* or *liberal/ liberalism*. But *Marxist, Stalinist* and *Nazi* should be capped

community beware overuse in phrases such as the international community, the black community etc

companies there was once a useful distinction to be made between *company* and *firm*; the latter implied a business partnership, as in the legal or accountancy professions, estate agents etc. The words now seem to be used more or less interchangeably to cover almost any sort of enterprise, not least because the shorter word has obvious advantages for headlines

company names and brand names Follow the style and spelling that the company prefers unless it is ugly, distracting or absurd; use common sense. In practice, given the irritating prevalence of initial minuscules and mid-word caps in the modern corporate world, this will mean applying conventional orthography to many names that the companies themselves choose to write differently. So, use all caps only if a name consists of (and is pronounced as) a series of initials: BMW, IBM, EDF etc. Otherwise generally (and if in doubt) use an initial cap followed by lower case as for any other name, even if corporate branding is all upper or lower case or has capitals in odd places: Adidas (not adidas), Amazon (not amazon), Ikea (not IKEA), Easyjet, (not easyJet), Moneysupermarket (not MoneySuperMarket), Talktalk (not TalkTalk), Talksport (not talkSPORT) etc. An exception is made for the small number of household name global brands that have a capital as their second letter: iPad, iPhone, eBay; these may be written thus, and there seems no need to give them an extra initial capital even when they start a sentence or headline (something they should do only if it cannot be avoided). Prefer to ignore spurious typographical symbols in contrived or gimmicky spellings: Yahoo not Yahoo!, Eon not E.ON, Fevertree not Fever-Tree etc. Abbreviate to Co in, eg John Brown & Co. Company is singular. No full points in company titles, as in WH Smith and J Sainsbury. Usually no need to add Ltd, plc, LLP etc

company, ship's all the officers and men

comparatively, relatively avoid using as synonyms of *fairly* or *middling*

comparatives use correctly to indicate the numbers involved: *older* (of two), *oldest* (of three or more); similarly *younger*, *youngest* etc

compare with/to *compare with* (the more common use) when differences or contrasts are the point: "compare the saints with the devils" or "compared with last year's figures" etc. *Compare to* for likenesses: "compare this image to a damsel fair"

comparisons beware of those which are confusing, incomprehensible or meaningless: to say that something is five times bigger than something else may make sense (if not precisely the same sense as saying that it is five times the size, so take care); to say that something is five times smaller is to baffle any reader who thinks about it for long

compass points generally take lower case (and no hyphen in compounds). So *north, south, east, west; southeast, northeast, northwest, southwest.* Likewise, lower case for general locations: the west of Scotland, the north of England, south Wales. Caps for proper names of specific places, eg counties, regions and, exceptionally, where clarity, common sense or familiar usage demands: *East Anglia, Northern Ireland, North Yorkshire, West Yorkshire, South Yorkshire,* the *East Riding of Yorkshire* (also *East Yorkshire,* not a county but once a local government district, still a parliamentary constituency, and odd lower case if the Yorkshire counties are all capped); the *West Midlands,* the *East Midlands* (the latter not a county, but one of the nine English regions, formerly Government Office Regions, used for official statistical purposes: *the South East, London, the North West, the East of England, the West*

Midlands, the South West, Yorkshire and the Humber, the East Midlands, the North East). Recognised geographical and cultural areas taking caps for clarity include the *Western Isles*, the *East End/West End* of London (following common usage; but *east London, west London*), the *West Country* etc.

Overseas, cap the following: *the Midwest* (US), *the Deep South, North America, South America, Latin America, Central America*; lower case *west Africa, north Africa, east Africa, central Africa* (but *Central African Republic*), *southern Africa* (but *South Africa*); upper case *North and South Atlantic*, the *Middle/Far East, sub-Saharan Africa* and *south India* (except in the *Church of South India*)

compensation not to be encouraged as a pompous word for pay in the case of top executives

complement completing something

compliment praise or tribute

complimentary approving, congratulatory; also the spelling you want for "free of charge"

comprehensive spending review all lower case

comprise means to consist of, be composed of. Avoid the ugly "comprising of", beloved of estate agents

comptroller general lower case

concertgoer as with *cinemagoer, operagoer, partygoer, theatregoer*, but *concert hall*

confectionery sweets, cakes etc. A *confectionary* is (or may be) a place where confectionery is kept or made; this is a word you will rarely need, not least because *confectionery* will happily cover this sense too; if you insist on using it, readers will think you cannot spell

Confederacy cap for the southern states in the American Civil War

conference keep lower case in Labour Party conference, Liberal Democrat conference etc

congestion charge lower case

Congo take care to distinguish between the *Democratic Republic of Congo* (formerly Zaire, and before that Belgian Congo) and the far smaller *Republic of the Congo*, which may also be referred to as *Congo (Brazzaville)*, and was formerly a French colony

Congress (US) but *congressional* lower case and *congressman* also lower case, except when used as a title with a name, eg Congressman John Waldorfburger; but generally try to avoid this US construction and say John Waldorfburger, a congressman from Minnesota etc

conjoined twins the proper medical term for Siamese twins

conjunctions avoid unnecessary buts, ands, howevers, yets. Always revise a sentence to see what conjunctions could be removed; two sentences may be better than one

conjuror prefer to conjurer

conman one word, as *hitman*

connection

consensus never concensus; the word is a cliché that should be avoided wherever possible. Furthermore, since consensus means general or widespread agreement, do not use tautologies such as general consensus, broad consensus, wide consensus, consensus of opinion etc

Conservative Party *Conservative central office* (lower case), second mention *central office* (never CCO); *Conservative chairman, manifesto* etc; *Tory* is permissible as a less formal alternative, *Tory party* (lower case p). Abbreviate in lists etc to C (not, for obvious reasons, Con)

considerable avoid its use as a lazy adjective implying emphasis

consistency a virtue promoted by this guide, but not one to be pursued at the expense of clarity, elegance or common sense

consortium plural *consortiums* (not consortia); as a general rule, use the -ums plural

constituencies, parliamentary generally, follow the format of place name first and then compass point, area etc, eg Ilford South (not South Ilford), Sheffield Hallam (no comma)

constitution of a country is lower case whether it is an actual document or not: the American constitution, the British constitution

consult never say "consult with". See also **meet**

Continent, the referring to mainland Europe, but lower case *continental*

continuous means without intermission; *continual* means frequently recurring

contractions generally avoid in news reports. Permissible in features and less formal contexts. Beware of ambiguity: "he's" can mean "he is" or "he has"; the latter meaning is usually better spelt out. Never confuse it's and its

contract out has no hyphen

controller of Radio 1 etc no longer cap C

controversial a word almost always best deleted

convener not convenor

convertible (not -able), noun and adjective

conveyor belt a *conveyer* is a person who conveys

cooling towers pictures of these should not be used to illustrate stories about air pollution. They emit water vapour, which is harmless

co-operate, co-ordinate etc hyphenate for clarity; but no hyphen when further prefixed, eg *uncooperative, uncoordinated, non-cooperation*

co-production, co-producer etc use hyphen to avoid ambiguity with copro-, as in dung

copycat no hyphen

copyright (sole right in artistic work etc); *copywriter* (advertising)

cornettist

cornflakes generic

Coronation cap when referring to a specific ceremonial event, such as Elizabeth II's in 1953, but lower case in adjectival uses, eg coronation ceremony, coronation broadcast, coronation oath

coroner's court at inquests, the coroner is lower case, as in the Westminster coroner. Juries return the verdict, the coroner records it. There are no coroner's inquests in Scotland; violent deaths are reported to the procurator fiscal, who may hold an inquiry

correspondents wherever possible, write the political correspondent of *The Times*, the Moscow correspondent of *The Times* etc; but the *Times* political correspondent, the *Times* Moscow correspondent etc are permissible.

In an age that prizes first-person accounts there is mercifully little temptation for reporters to refer to themselves ponderously as "your correspondent". Any writer tempted to do so in jest should heed the 1959 edition of this guide: "The use of 'your correspondent' for droll effect flops nine times out of ten"

cortège use accent

coruscating (not corruscating) means sparkling or scintillating, not abrasive or corrosive. The word often meant by this malapropism is *excoriating*

councils cap only the place even in full title, eg Birmingham city council

council tax replacement for *poll tax/community charge*, so use the last two only in their historical context

counsel is both singular and plural in court contexts. Do not say "counsels for Mr X and Mrs Y"

counterproductive, counterattack, countertenor, counterterrorism etc one word

counties spell out names except in lists. Do not add -shire to Devon (except in Devonshire cream or the Duke of Devonshire),

Dorset, Somerset. Irish counties should be rendered as Co Donegal (cap C, no full point); Co Durham takes the same style. Take great care with new, reorganised or abolished counties

county abbreviations these may be used to save space, but only in special circumstances such as postal addresses at the end of letters, in listings etc. Do not use them in ordinary text, eg News, Business, Sport etc body text

coup d'état (note roman, accent) normally write just coup. Note coup de grâce (roman, accent), coup de théâtre (roman, accents)

couple treat this collective noun as a plural, eg "The couple are coming to terms with their plight"

court martial plural *courts martial, Courts-Martial Appeal Court;* verb, *to court-martial*

Court No 1 etc in a legal context

Court of Appeal always use the full title at first mention and wherever possible thereafter, but *appeal court* (lower case) may be used sparingly

Court of Arches is the court of appeal of the Province of Canterbury in the Church of England. Do not say Arches Court

Court of St James's

Court of Session, Edinburgh not Sessions

court reporting If in the slightest doubt, consult a lawyer.

Criminal cases Lawyers appear *for the prosecution, for the defence* (avoid "prosecuting", "defending"). To *admit* or *deny* an offence is preferred to "pleads guilty" or "pleads not guilty", although the latter form is not banned. Seek legal guidance before naming anybody under 17 in any court case. Do not report details of sex offences involving children and do not allow sex trial reports to become salacious. Also, do not identify any victims of alleged sexual offences or give information that, with other information available elsewhere, might allow so-called jigsaw identification. When reporting evidence take care with phrases such as "the court was told *how* ....", which may assume or imply truth in what was said. At the end of a court report say if the trial, or the hearing in a civil case, continues. Always give the verdict at the end of a trial or hearing. Prefer legally precise terms such as "not guilty" to eg "cleared", except in headlines. Beware of misusing "majority verdict"; this can refer only to a conviction, not an acquittal. Defendants take their Mr, Mrs etc until they are convicted or admit guilt in the course of recognised proceedings; murder victims should be given the dignity of an honorofic.

Civil cases The parties in civil cases are the *claimant* (formerly the plaintiff) and the *defendant*. Say "counsel for Mrs Y" rather than "counsel for the claimant" etc. In judicial review the person challenging the decision is the *applicant*.

Appeals In criminal cases the defendant becomes the *appellant*; the respondent is usually the Crown. Say "counsel for Mr Smith" rather than "counsel for the appellant". In civil appeals either the claimant (formerly the plaintiff) or the defendant can be the appellant; it is always better to identify the parties and then avoid the phrase "counsel for the appellant/respondent" wherever possible

courts cap the *High Court,* the *Court of Appeal,* the *Supreme Court,* the *European Court of Human Rights* etc; but lower case local courts (except the place name) even when specific, eg Birmingham crown court, Clerkenwell county court, Dawlish magistrates' court, Ashford youth court etc; in a general, unspecific context, referring to the institution, cap the *Crown Court* (it sits in about 90 centres, which may loosely be referred to as *crown courts,* eg Snaresbrook crown court; this is not strictly correct, but even the lord chief justice has been known to do it)

Court Service, the caps; not Courts

crack is a type of cocaine; the phrase crack cocaine is tautologous, but need not always be avoided on that account

crackdown not banned, but use as little as possible

crèche not crêche

credit card no need to hyphenate adjectivally, as in eg "credit card purchases"

creditworthy no hyphen; also *creditworthiness*

Creole is a person born in the West Indies or Latin America whose ancestry is wholly or partly European. It does not imply mixed race. Lower case *creole* as an adjective to describe food or culture

crescendo means getting louder, growing in force. Nothing rises to a crescendo. Plural is *crescendos*

Creutzfeldt-Jakob disease (abbreviate CJD). Note also *variant CJD* (with lower case v), abbreviated to vCJD. No longer call it new variant CJD

crime approach all crime statistics with caution; they can be made to show almost anything

crisis a greatly overworked word

criterion plural *criteria*; using the plural for the singular is illiterate

Croat for the people and language, *Croatian* for the general adjective

crosier prefer to crozier

Cross, the cap C

cross benches but *crossbenchers*, *crossbench* opinion

cross-Channel but *transatlantic*

Crown (in constitutional sense) may be capped for the sake of clarity; but in phrases such as crown property, the crown representative etc it should usually be obvious what is meant when lower case

Crown dependency eg Jersey, Guernsey, the Isle of Man

Crown Jewels caps

crucifix a cross or an image of a cross with a figure of Jesus Christ on it

cruise missiles but *Pershing missiles*; also lower case *stealth bomber*

crunch avoid clichés such as "reaches crunch point", "the situation came to a crunch"

crystallise

cul-de-sac hyphens; plural *cul-de-sacs*

Cup upper case in FA Cup final, European Cup final, World Cup final, Davis Cup final etc

cupfuls (not cupsful or cupfulls), also *spoonfuls* etc

curate's egg it was wholly bad, and the clergyman was being polite, but insisting on this is a lost cause. The phrase now almost invariably describes something of mixed quality. It is a dreadful cliché anyway, so best not used at all

cure-all hyphen (noun and adjective)

currencies convert to sterling on Home News, Sport and Features pages, usually at first mention of the foreign currency. Round up or down. On Business and Foreign News pages commonly used foreign currencies (in practice, dollars and euros only) need not be converted unless it seems helpful, and the headline should reflect the article's original currency rather than a sterling equivalent. Do not convert meaninglessly, eg a number of dollars spent in 1995 to a number of pounds at a 2009 exchange rate; additional information on historic rates and/or purchasing power should be given when possible

current avoid wherever possible as synonym of *present*. The word currently is almost always redundant and best deleted

curriculums plural, not curricula, but note *extracurricular activities*; *curriculum vitae*, CV abbreviated (plural, *curricula vitae*)

curtsy not curtsey; plural *curtsies*

cut-throat use hyphen

cybercafé, cybercrime, cyberpet, cyberpunk, cybersex, cyberspace, cybersquatting, cyberterrorism, cyberwar all one word; some new words with the prefix cyber- may need a hyphen if they look (even more) hideous without one

Cyprus, northern keep the lower case in northern, as the "state" is recognised only by the Turkish government

czar avoid; usual style is *tsar;* there seems no obvious reason to make an exception by allowing the czar form in the context of government-appointed co-ordinators such as drug czar, mental health czar etc, as we used to. See **Tsar**

Czech Republic use Czechoslovakia only in the historic sense. The two countries since their division are the *Czech Republic* and *Slovakia*

Dd

d abbreviation for died, no full point, eg d 1997. Likewise b for born: b 1906

dad and **mum** lower case in general context; reserve caps for when it is clear that that is/was the family name in use. Thus "I told my mum I would be late home" but "I told Mum I would be late home". Caps for the *Bank of Mum and Dad*

Dafydd is the correct spelling of the Welsh name. Daffyd Thomas, of *Little Britain*, is (perhaps consciously) a variant the Welsh are most unlikely to accept

Dail Eireann (no accents required) the lower house of the Irish parliament; usually just *the Dail* (cap D)

Dakar capital of Senegal; Dhaka is the capital of Bangladesh

dal prefer to dhal etc for a curry made from lentils or other pulses

Dales, the Yorkshire (cap); or just *the Dales*

Dalit, Dalits synonym (and now generally the preferred term) for *Untouchable(s)* in Indian caste system; may be worth explaining at first mention

dam cap in specific names, eg Aswan Dam, Hoover Dam, Pergau Dam, Three Gorges Dam; (similarly reservoirs: Island Barn Reservoir etc)

danceband, dancefloor one word; *dance music, dance lessons,* two

Dark Ages caps, but take care; the period after the fall of the Roman Empire is no longer considered wholly obscure and barbaric and the term is now rarely used by historians

dark net for clarity needs to be two words in refs to the hidden, anonymous and often sinister regions of the internet. Likewise, *dark web*

Darwin, Charles write the title of his great work as *On the Origin of Species* (usually omitting the words *by Means of Natural Selection*)

dashes versatile and often useful to set off a separate thought or mark a dramatic break — but not to be treated as a lazy alternative to more careful punctuation. One — or two — may be helpful; more will annoy — and confuse. Beware of overuse

data strictly plural, but common usage (which we may as well follow) now tends to treat as singular

databank, database

date line two words as shorthand for the *international date line*

date rape beware of this phrase, which trivialises an unpleasant crime; in many cases the intended meaning is *drug rape* (involving, eg the spiking of a victim's drink with narcotics such as Rohypnol)

dates Monday, April 18, 1994 (never 18th April); but April 1994. When citing periods of years, say 1992-93 (not 1992-3); for the turn of the century/millennium, write 1999-2000, then 2000-01, 2003-09 etc. If using "from", you need "to"; eg from 1939 to 1941 (not from 1939-41); for decades, the *Forties*, *Eighties*, *Nineties*, upper case (or *1940s*, *1980s*, *1990s*); not the '40s, '50s, '60s. For decades in people's ages, lower case ("she was in her forties, eighties, nineties" etc). Common usage says that the 20th century/millennium ended on December 31, 1999, even if some readers (obsessively, and no doubt rightly) disagree

da Vinci, Leonardo Leonardo for short, never da Vinci; but note *The Da Vinci Code* for the book and the film

Day upper case in Christmas Day, Boxing Day, Easter Day, Thanksgiving Day, New Year's Day etc

DayGlo caps, no longer hyphen, proprietary

day one as in "it's been happening since day one"; ugly usage anyway, so best avoided

days/months if abbreviated, and only in listings etc, not in general body copy, use: *Mon Tues Wed Thur Fri Sat Sun; Jan Feb Mar Apr May Jun Jul Aug Sept Oct Nov Dec*

daytime but *night-time*

day trader, **day trading** no need to hyphenate

day trip but *day-tripper*

D-Day was on June 6, 1944; it seems to need a hyphen, where VE Day and VJ Day do not

deaf and dumb avoid this phrase, which is nowadays deemed offensive. Likewise, avoid deaf mute. The best alternative to either phrase is *profoundly deaf*

deafblind (no hyphen) unable to hear or see

deal with denounced in a *Times* style guide half a century ago as "perhaps the dreariest verb in the language, a colourless substitute for some better word for which the writer has not taken the trouble to look"; that now seems harsh, but better words may still be worth looking for

death people die, and we must say so. Write simply that someone has died; never use horrid genteelisms ("passed on", "passed away") unless unavoidable in direct quotes

deathbed no hyphen, one word, as *sickbed*

death row (as in American prisons), lower case; hyphen as adjective, eg death-row campaigner

debacle accents unnecessary

debatable prefer to debateable

debate US usage allows eg two politicians to debate each other; English usage still prefers them to *debate something with each other*

debut (no accent) is most widely understood as a noun; avoid using it as a verb, not least because it looks nasty when conjugated (debuted?); instead write, eg "He made his debut..."

decades use either the Sixties or the 1960s (similarly as adjectives); not 60s or '60s. For people's ages use lower case, ie "I am in my fifties" etc. See **dates**

decimals do not mix decimals and fractions in the same story

decimate by strict etymology might mean to kill one in ten; it is now more widely used (to the annoyance of zealots) as a non-specific indication of heavy casualties or damage. Opportunities to write about the killing of precisely one in ten being fairly rare, there is no compelling reason to resist the more general use

deckchair as *armchair* (no hyphens)

decor no accent

Deep South caps seem clearer for this geographical and cultural region of the US

de facto roman

defecate rather than defaecate

definite article do not omit, tabloid-fashion, when adding descriptions in front of names; so write, eg the film star Greta Garbo, the industrialist Alfred Krupp, the Chelsea forward Diego Costa, the Labour leader Jeremy Corbyn. Use common sense, however, when the description comes after the name; the article may seem clumsy and will rarely be needed, eg Sir Alan Moses, chairman of the press regulator Ipso; JK Rowling, author of the Harry Potter novels etc.

The modish tendency of cultural institutions to drop the definite article from their names in corporate branding seems now almost universal: Tate, V&A, Southbank Centre, Arnolfini, Royal Festival Hall etc. There is not a great deal to be done about this, but there is no need to embrace it with any enthusiasm. If it feels more natural to refer to "the Tate" or "the Festival Hall", then do so

defuse means to remove the fuse from, or reduce tension in an emergency etc; never confuse with *diffuse*, which means to spread in all directions, scatter etc, or (as adjective) verbose, not concise, spread over a large area etc

de Gaulle never cap de in this name unless at the start of a sentence or headline

degrees (educational) a *bachelor's*, a *master's*, a *first*, a *second*, an *upper second* (a 2:1), a *lower second* (a 2:2), a *third* etc. Abbreviations as follows: doctorates of literature (or letters), DLit, DLitt, LitD etc; Oxford and York have DPhil instead of the more usual PhD. Oxford has DM for the more usual MD. Cambridge has ScD for doctor of science. No full points in degrees

degrees (weather) omit degree sign in temperatures, eg 38C 68F

déjà vu accents but not italic

deliver, **delivery** perfect for babies, newspapers, milk on the doorstep, but beware meaningless overuse in government and business jargon and management-speak, eg "delivering positive outcomes" or "the key indicators of delivery are moving in the right direction". The word has become a cliché, so always try to think of an alternative and to convey what is actually meant; eg promises are *kept*, policies are *implemented*, public services are *provided*, improvements are *made*

demise strictly means the death of a person, or the failure of an enterprise or institution. Keep to these definitions and do not use to describe a fall from office or from grace. It is wrong to refer eg to the demise of Glenn Hoddle or, as *The Times* has more than once, of Peter Mandelson; both are still with us

Democratic Party (US) or *the Democrats. Democratic* is normally the preferable adjective to Democrat; note the *Democratic convention*

demonstration do not shorten to demo except in direct quotes

demonstrator thus

denouement no accent

deny does not mean the same as *rebut* (which means argue to the contrary, producing evidence), or *refute* (which means to win such an argument); show that you understand the difference

dependant noun, eg "a man with no dependants"; *dependent*, adj, eg "a man dependent on his family" (dependent is also standard for the noun in US usage and is increasingly becoming so in English; but it seems a shame to lose a perfectly good word, so we should try to preserve the distinction)

deprecate to disapprove of, deplore; *depreciate* generally to diminish in value. Because most people do not really deplore or disapprove of themselves and because depreciate may also mean disparage or belittle, Fowler prefers self-depreciation to self-deprecation. A generation of schoolmasters seems to have taught that he was right, but to follow him and them at this remove seems pedantic and perverse, and it baffles almost all readers: write *self-deprecation*, even if you have to grit your teeth

Depression, the cap for the 1930s economic slump

deputy prime minister similarly, *deputy governor of the Bank of England*, lower case

deputy speaker lower case; there are several of them in parliament, and the meaning will always be clear (but *the Speaker* gets a cap for clarity)

Derry generally use Londonderry; but Derry city council, and Derry when in direct quotes or in a specifically republican context

de rigueur roman; spell it right, not de rigeur

descendant absolutely not to be confused with an ancestor, as sometimes — inexplicably — seems to happen; also to be distinguished from a mere successor, eg when writing about monarchs

desktop (computer, publishing) no hyphen

despite perfectly acceptable, and virtuously shorter, alternative to *in spite of.* But do not say "despite the fact that"; use *although* instead

despoil means pillage, plunder, ravage; it is not a more exciting word for spoil; note *despoiled* (not despoilt); *despoliation* (not despoilation) or *despoilment*

détente accent

Deutsche Bank German commercial bank not to be confused with the Deutsche Bundesbank, or Bundesbank, the German central bank

deutschemark/deutschmark prefer not to use either form, nor D-mark. Use simply *the mark,* or with figures, DM500 (all now in historical contexts)

Devil, the (cap); but *devils* (many, lower case), *devilish, devil-may-care*

Devon write north Devon, south Devon (lower case) for these geographical and postal areas

dextrous prefer to dexterous

diabetes type 1, type 2 etc, no cap, no hyphen

diagnose strictly speaking illnesses are diagnosed, patients are not. Thus it is better to write "He had cancer diagnosed" than "He was diagnosed with cancer". The latter is now in common use, however, and is perfectly acceptable if the alternative seems awkward

Diana, Princess of Wales was in her lifetime at first mention always thus in *The Times*; subsequently the princess. Twenty years on from her death, however, the formulation *Princess Diana*, once eschewed as "tabloid", may well be one of the clearer and less cumbersome ways to make passing reference to her when the need arises; use it if it seems helpful. Princess Di or Lady Di remain more or less banned (except in reported speech). Say *the late princess* where appropriate.

Note *the Diana, Princess of Wales Memorial Fund* (one comma only)

diarrhoea thus

diaspora no need to cap

dice use as both singular and plural except in eg "the die is cast", which should generally be confined to quotations

Dictaphone is a trade name and must be capped

didgeridoo

die prefer to write "to die of, eg cancer" rather than "to die from ..."

diehard no hyphen

dietician now the much more common form; prefer to dietitian

different from prefer to *different to*, although, *pace* Fowler et al, there is no need to make a fetish of this; avoid the Americanism "different than". Likewise, *differ from*

dignitaries

diktat

dilate dilation means normal widening, as in pupils of the eye; *dilatation* is widening by force, as in child abuse cases. Take care

Dinky Toys cap T (trademark), but Dinky on its own can be sufficient

diocese lower case both for a specific organisation such as the diocese of Chichester and in general use; also lower case *diocesan*

diphtheria, diphthong note ph

Diplock court a non-jury court (named after the judge Lord Diplock) used in Northern Ireland to try terrorist cases during the Troubles; abolished in 2007

diplomatic service lower case, as civil service

directly, direct adverbs with long histories. In most senses use directly; reserve direct for meaning "straight in direction or aspect, without deviation", eg "the taxi took him direct to the airport"; or "without intermediaries", eg "she appealed direct to the mayor". Always use directly before an adjective, eg "directly liable". Directly has a temporal as well as a spatial sense; it may mean immediately or at once (eg "I'll do it directly"). It would be a pity to see this latter usage disappear altogether, but be aware that it will strike some readers as quaint and the meaning may sometimes be unclear (as in eg "I'll go there directly")

directives (in EU) lower case even when naming specific regulations, eg the European working time directive

director-general lower case, of the BBC, CBI, Institute of Directors, Fair Trading and the regulatory bodies etc

director of public prosecutions (DPP)

Directory Enquiries the operator-assisted number-finding service may have been styled thus in the days when telephones were the monopoly of the GPO but, except in specific historical references, we should now follow our usual style and refer generally to *directory inquiries, directory inquiry services* etc

disabled common usage changes quickly, so take care. Beware the offensive use of medical metaphors and the lazy misapplication of terms relating to physical or mental health; beware too the more absurdly patronising euphemisms, eg differently abled. Above all be sensitive

disc musical, recording, or shape, eg disc jockey, compact disc, disc brake; but *disk* in some computing senses, eg disk drive, floppy disk. In general, non-technical contexts, eg when reporting the loss of government data that had been kept on CD, write disc

discernible not -able

discomfit take care with this verb; it means primarily to thwart, defeat or rout, but by extension can mean thoroughly to embarrass or disconcert (noun *discomfiture*). It has no connection with the much weaker *discomfort*, which means to deprive of comfort or make uneasy

discreet means tactful, circumspect (noun *discretion*); *discrete* means individually distinct (noun *discreteness*)

disinterested means impartial, unbiased (noun *disinterest*). It seems a shame to use it interchangeably with *uninterested*, which means having a lack of interest; such usage is now widespread, but there is no reason to encourage it. When Gordon Brown, as prime minister, said in the House of Commons (February 11, 2009) that "the Conservative Party seems to have a huge disinterest in the environment", he sacrificed a useful distinction and wasted a valuable word

disorientate not disorient

dispatch not despatch, including *dispatch box*

dissociate not disassociate

distil, distilled, distillation

divorcé, man; **divorcée**, woman; use *divorcees* (no accent) in reference to both men and women

Diwali the Hindu festival of lights

DIY no need to spell out do-it-yourself at first mention

D-notice an official request to news editors not to publish items on specific subjects for reasons of national security. Since 1993 these have in fact been called *DA-notices* (defence advisory notices); they should be referred to as such except in historical contexts

do a good word; use it

doberman breed of dog; more fully, *doberman pinscher* (lower case)

Docklands in London, docklands elsewhere

doctor prefer to confine the title Dr to medical practitioners. If a person has a doctorate in a non-medical subject from a reputable institution and wishes to be known as Dr Smith he or she may be so titled in *The Times*, particularly in contexts (eg science or education reports) where academic qualifications and expertise have relevance. On the whole, however, there is little to be said for a German-style flourishing of doctorates in public life, and we should resist

Doctor Who the television programme goes in italics but the time-travelling protagonist is called simply the Doctor (not Doctor Who) with a cap D and in roman

docusoap, docudrama etc no hyphens

dogfight as *bullfight, cockfight* etc

dogs we like dogs, but we are not the Kennel Club. As in most other areas, we should aim to keep capitals to a minimum:

Capitalise proper nouns (or adjectives derived from them) when used as modifiers in the name of dog breeds: *German shepherd, Irish wolfhound, Afghan hound, Basset hound, French bulldog, Airedale terrier, Sealyham terrier, West Highland terrier, Yorkshire terrier, Jack Russell terrier, American pitbull, Rhodesian ridgeback, St Bernard* etc; also capitalise any additional qualifying adjective that forms part of the name: *Old English sheepdog, Great Dane, Cavalier King Charles spaniel* etc; lower case the accompanying common noun (dog, spaniel, terrier, hound etc).

However, where an adjective derived from a proper noun is in everyday use as the one-word name of a familiar breed, then it may be treated as a common noun and should be lower case: *alsatian, dalmatian, labrador, chihuahua, pekinese, doberman, rottweiler, weimaraner* etc.

Generally, all other breed names lower case: *poodle, whippet, boxer, border collie, greyhound, dachshund, corgi, pointer, setter, golden retriever, schnauzer, pug, foxhound.*

This should also work for cats

dog whistle noun; **dog-whistle** (hyphen) for adjective, eg dog-whistle politics, and verb

dollars with figures use $5 (when American), A$5 (Australian), C$5 (Canadian), S$5 (Singapore) and so on. Beware: in some South American countries (Argentina and Chile among them) the $ sign is used to represent the peso

doll's house not dolls'

Dolly the sheep lower case s

Domesday Book roman, like Magna Carta, but *doomsday* in general or biblical sense

dominatrix plural (should you need it) *dominatrices*

Dominican Republic neighbour to Haiti on the island of Hispaniola. *Dominica* is one of the Windward Islands. Both are sovereign states

dominoes but note Derek and the Dominos, the band formed by Eric Clapton

don as in to put on clothing — "he donned his jacket and tie" — is a corny and outdated expression far removed from ordinary speech. Avoid it

donate *give* or *present* may be preferable

doppelgänger ghostly duplicate of a living person. Note lower case and roman, anglicised version of German *Doppelgänger*

do's and don'ts ugly, inconsistent, but clear and understood; the alternatives seem worse

dotcom no hyphen for colloquial reference to internet companies, eg the dotcom bubble

-dottir no accent on the Icelandic female surname suffix

double bass the instrument

double entendre plural *double entendres*, roman

doveish not dovish, a rare instance (cf **ageing**) where we prefer the middle e

down avoid unnecessary use after verbs, as in close down, shut down. See **up**

Downing Street write 10 *Downing Street* (or 11 ...), or simply *No 10*; note *Downing Street policy unit*

downmarket no hyphen, as *upmarket*

downplay prefer *play down*

Down's syndrome never say mongol and note lower case s for *syndrome*

down to a T thus, but best avoided

downtown a North American term, and now somewhat Antipodean as well, for the central or lower part of a city, especially the main commercial area. Do not use inappropriately, except for deliberate comic effect. The phrase downtown Manhattan is meaningful, given the geography and culture, but downtown Walsall and downtown Baghdad, for example, are not

down under lower case, as a colloquialism for Australasia (especially Australia)

drachmas not drachmae (now historical contexts)

draconian lower case

draftsman (legal), but *draughtsman* (art, design)

drama, dramatic best confined to the theatrical context; in news reports resist the tendency to turn any event into a drama and to make every development dramatic (the latter a fairly dismal cliché anyway); readers can decide these things for themselves

dreadnought

dreamt not dreamed

drier is the comparative of dry; *dryer* is the noun, as in tumble dryer

drily prefer to dryly

drink-drive, drink-driver, drink-driving The legal alcohol levels in England, Wales and Northern Ireland are: blood, 80 milligrams per 100ml; breath, 35 micrograms per 100ml; urine, 107 milligrams per 100ml. The levels in Scotland are: blood, 50 milligrams per 100ml; breath, 22 micrograms per 100ml; urine, 67 milligrams per 100ml. See **alcohol**

drivers no hyphens in *taxi driver, bus driver, car driver* etc

drop a bombshell avoid

dropout noun or adjective, as in students; *drop-out* (rugby); and *to drop out* (verb)

drug dealer, drug dealing, drug smuggler, drug smuggling, drug taking drug (singular) and no hyphens as nouns; but hyphenate adjectives, eg a drug-dealing cartel, a drug-smuggling gang

drug names cap trade name, eg Valium; lower case generic name, eg diazepam

drugs do not confuse narcotics (which include cocaine and heroin) with other illicit drugs such as cannabis, LSD and amphetamines

druid(s) no cap

dry clean, dry cleaners, dry cleaning etc

drystone wall

dual of two, eg dual carriageway; *duel* (fight)

dual nationals try to avoid this officialspeak for *people with dual nationality*

Duchess of York she ceased to be a member of the royal family upon her divorce in 1996. After her first mention as Duchess of York, refer to *the duchess* (lower case) subsequently. Columnists and feature writers (not news reporters) may have occasional recourse to *Fergie* if it suits their purposes

duct tape two words

Dutch another of those adjectives from proper nouns that looks more natural with a capital letter, even in idioms where a connection with the Netherlands now seems remote or obscure: Dutch courage, Dutch bungalow, go Dutch etc

due to in an ideal world we might use "due" only as an adjective and insist on attaching it always to a noun. So we would write, eg "His absence was due to illness" and never "He was absent due to illness". The latter usage, beloved of railway announcers, treats "due to" as a compound preposition equivalent to "because of" or "owing to". It may offend purists, but it is both widely used and easily understood; there is no reason to take elaborate measures to avoid it

duffel bag, duffel coat

Duke of Edinburgh say the duke (lower case) or Prince Philip after first mention; only the Queen retains her cap at second mention; other royals follow style for aristocracy

dump do not use as synonym of dismiss or sack

Durham say Co Durham for the county and (if any question of ambiguity) Durham city for the city

duty-free hyphenated, noun or adjective

dwarf as plural write *dwarfs* (not JRR Tolkien's affectation *dwarves*); avoid politically correct circumlocutions such as "person of restricted growth"

dyke (embankment), not dike

dysentery not, eg dysentry or disentery

dyspepsia

Ee

each, every (one) although singular, there is a growing tendency to use them with plural pronouns, as the plural is increasingly becoming a way of saying "he or she", or "his or her". Hence, "everyone has what they want", "each of us has our secrets", but "everyone has secrets". We must learn to live with this

earlier this word is often redundant, because the tense of the verb says it all; similarly *later*

early hours the phrase "in the early hours of the morning" can usually be shortened to "the early hours" or, better, "early yesterday/today"

earned never earnt, which is a formation not recognised by reputable dictionaries

earring no hyphen

Earls Court no apostrophe, even though the signs at the Underground station have one

earth cap in astronomical sense and when clearly referring to the planet (life on Earth, first man to orbit the Earth etc); lower case for the soil and generally in idioms; down to earth, back to earth with a bump etc

earthquake can abbreviate to *quake* especially in headings. See **Richter scale**

east, eastern etc almost always lower case

East End, West End of London; but east, west, north, south, central London; also outer London, inner London (but historically the Inner London Education Authority, ILEA). Greater London probably needs a cap for clarity.

Note that the East End is generally confined to four postal districts: E1 (Whitechapel, Wapping, Stepney, Mile End), E2 (Bethnal Green, Shoreditch), E3 (Bow, Bromley-by-Bow), E14 (Limehouse, Poplar, Millwall, Isle of Dogs)

EastEnders the TV soap opera; an *Eastender*, someone from the East End

Easter Day (or *Easter Sunday*) is the Sunday between *Good Friday* and *Easter Monday*. But note that the Saturday before Easter Day is *Holy Saturday* (not Easter Saturday, which is the Saturday after Easter). The week leading up to Easter Day is *Holy Week*; the week after is *Easter Week*. This may be a lost cause, but it is worth trying to get it right

eastern Europe lower case, similarly now *eastern Germany* for what was East Germany before reunification

easygoing one word

eau de parfum plural *eaux de parfum*; likewise, *eau de vie*, plural *eaux de vie*

eBay avoid at the start of a sentence, as it looks especially strange typographically, but if there is no alternative then write e*Bay* in that context as in others. It is also permissible to write eBay thus at the start of a headline, but try to avoid. Apply these rules to similarly familiar trademark global brands such as iPod, iPhone etc. See **company names**

ebitda earnings before interest, tax, depreciation and amortisation; where possible spell out at first mention; try not to inflict this one on the general reader anyway, and certainly not without explanation

ebola lower case the virus, even though it takes its name from the Ebola, a river in the Democratic Republic of Congo

ebook generally no hyphen in these ewords, unless they are thoroughly unfamiliar or very difficult to read without:

e-cigarette is the most common exception; without a hyphen it looks nasty and hard to pronounce. As a general guide use a hyphen if new or unusual coinages seem to benefit: *e-petition, e-mediation, e-arbitration.* Much will depend on familiarity and common use; email was once inconceivable without a hyphen and now looks quite odd with

EC must NOT be used as an abbreviation for the European Commission in text or headlines. EC remains the short form only of the European Community, although in almost all contexts now EU is preferred

e-cigarette hyphenate this, unlike most ewords, as it otherwise looks ugly and hard to pronounce

ecofriendly hyphen no longer necessary in this adjective. A hyphen can make some of the eco- compound noun coinages less hideous and easier to understand until they seem familiar enough to work without: *eco-hotel, eco-region, eco-species, eco-terrorist, eco-town, eco-tourist, eco-type, eco-warrior.* Two established exceptions are *ecosphere, ecosystem;* others may lose their hyphens in time

E. coli italics in text, but roman and no point in headlines; in full, *Escherichia coli.* Note the O157 strain (letter O, not a zero)

ecommerce

Ecstasy (cap) the drug

Ecuadorean not -ian

ecumenical not oecumenical (including the Ecumenical Patriarch of Constantinople, should he come up)

editing be wary of overediting. It risks making everything in the paper sound the same and, worse, it may introduce mistakes. Essential facts must be concisely conveyed; style and usage should be consistent and clear. Writers may nonetheless be allowed an individual voice, at least if they have first taken the trouble to check and revise their own work carefully

editor lower case job title at all times, including first mention of editors of well-known leading publications, such as the editor of *The Times*, editor of the *Daily Mirror*, editor of the *Yorkshire Post*, editor of *The Spectator*. Similarly, editor-in-chief

educationist not educationalist

EEC the European Economic Community, forerunner of the European Union

eg no points; a comma may often be helpful before, eg when used like this, but it is not always essential; similarly no comma is needed after ie but one may be helpful before

effete is a good word for exhausted, worn out, ineffectual; its use as a clever-sounding (and unnecessary) synonym for effeminate may now be too widespread to resist, but there seems no reason to encourage it

Eid al-Adha literally the festival of sacrifice, marking the end of the annual pilgrimage, the **haj**, to Mecca. Write Eid al-Adha in full at first mention, not simply Eid

Eid al-Fitr literally the festival of fast-breaking, marking the end of the fast of Ramadan. Write Eid al-Fitr in full at first mention, not simply Eid. (When Eid alone is written, this is usually the festival that is meant)

Eire do not use except in quotes and historical context

eisteddfod lower case except when naming a particular one in full, eg the International Eisteddfod at Llangollen; plural *eisteddfodau*

either takes a singular verb when both subjects are embraced: "Either is good enough"

eke, **eking**

elbowroom one word, similarly *headroom, legroom*

elderly, **aged**, **old** be extremely sensitive in the use of these words. People are living longer and remaining active longer; many dislike being described in language that makes them sound older than they feel. As a guide, never use any of these words for anyone under pensionable age, and be aware that there are many over this age for whom "elderly" is not a remotely appropriate adjective. For almost all those under 70, perhaps even under 80, a safer, less loaded alternative might be "older people". See **pensioners, retiree**

-elect hyphenate, lower case, as in "Donald Trump, the president-elect of the United States" in the period between the election and the inauguration

electoral college no need for cap in US election context

electrocardiographs are machines for measuring heart function; *electrocardiograms* are the tracings made by them

electrocute means to kill by electric shock, not merely to suffer an electric shock

Elgin Marbles caps when named in full; at subsequent mentions, *the marbles*

elicit means to evoke, bring to light, or draw out; never confuse with *illicit* (unlawful, forbidden)

elite roman, no accent

ellipses see **punctuation**

email cf *ebook, ecommerce* etc

embarkation prefer to embarcation, unless writing French. You embark *in* (not on) a ship

embarrass(ment) but note the French *embarras de choix, embarras de richesses*

embassy lower case, eg the French embassy in Rome, thereafter the embassy

émigré roman, two accents

éminence grise roman, accent

Emmys plural of the Emmy awards

emphasise no longer any preference for this to the shorter *stress* in phrases such as "he emphasised the importance", "she emphasised that the ruling was final"; "he/she stressed etc" is also fine

empire cap as in British or Roman Empire; similarly, cap *emperor* when a specific name, eg Emperor Claudius, otherwise, the emperor

employment tribunals have replaced industrial tribunals. They end with a *judgment* or a *decision*, not a verdict. Only juries in court hearings, or magistrates hearing cases summarily, deliver a verdict. See **tribunals**

encyclopaedia not the American encyclopedia

endgame one word

energy measured in watt-hours etc, whereas power is measured in watts, megawatts etc, eg a 60W lightbulb. Beware confusing energy and power. See **kilowatt-hour**, **power**

engineers restrict use to white-collar workers with engineering qualifications; do not use with reference to unqualified mechanics, repairmen, manufacturing workers, platelayers etc. Engineers also dislike being mistaken for scientists, particularly when it means that scientists get the credit for engineering feats

England, **English** do not use these when what you mean is *Britain, British*

enormity does not mean great size; it means the quality or character of being outrageous, or extreme wickedness or serious error. Do not misuse. If you want a word for great size, use *immensity*

en route not italics

ensign the white ensign is the ensign of the Royal Navy and the Royal Yacht Squadron; the red ensign is the British Merchant Navy's flag; the blue ensign is flown by Royal Fleet Auxiliary vessels and by certain yacht clubs. There is no such thing as the royal ensign; however, the royal standard will fly from one of the Queen's homes when she is there

en suite two words, no hyphen, no italics, both as adverb and adjective

ensure means to make certain; you *insure* against risk; you *assure* your life. The verb *ensure* usually needs "that" after it if accompanied by a following verb (eg "he tried to ensure that the policy was adopted"); but omit "that" if followed by a noun (eg "he tried to ensure its success")

enthral

epicentre the point on the Earth's surface directly above the focus of an earthquake or underground nuclear explosion. The epicentre cannot be "5km below ground" (that would be the *hypocentre* or *focus*). Take care, especially in graphics

eponymous means "giving its name to ..." so "Hamlet, the eponymous prince" (ie giving his name to the play) is correct; "*Hamlet*, the eponymous play" is wrong; even used correctly, it sounds pompous, so better avoid

Equator (cap), but *equatorial* in general sense

escalate, **escalation** avoid these ponderous clichés; say *rise, grow, get worse*; transitive use ("I shall escalate your complaint") should be left to customer services departments

escapers never escapees

Eskimo is now widely regarded as a derogatory term. Use *Inuit* instead, except in occasional historical contexts. Note, Inuit is the singular and plural noun

establishment generally may be lower case in references to the perceived leaders of society, the establishment, unless (rarely) a capital seems helpful to clarify meaning (eg in the unlikely event of needing to write that "the Savoy Grill is an establishment much favoured by the Establishment"). Always lower case in the medical establishment, the legal establishment etc and in reference to the establishment of the Church of England; anti-establishment also lower case, as it is clear enough what it means

estuary lower case Thames estuary, Severn estuary, estuary English

Eta (not ETA), the Basque separatist organisation

"ethnic cleansing" use quotation marks in writing this euphemism for the enforced removal of people from a place based on their ethnicity

eticket another unhyphenated eword, ugly but generally understood

Eucharist cap

EU referendum on June 23, 2016 the question posed was not one requiring a "yes" or "no" vote, and reference to such should be avoided. In referring to a vote for Remain or Leave, render it thus, capped and with no quote marks: eg "he was campaigning for Remain but has switched to the Leave camp"

euro the European single currency takes lower case (as franc, pound, mark, peseta etc), as do all compounds derived from it; compounds derived from Europe rather than the euro (eg Eurosceptic) are upper case

eurocheques, eurobonds lower case, no hyphen

euroland lower case, vernacular term for European single currency area; also *eurozone*

Europe western, eastern, central, northern, southern (all lower case, except geopolitical Eastern, Western in historical Cold War context). Geographically at least, Europe includes the British Isles, so do not use the name unthinkingly as equivalent to *the Continent* or a synonym for the EU. Use common sense, however. Prefer to say that Britain exports to *the rest of* Europe, or to the EU; but if you say you spend your holidays in Europe, no one will think you're talking about Skegness

European arrest warrant

European Commission cap when naming in full. Otherwise lower case, eg a commission ruling, the commission ruled; *the commissioner* can be lower case even when referring to a specific person (eg Margrethe Vestager, the competition commissioner; thereafter, the commissioner). The president of the European Commission is lower case

European courts take great care not to confuse EU and non-EU institutions; the European Court of Human Rights is not an EU body

European Economic Area (EEA) the European tariff-free zone, comprises all the members of the EU plus Norway, Iceland and Liechtenstein. Other EU-EEA areas of co-operation include education, research, environment, consumer policy and tourism

European parliament lower case parliament; also lower case members of the European parliament (MEPs), or Euro MPs

European Union (EU), European Community (EC) the first is the preferred phrase except where the context is trade. If we have to use *the Union*, it should be capped for clarity, but wherever possible use EU. Use *Common Market* and *EEC* (the European Economic Community) only in historical context

Eurosceptic (not hyphenated), and similarly cap *Europhobia*, *Europhiles* etc; compounds derived from Europe take a cap; those from the currency (euro) lower case

Eurotunnel (one word) is the company that owns and operates the Channel tunnel. *Eurostar* operates the passenger trains that run through the tunnel. Note that *Eurotunnel trains* carry cars, coaches and lorries through the tunnel between Folkestone and Calais only; they run a shuttle service and although the logo of Le Shuttle still appears on their locomotives, their formal name is Eurotunnel trains

Eurovision Song Contest caps

eurozone the single currency area. See also **euroland**

euthanasia be aware that *mercy killing* is a loaded euphemism with which some readers would take issue. Note the assisted dying (lower case) bill as a shorthand for the Assisted Dying for the Terminally Ill Bill, introduced by Lord Joffe. The organisation Dignity in Dying was formerly the Voluntary Euthanasia Society. If it must be used, prefer *euthanase* (to euthanise) but otherwise avoid this verb

evangelical(s) keep lower case in general church contexts except when part of an official title such as the Evangelical Alliance

eve cap in eg Christmas Eve

evensong lower case

eventuate avoid this bad word; use *happen* instead

ever is rarely necessary; avoid phrases such as best-ever, fastest-ever, and say simply *best* and *fastest*, qualifying (where appropriate) with *yet*

ex- prefer *former* in most contexts, as in *former Yugoslavia*, although *ex-serviceman* is unavoidable, *ex-wife* is usual and *ex-* is generally fine for headlines

examinations 11-plus, 7-plus etc; also A levels, but A-level results etc (hyphenate only when adjectival); also AS levels, A2s. GCSE, the General Certificate of Secondary Education, need not normally be spelt out

excepting do not use when *except* or *except for* is possible

exclamation marks nearly always unnecessary!!!!!

exclusive do not overuse with story or interview. The phrase "in an interview with *The Times*" is generally sufficient

excoriating the word that may be meant when *coruscating* is written

ex dividend (not ex-dividend) in financial contexts

execution take care; as with *assassination*, do not use as a synonym of killing or murder. On occasion, the phrase "summary killing" may be appropriate. Legally, an execution is a judicial killing after due process of law

Executive in the Scottish, Welsh and Northern Ireland contexts, when used as a noun meaning the government, a cap may occasionally be required for clarity to distinguish the body from an individual executive person; but lower case when possible (context will usually make meaning clear) and always when adjectival

exhibitions titles of art exhibitions in italics

existing use *present* where possible as an alternative

ex parte lower case, roman, no hyphen

expatriate noun, verb or adjective: not ex-patriate and certainly not expatriot. The noun is often shortened to *expat* — it does not take a hyphen

expert if someone is eg a lawyer, then avoid writing the imprecise "legal expert"; on the other hand, a phrase such as "an expert on constitutional law" could be appropriate and precise. Do not overuse; "experts warn" etc might be all right in headlines or intros but readers deserve to be told very early in the story just who these vague "experts" are and in what their expertise consists. See **research shows that** ...

extinct means, of an animal or plant species, having no living representative; having died out. Biologists do talk of local extinctions, ie when a species has died out in a particular habitat, and we can follow that usage, eg "The creature is extinct in Britain." In the UK context, the smallest area specified would normally be a county. More generally, extinction means the total elimination of a species worldwide, eg the dodo

extramarital no hyphen; similarly, *extramural, extracurricular, extrasensory* etc

extra virgin olive oil no need for a hyphen between the first two words

exuberant (not exhuberant), but *exhilarate, exhort* etc

eye of a storm do not refer tautologically to "the calm in the eye of the storm"; also note that the eye, as a quiet area, is a singularly inappropriate metaphor for a focus of high activity or frenetic action

eye to eye no hyphens adverbially, as in "seeing eye to eye"; but hyphenate eye-to-eye should you ever contrive to use it adjectivally

eyeing

Ff

façade use the cedilla

facelift use sparingly in its metaphorical sense, where it has become overworked. Fine in its cosmetic context, of course

faceted, faceting prefer single t

factsheet

fact that often — perhaps almost always — an unnecessary circumlocution, so avoid (eg "owing to the fact that" means *because*)

FA Cup, FA Cup final

Fairtrade (one word, cap) referring to the mark sanctioned by the Fairtrade Foundation on goods; *fair trade* (lower case, two words) for the general concept

fairytale no hyphen

falangist in Spain; *phalangist* in Lebanon

Falklands conflict, the lower case, preferred formula because war was never formally declared; this was an important point at the time, but seems less so now; if the word war is to be used, as it often is, write Falklands war (lower case)

fallacy means a faulty argument, not an erroneous belief

fallback (noun) one word, but *fall back* (verb)

fallopian tubes lower case

fallout noun, one word

fall pregnant avoid this phrase, which suggests illness; write *become pregnant*

family one of the collective nouns that is preferable as a plural, eg "the family are rearranging their holiday". Likewise, use the plural for couple, music bands and groups, the public, sports teams.

Beware when using "families" to break down big numbers and humanise the impact of government policies (budgets, tax changes etc); by all means explain what a financial measure "will cost every family", but first make sure that every family will actually have to pay

Farc (not FARC) the Revolutionary Armed Forces of Colombia

Far East encompasses the following: China, Hong Kong, Japan, North and South Korea, Macau, Mongolia, Taiwan; cap the region for clarity

farmers' market

farther is applied to distance (literal or figurative); eg "nothing could be farther from the truth"; *further* means i*n addition to, another, more,* eg "a further argument against consistency". The distinction may be eroding, with *farther* in danger of being lost; some further effort to preserve it seems worthwhile

fascia not facia

fascism, fascist cap only in a specific party political sense. More generally, eg as a term of abuse, always lower case

fat cat no quotation marks, no hyphen. Hyphenate as modifier, eg fat-cat salaries

Father (as in priest) prefer to avoid the ugly abbreviation Fr before a name; be aware that some Anglican clergy like to be known as Father; do not assume that everyone so called is a Roman Catholic priest

father of two, mother of three no hyphens. Do not define people by their relationships unequally: do not say "a mother of two was jailed" where you would not say "a father of two ..."; do not say "a grandmother was attacked" — she may be no older than 40

Father's Day not Fathers'

fatwa (not italic), a Muslim religious edict, not a sentence of punishment; it is not synonymous with a death sentence

fault lower case in geological context even when referring to a specific fault in the Earth's crust, eg San Andreas fault; also note *fault line* (two words)

Fed, the (US) say Federal Reserve (Board not usually necessary) at first mention; keep upper case for clarity; lower case the chairman of the Fed, as with governor of the Bank of England, president of the Bundesbank etc

fed up *with* may be preferable to the more informal *of*, but both are widely used and understood

feelgood factor no need for quotes (but a phrase best avoided anyway)

fellow lower case even in specific titles such as Dr Arthur Brown, a fellow of Magdalen, or in the more obvious fellow of the Royal College of Surgeons (FRCS), unless there is a real risk of confusion; in general sense, "a group of fellows in the quadrangle", "a research fellow", lower case; keep fellowship lower case

feminine designations such as authoress, poetess, sculptress, wardress, should be avoided. But *actress* remains widely accepted (not least by most actresses) and should be used

feng shui two words, roman

ferris wheel

Festival Hall, the prefer to use Royal when first (or formally) naming the venue; fine to drop the adjective subsequently or in informal use; resist the Americanising tendency (promoted by the venue's management) to drop the "the"

festivals use capitals for the full names of festivals, eg the Edinburgh International Festival, Reading Festival, otherwise lower case, eg the Edinburgh festival, Cheltenham festival (racing, literature) etc; after first mention, the festival (lower case)

fête with accent

fewer in number, and generally with plural nouns (fewer people, fewer goals, fewer pointless rules); *less* in size or quantity, and with singular nouns (less confusion, less meat, less work). Treat duration, distance etc like size, ie use less: the thing being measured is singular (time, space) even if the units (years, miles) are plural; they were married for less than five years; Canary Wharf is less than three miles from Wapping. This is an area where prescriptive zeal should not trump common sense and an ear for what sounds natural and right; so that's one less thing to worry about

fiancé (man), **fiancée** (woman)

Fianna Fail, **Fine Gael** the Irish political parties

Fide (not FIDE), the world chess body

Field of Cloth of Gold, the not the Field of the Cloth of Gold; cloth of gold is a material

Fifa the governing body of world football, the Fédération Internationale de Football Association

fifty write *50-50 chance*; note *Fifties* (cap) for the decade, but "she was in her fifties" (age, lower case, not 50s)

fighting for his/her life avoid this cliché. Instead say *critically ill/ injured*

fig leaf two words

file sharing (noun); *file-sharing* (adj) eg a file-sharing program

filibuster not fillibuster

Filipinos, Filipinas (women), **the Philippines** the correct adjective for that country's institutions, officials and similar is *Philippine*, ie the Philippine government, the Philippine president, the Philippine election

films titles in italics; note *film-maker*

film star two words

final-salary scheme with hyphen

firearms do not confuse bullets with shotgun cartridges (containing pellets); a gunshot wound is markedly different from a bullet wound

fire brigade lower case in general context, but cap specifics, eg Kent Fire Brigade

firefight should not be used as a synonym of military skirmish or exchange of fire; *firefighters* try to extinguish flames. Note that we should refer to firefighters rather than firemen, as a substantial number in the fire service are women

fire service lower case as the *ambulance service, civil service, police service, prison service, probation service* etc

firing line in military terms, the group doing the shooting, with their targets being in the *line of fire*. In common usage, the strict sense of firing line is almost never needed and the distinction is now quite lost; there seems little reason to object

firm try not to use as a synonym of company or business, except in headlines

first serves as an adverb; avoid firstly. If a list of priorities is essential in a story, write *first* and then prefer *second, third* etc as the shorter adverbial form. Never say first-ever. Use *first-class* (for service, hotel etc) generally including for postage stamps

first aid noun, no hyphen; but hyphenate when adjectival, eg first-aid qualifications

first lady no need for caps even in US context (to which the term should in any case ideally be restricted)

first world like third world, lower case; both better avoided anyway in favour of developed/developing world

First World War not World War One; similarly, Second World War but World War Three permissible. See **wars**

fjord not fiord

flair as in talent, must never be confused with *flare*, as in fire, fashion etc

flatfish eg brill, dab, megrim, plaice, sole, turbot and other species of bony fish that are asymmetrical as adults; but write *flat fish* to describe skates, rays, monkfish and other species, whether cartilaginous or bony, that are symmetrical but compressed *dorsoventrally* (an adverb worth using, should the opportunity arise)

flat-owners hyphen, but *homeowners*

flat-screen hyphen as in flat-screen television

flaunt means to make an ostentatious or defiant display, eg "she flaunted her finery"; to *flout* is to show contempt for, eg "he flouted the law". To confuse them is ignorant

flavonoid any of a group of organic compounds that pigment fruit and flowers

fledgling without the second e

fleur-de-lys not lis

flight numbers cap in stories where the number of the flight is relevant, eg Flight 103 (in the Lockerbie disaster), Flight 93 (on 9/11)

flight path two words

floodlighting but *floodlit*

floodwater one word

flotation (shares) but *floatation* (tanks)

flout not the same as *flaunt*

flowerbed one word; also *flowerpot*

flu (no apostrophe) acceptable for influenza

flunky prefer to flunkey; plural *flunkies*

flyer whether a pilot or a handbill. A *high-flyer*

flying boat an aircraft that can land only on water, eg a Sunderland; not to be confused with an amphibian aircraft that also has landing gear, and so can land on terra firma as well as water, eg a Catalina

Flying Squad upper case this one for clarity; but *fraud squads, vice squads, drug squads, crime squads, regional crime squads*

focused one s

foetus, foetal not fetus etc; similarly, *foetid* not fetid

fogey plural *fogeys*

folk song, folk singer no longer use hyphens

following avoid as a ponderous synonym of *after*

font prefer in the typographical sense to *fount*

food and drink cap proper nouns (or adjectives derived from them) when they form part of a name; this will give capitals in some places where they may seem fussy or otiose, but it will spare readers the irritation of a lower case letter on words which in themselves (as words) seem naturally to demand a capital: Bakewell tart, Cornish pasty, Eton mess, Lancashire hotpot, Worcestershire sauce, Yorkshire pudding etc; lower case for what have become in English common nouns: hamburger, frankfurter, sandwich etc; see **cheeses, wines**

foodie

foolproof no hyphen

foot-and-mouth disease

for-, fore- the general rule is that the e is added only when the prefix has the meaning of *before*. Thus "he *forbears* (he refrains) from criticising his *forebears* (his ancestors)"; *forgo* (go without), *forego* (go before, as in foregone conclusion). Take particular care with *forswear* and *foresee(able)*, both frequently misspelt

forced to always look twice at this phrase: "The police were forced to call in troops in support ..." Is "forced to" giving the correct impression?

forces say the armed forces where possible

foreign appellations *The Times* no longer routinely uses local honorifics (M, Mme, Mlle, Herr, Frau etc). Use English styles

(Mr, Mrs, Ms, Dr) for all nationalities, except where it is possible/appropriate to use a local title (eg Ayatollah, Begum, Chief, Pandit, Sheikh, General, Bishop, Professor, Baron etc);

NB in Burma, U means Mr, Daw means Mrs; in China, use the first Chinese name as surname, eg Deng Xiaoping becomes Mr Deng

foreign immigration avoid this tautology in stories about movements of people from one country to another, despite its popularity with those who disapprove of the phenomenon

Foreign Office prefer this at first and subsequent mentions, reserving its full title, Foreign and Commonwealth Office, for when the context demands it (such as a story in which FCO crops up in many quotes). Historically, it was the Foreign Office pre-1968 (with the Commonwealth Office separate), and the Foreign Office is how the combined institution is most commonly known today

foreign places as a general rule use the spellings in *The Times Atlas of the World*, including Chinese place names. However, *The Times* retains the anglicised spellings of many familiar (and especially European) cities and countries, such as Brussels, Cologne, Cracow, Dunkirk, Florence, Geneva, Gothenburg, the Hague, Lyons, Majorca, Marseilles, Mexico City, Minorca, Moscow, Munich, Naples, Prague, Rheims, Rome, Venice. Be aware that our practice in this area remains always under review, and may change; there was a time, not so very long ago, when we happily wrote of Brunswick and Leghorn

foreign words write in roman when foreign words and phrases have become essentially a part of the English language. Retain accents on such words when they affect pronunciation or meaning. Unfamiliar foreign words should be in italics, translated in brackets if necessary. Avoid pretension: use an English phrase wherever one will serve. Beware the temptation to overload even travel pieces with the local names for things; a little exotic colour goes a long way

forensic means pertaining to the courts. A forensic expert could be a solicitor or a biochemist; make your meaning clear by writing *forensic scientist, forensic medicine* etc. Prefer not to use forensics as a shorthand for forensic science tests or the like. This is almost a lost cause, but not one that should be given up

for ever means always; *forever* means continually (eg "we are forever getting them confused")

for free resist if possible this illogical if popular construction of preposition and adjective. "For cheap" or "for expensive" would not be contemplated. You should generally be able to get by with just *free* (adjective); if not, prefer *for nothing* (preposition and noun), *without charge, at no cost* etc; you will be in a minority, but you will be right

forklift truck

former it is better not to describe someone as "the former something" if, at the time under discussion, they still were whatever it was. So, in less abstract terms, Tony Blair is better described not as "the former prime minister who led Britain to war in Iraq" but as "the prime minister who led Britain to war in Iraq"; what matters is that he was prime minister then, not that he is no longer prime minister now. Similarly, it makes more sense to say that "Chris Huhne's wife took driving licence penalty points on his behalf" than to say it was "his former wife"; he and Vicky Price have since divorced, but they were still married at the time of the offence. This may seem an unnecessary fuss — in most cases it will be perfectly clear to the reader what is meant — but the extra precision then allows us to make a small but occasionally useful distinction in referring eg to "the assassination of the former prime minister of India, Rajiv Gandhi" (prime minister from 1984 to 1989, he had left office by the time he was killed in 1991)

formula plural usually *formulas*, but *formulae* in mathematical and scientific contexts

Formula One can be F1 at the second mention

for Queen and country, for King and country cap as the monarch being served is always specific

for real avoid this ugly, transatlantic cliché. Say what you mean: *real, genuine, in reality, really* etc

fortuitous does not mean *fortunate*. It means *by chance* or *accidental*. Do not misuse

forum plural *forums*

four-letter words avoid wherever possible. If there is no alternative (eg in direct quotes that are essential to the story) soften them with three asterisks: f***, f***ing, c*** etc. Many readers are much less tolerant of obscenity than some regular *Times* columnists would like to believe. See **obscenities, racist language, swearing**

Fourth Estate for clarity caps referring to the press in Britain, as part of the body politic (the first three being the lords temporal, lords spiritual and commons)

Fourth of July or *US Independence Day* (not 4th)

four-wheel drive (for the power system), but a *four-wheel-drive vehicle*

foxhunt, foxhunting no hyphens, as *foxhound, foxhole, master of foxhounds* (lower case). Note the Hunting Act 2004

fractions do not mix fractions, decimals and percentages in the same story. Compounds such as half-hour, half-dozen etc take a hyphen; half an hour, half a dozen do not. Follow style for whole numbers and write out up to and including ten (only exception is percentages). Hyphenate when fractions are adjectival — "two-thirds full", "a two-and-a-half-year contract" — but not as nouns — "two thirds of the bus was empty". Such expressions usually take the plural verb, eg "three quarters of the children prefer horror films"; the same applies even in "a third of the children prefer blancmange"

franc lower case for the currency, and abbreviate as, eg Fr40; specify in historic and other contexts if not French, eg BFr40 (Belgian), SwFr40 (Swiss)

franchisor no longer franchiser; nasty word either way

Frankenstein foods do not use this pejorative phrase (or the contraction Frankenfoods) to describe genetically modified (GM) foods, except in direct quotations

fraud squad lower case

freak wave always treat this phrase with profound scepticism. Coasts can be dangerous and people may drown because of their lack of familiarity with how big normal waves are. Scientifically, there are such things as freak waves, but they are far less common than landlubberish media reports sensationally suggest. Beware

freebie permissible as colloquialism for a handout, free trip etc; no longer seems to need inverted commas

free churches, free churchman etc, lower case these nonconformists, but cap specific institutions, the Free Church of Scotland, Hampstead Garden Suburb Free Church

Freedom of Information Act spell out in full at first mention, thereafter simply the act. As a concept, freedom of information may be abbreviated to FoI; the act gives everyone the right to ask any public sector organisation for all recorded information on any subject, known as an FoI request

free fall two words

free kick

freemasonry, mason, masonic but *the Freemasons* in specific references

French many hours could be (and have been) spent attempting to distinguish beans from fries and windows from horns. Rather than worry about whether something is "really" French or not, and whether it therefore "really" needs a capital letter, it seems simpler to consider that *French* (as an adjective derived from a proper name) is a word that of itself and in almost every context just looks more natural capped; so cap it

French names prefer the more anglicised style for street names, capitalising rue, place etc: Rue Royale, Place de la Victoire, Boulevard des Montagnes. No need to hyphenate place names such as St Malo, St Etienne etc

frescoes not frescos

freshers week no apostrophe needed

"friendly fire" this euphemism should be in quotes in headings and at first mention in copy

Fringe, the Edinburgh always cap to avoid confusion, whether as noun or adjective (eg a Fringe puppet show on the Royal Mile)

Frisbee cap, unfortunately, as it is a proprietary name; flying disc might be a rather awkward generic substitute

front bench, the (noun); but *frontbencher, frontbench power* etc

frontline (adjective, as in the frontline states), but *the front line* (noun)

frontman one word

frontrunner no hyphen

FTSE 100 index (do not hyphenate FT-SE), also *FTSE all-share index*; both can be shortened to the FTSE 100 or the FTSE all-share

fuchsia spelt thus, because named after Leonhard Fuchs, a German botanist

fuel is becoming a greatly overworked verb, especially in headlines; always seek other options such as *raise, increase, add to, drive,* even *boost*

Führer not Fuehrer

Fujiyama or *Mount Fuji*, not Mount Fujiyama

fulfil, **fulfilment** but *fulfilled, fulfilling*

-ful, **-fuls** so *cupfuls*, not cupsful

full points no need for full points after initials, or space between initials, whether for individuals or for companies. So FW de Klerk, PJ Harvey, TS Eliot, WG Grace, as well as WH Smith, J Sainsbury, *ET the Extra-Terrestrial*. See **companies**, **initials**

full-time (adj), but *full time* (noun, as in football)

fulsome be careful, and sparing, with this word. It is widely (but alas not universally) held to mean excessive or insincere, rather than lavish or abundant. Many readers will therefore understand "fulsome praise" to be praise that is overdone or hypocritical, when all that the writer may intend is *generous* or *warm*. A word so open to misunderstanding (or misuse) may be best avoided altogether. "Fulsome praise" is a dreadful cliché anyway, sincerely meant or not

fundholders as in NHS

fundraising, **fundraiser** no hyphen

further seems to have replaced farther in most senses; preserve the distinction if you can get it right (see **farther**)

fury avoid the temptation to overuse this hyperbolic word, particularly in the lazy tabloid headline construction "Fury as ..." Real "fury" is rarely expressed or intended; anger, irritation or even mild disappointment are more likely responses to most of the things that are written about in this way

fusillade

Gg

Gaddafi, Colonel (Muammar) the now dead Libyan leader; Colonel Gaddafi at second mention. Note spelling, and that he was not president

gadwall a species of duck; plural is *gadwalls*

gaff is a hook or spar, also slang for a house; *gaffe* is a blunder or indiscretion. Note to *blow the gaff* (let out a secret)

gallon the US gallon is not the same as the imperial gallon so extra care is needed when converting American pump prices to British ones. The US gallon is 3.785 litres; the imperial gallon is 4.547 litres

Gambia, the keep the definite article, as part of the country's official name

gambit is a technical term in chess, meaning an opening involving a sacrifice in return for general advantage. Thus "opening gambit" is a tautology (and a pleonasm, and a cliché). Take care with its use as a metaphor, and use sparingly. Note *endgame* (one word)

game plan

game show, chat show, quiz show, talk show etc. No hyphens for nouns or adjectival use, eg game show contestant

the gardai is the formal name by which the Irish police force is generally known in Ireland. Use this term, lower case, to refer to the force generally or to police officers (plural). An individual officer is a *garda*. The word garda is sometimes used as an adjective, as in "garda pay reform", "garda recruitment" etc; use lower case. The phrase Irish police is acceptable

garrotte

gas, gases (noun); *gassed, gassing* (verbal use) and note *gases* (not gasses) for present tense, eg "doctor gases patient"

gasfield as *coalfield, oilfield*

gastropub

-gate use, serious or jocular, of this tired Watergate-derived suffix to designate any new scandal is lazy and to be discouraged

gateau

Gatwick sufficiently well known not to need airport in title

gavel used in Britain by auctioneers, not by judges, so likely to be an unwise choice of illustration for legal stories. Beware

gay fully acceptable as a synonym for homosexual or lesbian

gay marriage do not put in quotation marks

GDP gross domestic product. In most contexts, sufficiently well known not to need spelling out

gelatine rather than gelatin

Geldof, Bob never call him Sir Bob Geldof, as he is an honorary KBE (as an Irish citizen) and so may not use the title

gender is a term of grammar; prefer not to use as a synonym of a person's sex, although this may be a lost cause

general election always lower case. The Fixed-Term Parliaments Act 2011 introduced a system of five-year fixed terms. It allows the prime minister to alter the date by up to two months. An election can be called before the end of the five-year term if a motion of no confidence is passed and no alternative government is found; or if a motion for an early election is agreed by at least two thirds of the House

General Medical Council note the *fitness-to-practise panel*

general secretary (of the TUC or of individual unions), keep lower case

General Strike of 1926 (caps)

General Synod of the Church of England, thereafter the synod

Geneva conventions plural

Gentile(s) cap

gentlemen's club prefer to gentleman's; also *gentlemen's agreement*

geriatric does not mean elderly, but is applied to medical treatment for the elderly, eg geriatric hospital. Never use as a term of abuse

German in German all nouns take an initial capital letter. They should be allowed to do so when borrowed for local colour, unless they have passed into English usage to the point where they no longer need to be written in italics (eg zeitgeist, schadenfreude). Use umlauts as required. Cap *German* as an adjective in eg *German measles, German shepherd dog* etc

Germany full title is the Federal Republic of Germany. If referring to the area that was East Germany, say eastern Germany or the former East Germany; similarly, western Germany or the former West Germany. Ossis, Wessis permissible vernacular for inhabitants of the two parts. When plural, use the two Germanys, not Germanies. Reunification was in 1990. In the postwar period sporting teams etc represented West Germany and East Germany separately

gerrymander

get, **got** often a lazy verb for which an alternative should be sought

ghetto plural *ghettos*

ghillie rather than gillie

giant killer, **giant killing** (nouns), but *giant-killing* (adj)

gibe means taunt or sneer; gybe means to shift direction or change course, particularly in sailing. Use neither; for the sake of simplicity, prefer *jibe* (a variant of both)

gig perfectly acceptable for a musical event, as *rave*

gipsy no; use *gypsy/Gypsy*

girl do not use as a synonym of *woman* except in informal contexts or direct quotes

girl band two words. Note also *boy band*

girlfriend one word, as *boyfriend*

girlie not girly

giro lower case, as in benefit payments, cheques etc

Giuseppe the standard spelling for the Italian equivalent of Joseph

giveaway (noun or adjective), one word, as *takeaway*; but to *give away*

glamorise, glamorous, but **glamour**

glasnost not italic

glassmaker

Glen Coe the valley; but *Glencoe* for the battle, the village and the pass

glisters, all that ... Shakespeare did not write "glitters" in reference to what is not gold; better to quote precisely or not at all (*The Merchant of Venice*, Act II, scene vii)

Glorious Twelfth, the caps, for the August start of the grouse-shooting season

glueing prefer to gluing

glühwein lower case, roman, accent

glycerin no need for terminal e; likewise *nitroglycerin* and *trinitroglycerin*

go-ahead, give the prefer *approve*, shorter and preferable to this cliché

goatherd one word

gobbledegook

God cap when referring to just one, in any religion. No need for he, his, him to take cap unless there is a risk of confusion. Many gods, use lower case, as in *the Greek gods*. Bear in mind that there are readers who dislike the use of "God" as an expletive or exclamation

goddam

godforsaken, **godless** lower case, but *God-fearing*

godparents, **godfather**, **godmother**, **godson**, **goddaughter**, **godchild**

Goebbels, Joseph -oe- not umlaut. Similarly, *Hermann Goering*

-goer as a suffix, run on as one word, as in *churchgoer, cinemagoer, operagoer, partygoer, theatregoer* etc

going forward now widely and horridly used to mean *in future*; avoid

go-kart use hyphen

gold 24-carat gold is pure; 9-carat gold would have 9/24th gold in the alloy with other metals

Golden Globes note that, contrary to the cliché, these film awards are not reliable pointers to Oscar success

Golden Jubilee caps for the Queen's celebration in 2002, lower case in general context

Golders Green no apostrophe

goldmine, **goldmining**

gold rush two words as noun, but hyphenate adjectivally, eg gold-rush fever

gold standard lower case

goodbye

good-time Charlie

goodwill one word, whether used as a noun or adjective

Google cap noun; *google* lower case verb; *googling, googled* etc; as per *Hoover/hoover, Twitter/tweet, Skype, skype*

gorilla

Gothenburg not Göteborg

gothic not Gothick, and lower case for whatever meaning, including architectural, artistic, fashion, literary, musical and tribal; likewise *goth* (except for the East Germanic tribe who troubled the Romans, who are capped)

gotten do not use except in direct quotes or, if you must, in *ill-gotten gains*

gourmandise

government lower case all governments, British and overseas, even when referring to a specific one. Also lower case government in all adjectival contexts

government departments cap when giving full title (eg Department of Health), lower case when abbreviated, as in health department etc. Prefer to use the fuller form if possible with British government departments, at least at first reference

governor lower case, whether of the Bank of England, of the Falkland Islands, of a US state or of a prison

governor-general takes a hyphen everywhere except Canada

Graces *The Three Graces* (Canova's statue)

grade II listed, grade II* listed etc no hyphen or caps

graffito singular; plural *graffiti* (but generally used as singular, with singular verb, except in specialist — eg art historical or archaeological — contexts; no point fighting this)

gram not gramme; similarly, *kilogram*

Grammy, Grammys

grandad but *granddaughter*

grand jury lower case, in US contexts

grandmaster (chess) lower case

grand slam noun, lower case; *grand-slam* adjective, lower case, hyphen

Grand Tour, the caps, for the upper-class cultural trip round Europe

grassroots (adjective), the *grass roots* (noun). Try to use this cliché sparingly

grave, turn in his/her dismal hackneyed phrase, best avoided, and definitely not to be used if the person is not dead

gravlax (rather than gravadlax) dry-cured salmon, marinated in salt, sugar and spices

great and the good, the (all lower case, and quotes usually unnecessary); not one to overuse

Great Britain or **Britain** = England, Wales, Scotland and islands governed from the mainland (ie, not Isle of Man or Channel Islands). *United Kingdom* = Great Britain and Northern Ireland. *British Isles* = United Kingdom and the Republic of Ireland, Isle of Man and Channel Islands. *Britain* is widely used as another name for the United Kingdom or Great Britain, and pragmatically we accept this usage

Great Dane upper case. See **dogs**

Greater London Authority (GLA at subsequent mention) is the strategic government for London, consisting of the mayor of London and the London Assembly, backed up by a staff of 400. *The London Assembly* (not the Greater London Assembly, and subsequently *the assembly*) is an elected body of 25 members providing checks and balances on the mayor of London

greater or lesser degree lesser is not correct but is common usage

Great Ormond Street Hospital for Children (no longer Sick Children), but Great Ormond Street Hospital acceptable

Great Train Robber(s), Great Train Robbery on August 8, 1963, in Buckinghamshire

Greco- not Graeco-

green belt lower case, but *greenfield sites* (similarly *brownfield*)

green line lower case, demarcation line between hostile factions in, eg Jerusalem, Beirut, Cyprus; likewise, *green zone*

green paper lower case in official government sense (often precedes a white paper)

Green Party or the Greens, but *green issues* etc, lower case, for generic environmental matters

Greenwich Mean Time (GMT) thus; likewise, *British Summer Time* (BST). Follow a similar style for overseas time zones, eg *Eastern Standard Time* (EST)

green zone lower case as *green line*

grenade no need to write hand grenade; but qualify if delivered in another way, eg rocket-propelled grenade

griffin prefer to griffon or gryphon

grisly means horrifying, repugnant; *grizzly* means greyish, grizzled, or is a short form of *grizzly bear*

grottoes

ground(s) for at least half a century *Times* style guides have suggested, even insisted, that ground, in the sense of reason, may not be used in the plural unless more than one is given: eg "on the ground (not grounds) of diminished responsibility", and "he gave up his job on the ground of illness" but "he gave up his job on the grounds of his failed marriage and illness". This seems an extraordinary superstition to have clung to for so long; it is time to abandon it (if only on the grounds that no one took much notice anyway). *On the* (plural) *grounds of* is idiomatic English, however few grounds there may be, while *on the* (singular) *ground of* sounds unnatural and odd. *Because of* may often be better anyway, of course

groundbreaking one word, and not one to overuse

G-string

Guantanamo Bay Cuba (no accent), avoid referring to it as Guantanamo, a city about 15 miles away that is not under US control. The name also applies to the surrounding province

guerrilla note double r and double l; beware of loaded terms for advocates of political violence

guest avoid using as a verb (Lady X will guest on the show; say Lady X will be among the guests, or Lady X is a guest)

guesthouse no hyphen

guidebook similarly, *chequebook, formbook, stylebook, textbook* etc

Guides (not Girl Guides) Girlguiding UK became the name in April 2002 for the Guide Association; the individual members are still known as guides, brownies and rainbows

Guildhall (London) not *the* Guildhall

guinea pig no longer hyphen

Gujarati person or language (not Guje-)

gulag loosely, labour camps; Gulag (cap) was the Soviet organisation that ran the prisons and forced labour camps

Gulf, the avoid Persian Gulf and Arabian Gulf in this politically sensitive area; other gulfs, eg of Aden or of Florida, will need to be identified

Gulf war, the do not write "the first Gulf war". Refer to the subsequent conflict as the Iraq war (lower case)

gunboat likewise *gunfight, gunfire, gunman, gunpoint, gunshot, gunsmith* but *gun dog*

gunned down avoid this Americanism, which means *shot*; if you mean *shot dead,* say it

gunrunner, gunrunning one word

gunwales not gunwhales; (pronounced gunnels, which is an alternative spelling, although not one we use)

gurdwara (lower case, roman) a Sikh temple

Gurkhas thus

guttural not gutteral

Guyana (formerly British Guiana, now independent); do not confuse with *French Guiana* (still a French overseas territory).

The adjective from Guyana is *Guyanese*, also the person. Note also *Surinam* (not Suriname), the former Dutch Guiana

Guy Fawkes Night no apostrophe, initial caps; similarly *Bonfire Night*

Gypsy/gypsy (not gipsy). Use the cap when referring to the ethnic group defined in law, but lower case if using in a lifestyle, fashion or general sense, as in "gypsy style is the look for spring". The other wandering groups in Britain are Irish tinkers, who prefer the name *Irish Travellers* (likewise now defined in law as an ethnic group and so, in this sense, to be capped); the *Scottish Gypsies/Travellers*; and the latter-day hippies sometimes referred to as *New Age travellers*; when discussing lifestyle rather than ethnicity, *travellers* is a useful generic term for these itinerant groups. Note (the) *Roma* is the term for Gypsies from the Continent, some of whom have sought asylum in western Europe. Do not confuse with Romanians. The singular and adjectival form is *Romany*, eg a Romany woman, but Gypsy can be used in the same way. Prefer *Romani* for the language

Hh

Hadrian's Wall is not literally the border between England and Scotland, so take care in writing phrases such as "north of Hadrian's Wall" when "north of the border" is meant precisely. But in lighter and/or historical pieces, of course, mention of the wall as a frontier may be appropriate. See **border**

haemorrhage means heavy and potentially dangerous bleeding, not simply bleeding. Beware of misuse in metaphor

Hague, the lower case t

hairbrush, haircut, hairdo, hairdresser, hairdressing, hairdryer, hairpin, hairstyle

Haiti, Haitian note that Haiti must not be described as an island; it is joined to the Dominican Republic and together they constitute the island of Hispaniola

haj pilgrimage to Mecca, lower case and roman

haka the Maori war dance, lower case and roman

half-hearted, half-mast, half-term hyphenate

half-time in a football match etc; the *half time* in business context (but *half-time results*)

halfway no hyphen

Halley's comet thus, but Bill Haley and his Comets

Hallowe'en

Hamas is an acronym in Arabic for the Islamic Resistance Movement; the Arabic word *hamas* means zeal, courage

handheld (computers etc) as *desktop, laptop, palmtop* etc

handmade, handbuilt no hyphens

handout as a noun, no hyphen; two words as a verb; likewise, *hangout*

hangar (aircraft), *hanger* (clothes)

hanged "The murderer was hanged at dawn", not hung. Clothes are *hung* on a washing line or a hanger

Hansard

hara-kiri

hardcore one word as adjective, eg hardcore pornography; but the *hard core* of the rebels (two words as noun); similarly, *hard core* (rubble)

hardline (adjective) but *taking a hard line*

harebrained

harem

Haringey is a London borough and council; *Harringay* a London neighbourhood

HarperCollins or **HarperCollins Publishers** a subsidiary of News Corp

Harris Tweed cap, trademark

harvest festival lower case

Hasidic prefer to Hassidic, Chassidic etc

Hawk-Eye note hyphen in electronic sports equipment for lbw, line decisions etc

hay fever no hyphen

headache avoid as a synonym of *difficulty*

headbutt noun or verb, no hyphen; this is preferable to butt, although it may appear tautologous. While butt can mean to strike or push (something) with head or horns, it has a variety of other definitions, including the anatomical; headbutt has the benefit of clarity

headcount no hyphen

headed avoid the Americanism he is headed, she was headed etc; write he is heading, she was heading etc

headhunt, headhunting etc no hyphens

headlines good headlines are not easy to write. They must make the busy reader stop and want to read; a dull or confusing headline will have the opposite effect. The best headlines intrigue, entertain and convey in a very few words the substance and essence of a story that may be nuanced, complex and highly sensitive. In doing so they must be accurate and impartial. They may not go beyond the facts of the story; headlines not supported by the text are a breach of the Editors' Code, by which *The Times* abides.

Some thoughts. Remember that the force of every headline is in the verb. Active is better than passive, concrete better than abstract, positive usually better than negative. Generally prefer to express one idea clearly than to link two with a tired conjunction such as *as*. Find the key words — vivid words — in the text and try to get them into the headline. Emphasise what makes this story interesting, surprising, important and new. Do not just duplicate the opening sentence of the text (but if the opening sentence gives you a terrific headline that fits, it may then sometimes be easier to remove the duplication by rewriting the text). Avoid the worst clichés and hyperboles such as bash, crash, shock, slam etc; but short words such as *bid* (for attempt), *crisis*, *hit* (adversely affect), *row* (clash or dispute) — all of which should appear only sparingly in text — are permissible in headlines, provided that they are not overworked. Acronyms and initials can be offputting in a headline; keep them to a minimum, and try not to start with them. Similarly, dull and offputting (but essential) words — ministers, experts, civil servants, government etc — are generally better deployed at the end: "We're all doomed, experts warn" is a more dramatic and immediate construction than "Experts warn that we're all doomed" (although it is to be hoped that neither of those headlines finds its way into print). Beware of names in headlines; they need to be instantly recognisable, and they should be there only if they aid understanding and make readers more likely to read. If words and phrases belong together — cost of living, elderly patients, young drivers, poor families, spy scandal etc — avoid splitting them across lines. Beware impenetrable jumbles of words that might be nouns, adjectives or verbs: *Miners strike deal bid shock.* Go easy on the puns; they are often more fun for sub-editors to write than for readers to read; a headline must make sense in its own right, not just allude to, or sound a bit like, something else.

Inverted commas are always single in headlines, straps and display panels on News, Sport and Business pages. Ideally they should not enclose words or statements that differ from those in the report; if a headline uses inverted commas around a summary or paraphrase rather than a direct quotation, great care must be taken to ensure that the effect is not inaccurate or misleading

headmaster, headmistress one word and lower case. Some schools have variants on the usual style: *head master, high master* etc; always check which is required, but these too are all lower case. The colloquial "head" is useful not only in headlines but as an alternative to all these variants (after first mention) in text; note that *head teacher* is two words except when part of the designated title

headroom one word; as *elbowroom, legroom*

heads of state when these are royal, such as King Abdullah of Jordan, after the first mention refer to them as the king (lower case). The cap at subsequent mentions applies only to the Queen (Elizabeth II). For overseas heads of state write, eg President Y of Ukraine (President and surname and country) at first mention, then the president (lower case) or simply Mr Y

head up (an organisation etc) avoid; write simply, eg "she will head the organisation"

healthcare one word

heart attack and *cardiac arrest* are not synonymous; do not change one to the other without checking what is meant

heartbroken, heartbreaking, heartfelt, heartstrings but hyphenate *heart-rending, heart-throb*

-hearted hyphenate, eg light-hearted

Heathrow sufficiently well known not to need airport in title

heatstroke one word. A condition resulting from prolonged exposure to intense heat, cf *sunstroke*, which is heatstroke caused by prolonged exposure to intensely hot sunlight

heatwave make one word

Heaven, Hell cap in religious context only

heavenly bodies cap the proper names of planets, stars, constellations etc: Venus, Arcturus, the Plough, Aries; for comets, lower case the word comet in, eg Halley's comet. *The universe* is lower case, as are *the moon* and *the sun*, unless caps seem better and more consistent in specific astronomical context (eg Night Sky column); generally, lower case for *the earth* (except in specific planetary context and when necessary to distinguish from soil; see **earth**). Use lower case for the adjectives *lunar* and *solar*, and phases, eg full moon, new moon; but cap *Martian* adjectivally and as a noun

hellhole one word

Hell's Angels apostrophe, despite evidence on jackets to the contrary

helping the police with their inquiries avoid this phrase: suspects rarely willingly help the police. Say "were being interviewed" instead

helpline one word. See **hotline**

help to (plus verb) is generally preferable, eg "he helped *to* make the cake", not "he helped make the cake", but this need not be treated as a rigid rule

hemisphere northern, southern, eastern, western

heraldry do not confuse *crests* with *coats of arms*. Most arms consist of a shield and a crest; crests are the topmost part of the coat of arms (think of the crest of a bird or a wave)

heralds the curious titles of the officers of the College of Arms seem to need capitals: Garter King of Arms, Somerset Herald, Rouge Croix Pursuivant etc

Her Majesty's pleasure detained at

Hezbollah (Party of God) in Iran and Lebanon; soft-hyphenate (on a line break) as Hezb-ollah

Hibernian means of or concerning Ireland, not Scotland, despite the Edinburgh football club of that name

hiccup not hiccough

hi-fi is an acceptable abbreviation (noun or adjective) of high fidelity, but *wifi* (lower case, one word)

high acceptable usage as a noun, eg "she was on a high". But avoid clichés such as "all-time high" and "hits new high"

highbrow, lowbrow

high command avoid its clichéd use, as in "Tory high command"

high commissioner lower case, eg the Indian high commissioner; thereafter, the high commissioner. Remember that Commonwealth countries and the UK have high commissioners serving in high commissions in each other's countries, not ambassadors serving in embassies

High Court upper court

highfalutin

high-flyer like *flyer*

high jinks

high-profile unappealing (and often redundant) adjective; there are many better words to use instead: *prominent, famous, celebrated, renowned, big* etc

high sheriff lower case

high street is lower case and no hyphen in general sense, as in high street prices, high street shops. But cap in specific names, eg Putney High Street

high-tech but *hi-tech* acceptable in headlines

Hindi for language context (the Hindi language); but use *Hindu* for religious or ethnic contexts (an adherent to Hinduism, or relating to Hinduism)

hingeing prefer to hinging

hip-hop hyphenate

hippopotamuses plural

hippy, hippies almost as old-fashioned as *beatniks*

historic, historical prefer *a historic event* rather than an historic. Also, take care with use of historical and historic; the former can refer only to past history, while the latter can refer to a contemporary event likely to be of long-term significance. But *a historic building* is now in common usage as a synonym of an old building. Say *historical sex-abuse cases*, not historic

hit try to avoid in text in sense of affected, eg "Homeowners were hit last night by an interest rate rise", or in the sense of attack, eg "The minister hit out at his critics". Sparing use of the verb in headlines is permissible

hitchhike, hitchhiker, hitchhiking etc, no longer hyphenated. Note *The Hitchhiker's Guide to the Galaxy*, by Douglas Adams

hi-tech is acceptable in headlines, but prefer *high-tech* in text

hitlist, hitman no hyphens

HIV is a virus, not a disease. Do not write "HIV virus" (tautology), but use a phrase such as *HIV-infected*. Write *HIV/Aids* when appropriate regarding the virus and the condition together. See **Aids**

HMS do not italicise in a ship's name, eg HMS *Ark Royal*, also roman (as is the name) when part of a shore-based establishment, eg HMS Collingwood; do not write *the* HMS Anything, as the article is redundant

hoards are stocks or stores (of treasure, for example); *to hoard* is to amass and store food, money etc; *hordes* are large groups or gangs (of wild beasts etc)

hobbit generic lower case, but *The Hobbit* is the title of the book

hobo prefer *hoboes* as plural

Hogmanay cap

hoi polloi means, literally, "the many", so it does not need "the"; common usage mostly says otherwise, but we should continue to resist. Roman, not italic

holidaymaker one word

Holland use *the Netherlands* (lower case t) for all contexts except sports teams, historical uses or when referring to the provinces of North and South Holland. The adjective is *Dutch*

Holocaust cap as in the mass murder of Jews and other ethnic and social groups in Europe by the Nazis

Holy Communion caps

Holy Grail (caps) when referring to the Last Supper; *holy grail* (lower case) when used figuratively (as *mecca*)

Holyroodhouse

Holy Week the week leading up to Easter (Easter Week is the week after)

homebuilder, homebuilding (one word) but note Home Builders Federation. See **housebuilder**

homebuyers, homeowners no hyphens

home counties, the lower case

homemade no hyphen

homeopathy no longer homoeopathy. Similarly, for other words with the prefix homeo-, meaning like, similar, eg *homeobox*, *homeostasis*, *homeotherm*

home town two words, but hyphenate in adjectival use, eg home-town memories

homogeneous means having parts all of the same kind; *homogenous* (rarely needed and if encountered most likely a mistake) is a term from biology meaning similar owing to common descent

Homo sapiens now italicise, as any other scientific names

Hon, the when referring to the children of peers, normally restrict this form of address (the Hon So-and-So) to the Court & Social page

honeybee one word

honeytrap one word

honour killing is a euphemism for murders by family members committed usually for socio-religious reasons. Most readers understand what it means, but we should not be seen to be adopting the phrase uncritically; if helpful, use with quote marks or add *so-called*

honours strictly speaking, people are *appointed* KBE, CBE, OBE, MBE etc. There is no need to speak strictly all the time, however; in less formal contexts it is quite acceptable to follow common usage for the sake of variety and to write that someone was made GCVO, was awarded the OBE, received (or even got) the MBE etc; this licence should not be overused, but it may be helpful when reporting large honours lists. Note that baronets, peers etc are formally *created*, not appointed etc. Privy counsellors, in an engagingly impressive formulation, are "sworn of the privy council", although we can just say that someone was made a privy counsellor, if we prefer. At investitures those honoured receive the insignia of the award, not the award itself. Normally (except on Court Page) omit honours and decorations after names unless somehow relevant

hoodie plural *hoodies*

hoof plural *hoofs*

Hoover is a trade name so must be capped as a noun; generically, use *vacuum cleaner*, or to *vacuum*. But as a verb use lower case, eg he hoovered up his food

hopefully except in very informal contexts, try to avoid in the sense of "it is hoped that", even though this usage is so widespread

Horse Guards Parade

horse race/racing two words, but *racing* alone is preferable; *riding* similarly preferable to horse riding (also two words). Note Horserace Betting Levy Board

horse trading two words

horsey

horticulturist not horticulturalist

hospitalise, hospitalisation Americanisms; prefer *taken to hospital, treated in hospital* etc

hospitals cap when the full title is given, eg County Hospital, Staffordshire (formerly Stafford Hospital); Birmingham Children's Hospital; Great Ormond Street Hospital

host avoid verbal usages such as "West Ham will host Aston Villa on Saturday"; use *play host to* instead. But a person can host an event

hotchpotch no hyphen. Note that *hodgepodge* is the preferred variant in North America

hotline one word; similarly, *helpline*

hotpants one word

hotspot one word

hot-water bottle note hyphen

hour and a half, an no hyphens as a noun; but hyphenate adjectivally, eg an hour-and-a-half break. Similarly for two and a half years, two thirds. But note twenty-three etc

housebuilder, housebuilding but note the Home Builders Federation (formerly the House Builders Federation). See **homebuilder, homebuyers**

house prices do not routinely round these up or down as you might other large numbers; the difference between a £1.75 million house and a £2 million house may feel quite significant to the purchaser and the vendor.

Think carefully when giving house prices in stories about victims of crime. This tabloid convention may be a usefully concise way of conveying the background to a story, but it offends some readers and should not be done casually

however when used in the sense of nevertheless, always needs a comma after it (and before, when in the middle of a sentence, eg "It was said, however, that the agent ..."). Note also the comma in the extended clause: "However many times I say this, there are people who ignore it." Do not attempt to use *however* as a conjunction between clauses when what you need is a new sentence (or *but*): "The pedant's sharp eye does not dim, however his misanthropy becomes even more marked as the years pass." This ungainly and unclear construction is quite common, and quite wrong

Howzat? the cricket appeal (from "How's that?")

human acceptable as noun as well as adjective; alternatively, *human being*

human rights European Convention on Human Rights; European Court of Human Rights. Both operate under the aegis of the Council of Europe, not the European Union (or EC); take particular care not to get this wrong

hummus note less-exotic preferred spelling for the now perfectly familiar chickpea dip

humongous

humorist not humourist

Hundred Years' War, the note apostrophe

hung parliament lower case

Huntington's chorea now properly known as *Huntington's disease*

hunting with hounds (not with dogs). Note the Hunting Act 2004. See **foxhunt**

hurricane cap as part of title, eg Hurricane Andrew; similarly, Tropical Storm Linda (caps)

hydroelectric no hyphen

hyena prefer to hyaena; but note that *Hyaena* is the scientific genus name

hyperbole eschew it. Few allegations are truly "sensational"; stock markets may fall without "panic"; a surprising revelation need not be a "shock" and in *The Times* there need never be a "bombshell". Emotive clichés add little to understanding; readers are intelligent enough to judge things for themselves

hyphens be sparing with hyphens, and run together words where the sense suggests and where they look familiar and right; eg *blacklist, businessman, goldmine, knockout, intercontinental, motorcycle, takeover* and *walkover*. Unusual hyphenations will be listed separately. However, a few guidelines can be specified:

1. Usually run together prefixes except where the last letter of the prefix is the same as the first letter of the word to which it attaches: *prearrange, postwar, prewar, nonconformist;* but *pre-empt, co-ordinate, co-operate, re-establish.*

2. Hyphenate generally in composites where the same two letters come together, eg *film-makers,* but an exception should be made for double r in the middle: *override, overrule* (not over-ride etc), and note *granddaughter* and *goddaughter.*

3. Generally do not use dangling hyphens: say "full and part-time employment" etc; but this does not apply to prefixes: "pre- or post-match drinks".

4. For hyphenation when qualifying adjectives, see **adverbs**.

5. Always use a hyphen rather than a slash (/) in dates etc: 1982-83 (not 1982/83).

On this as on much else Keith Waterhouse has wise advice: "Hyphens have a welcome tendency to wither away. When it looks as if the time has come when a compound no longer needs a hyphen, then allow it to throw away its crutch"

hypothermia state of being too cold; *hyperthermia* too hot

Ii

Iberian peninsula lower case

Ice Age see **ages**

ice cap no longer hyphenate

ice cream no longer hyphenate, similarly *ice lolly*. But hyphenate when the two are used adjectivally to qualify another noun, eg ice-cream cone

icon beware overuse in the sense of a person regarded as a sex symbol or a symbol of the latest fashion trends etc; likewise with the ghastly adjective *iconic*

Identikit is proprietary, so cap; but *photofit* lower case

ie use comma before if useful, ie like this, but not after. See **eg**

if whenever possible use the subjunctive after this, eg "if I were a rich man" (not "if I was a rich man"); more generally, aim to preserve the correct use of the subjunctive, which sometimes seems in danger of dying out

île circumflex whether lower case or cap, as in Île-de-France

illegal asylum seeker is a legally inaccurate phrase and must not be used. An asylum seeker is someone seeking refugee status or humanitarian protection, so cannot in law be "illegal". He or she can become an *illegal immigrant* only if remaining in the UK after having failed to respond to a removal notice

ill health no longer hyphenate; similarly *ill feeling* etc and any other simple adjective-and-noun construction

ill intentioned etc no hyphen in, eg "He was ill intentioned"; but *ill-intentioned* etc (hyphen) before a noun, eg "He had ill-intentioned motives"

immensity is mostly what is meant when *enormity* is wrongly used

impacted on avoid this Americanism

Imperial College London (no comma) is no longer part of the University of London (when it was known formally as Imperial College of Science, Technology and Medicine). It became a university in its own right in July 2007

imperial family no need to cap (cf *royal family*)

imply never confuse with *infer*. As the neatest definition has it, speakers imply, listeners infer. There is a school of higher pedantry that insists that it is acceptable to muddle the two, because Shakespeare did; take no notice, unless you want most readers to think you are illiterate

impostor (not imposter)

impresario

impressionist, post-impressionist generally lower case for the artistic movements when used as stylistic designations; may occasionally be capped to make precise art-historical point and/or to avoid confusion

impugn to challenge or attack as false; assail; criticise

impute to attribute or ascribe (something dishonest or dishonourable, especially a criminal offence) to a person; to attribute to a cause or source; commercially, to give (a notional value) to goods or services when the real value is unknown

in addition to prefer *as well as* or *besides*

inadmissible not -able

inasmuch as two words

inauguration but, for clarity, *Inauguration Day* (US)

include do not confuse with *comprise*; "breakfast includes toast and coffee", but "breakfast comprises cereals, toast, butter, marmalade and coffee" (ie, where the full list of elements is given)

indestructible not -able

index plural is *indices*, but *indexes* for books

Indian place names Where there are familiar English names for places, we do not need always to reflect every new local usage that may come along. Nevertheless, our preferences have changed over time and will continue to change; our practice must be kept under review. We now prefer Mumbai to Bombay and Chennai to Madras when naming the cities; but obviously not in eg culinary contexts (Madras curry, Bombay duck) or when referring to institutions and businesses which prefer the old name (the Royal Bombay Yacht Club, Bombay Bicycle Club etc). Continue to use Calcutta rather than Kolkata, Poona rather than Pune and Delhi rather than New Delhi, except where the new names form part of an official company name or similar title. If in doubt, put the alternative name in brackets

indispensable not -ible

Indo-China

Industrial Revolution, the caps

industrial tribunals were renamed *employment tribunals*. See also **tribunals**

inevitable do not use as a synonym of *customary, usual* or *predictable*

in fact can, in fact, almost invariably be omitted

infer do not confuse with *imply*; to infer is to draw a conclusion from a suggestion, to imply is to make the suggestion. Thus, we *imply* things when we speak, we *infer* things when we listen. The distinction may only have been clearly drawn in the past century or so, but it is a useful one, worth preserving

infighting one word, but *in-house* and *in-flight* (both with hyphen)

infinitives may be split if splitting improves clarity or avoids awkwardness

infrared one word, like *ultraviolet*

in happier times self-evident local paper cliché banned for captions to photographs showing grinning people now divorced, gravely ill or dead etc; "share a joke" is no better

initials where totally familiar, no need to spell out what they stand for at first mention (eg BBC, CBI, TUC, Nato etc). Generally, however, when writing about an organisation (or anything else) that may be referred to by its initials, at first mention give the full name (however cumbersome) with the initials in parentheses; the initials alone may be used thereafter, although sometimes a word such as "the organisation" or "the group" will be preferable, to avoid an ugly alphabet soup.

Where the initials can be spoken as a word, we write them as upper and lower case (even when companies or organisations may prefer caps), eg Nato, Gatt, Unesco, Eta, Rada, Riba, Ukip, Axa, Sane.

With names of companies and individuals, now omit points between the initials. WH Smith, J Sainsbury, PL Travers, TS Eliot, WG Grace (space between initials and surname; no space between initials)

injure, injury implies something more serious than *hurt*. Do not normally say someone received an injury; prefer to say they suffered or sustained an injury, or (simply) were injured. Injured or sick people should not be described as "satisfactory" or "critical", it is their condition that is satisfactory etc. Note that in a military context, eg on a battlefield, it is more normal to refer to *wounded* rather than injured; although a soldier would be injured in, eg a straightforward vehicle accident

innocent take great care with this word, and avoid phrases such as "the innocent victim of the attack" and clichés such as "innocent children". Best to stick to its literal sense of not guilty

innocuous thus

Inns of Court the order of precedence among the Inns, should you need it, is Lincoln's Inn, Inner Temple, Middle Temple, Gray's Inn

in order to simply wastes two words. Delete "in order"

in/out as in the in/out referendum on the EU: prefer a slash to a hyphen for either/or constructions

inpatients, outpatients no hyphens

inquire, inquiry not enquire, enquiry

insignia plural. Do not confuse insignia, eg for an MBE appointment, with regalia, strictly emblems of royalty

in so far as use the four words in this expression; insofar is the American version

install but *instalment*

instil

insure you *insure* against risk; you *assure* your life; *ensure* means to make certain

intelligence lower case as a noun even when referring to the security services, eg "he was in British intelligence"; "he was in military intelligence", "she provided useful intelligence to MI5"; also lower case for adjectival uses, eg "she was interviewed by intelligence officers". Only exception is in full names, eg Secret Intelligence Service (ie MI6, which is preferable anyway)

intelligence and security committee has members from both Houses of Parliament, who are chosen by the prime minister in consultation with the leaders of the two main opposition parties. The joint intelligence committee, which the ISC scrutinises, is part of the Cabinet Office. Its members are senior government department officials and heads of intelligence

intensive do not confuse with *intense* or *extreme*. It means concentrated, as in *intensive care*

inter to bury, not to be confused with *intern*, to detain

inter- as a prefix, normally no need to hyphenate, eg intercountry, interracial

interdependence

interesting avoid as an adjective; the reader will decide

interest rate cuts/rises no hyphens; avoid "hikes" for *rises*

interfaith

intergovernmental conference no hyphen. Abbreviation is IGC

intern as a verb, do not confuse with inter; *intern* (noun) is an Americanism that now seems to have passed into English usage, if only because it is much shorter than "young person on (often unpaid) work experience"

International Criminal Court, the (ICC), based in the Hague, has jurisdiction to prosecute individuals for the most horrific of crimes: genocide, crimes against humanity and war crimes. Its jurisdiction is complementary to national courts, and it acts only when countries are unable or unwilling to investigate or prosecute. Established by multilateral treaty, it is independent of the UN and was designed to replace the UN system of ad hoc tribunals, eg for Rwanda or the former Yugoslavia

international date line may be abbreviated subsequently to the date line

Internazionale the Milan football club; simply Inter Milan at first mention, thereafter Inter. The other big club in the city is AC Milan (shortened to Milan thereafter)

internecine can mean: (1) mutually destructive or ruinous; maiming both or all sides; (2) of or relating to slaughter or carnage; bloody; (3) of or involving conflict within a group or organisation

internet lower case, also *the net* for short

interpretive now prefer to interpretative

interred buried; *interned* = imprisoned. Do not confuse

intifada religious struggle or uprising, lower case and roman

intro there will be (carefully considered) exceptions, but as a general rule the opening sentences of a news report should clearly convey the essential facts of the story and make the reader want to read on. Do not try to cram in too much information; but do not wait until paragraph six to answer those obvious questions: who, where, what, why, when? Take care that you do not omit the key line that supports the intro. An opening assertion must be substantiated farther down

Inuit prefer to Eskimo. Retain Inuit as the plural

inverted commas should be used very carefully in headlines and as sparingly as possible in text. The 1959 edition of this guide enjoined its users to "avoid the kind of use which is meant to indicate that the writer dissociates himself in some unspecified way from the word he is using"

invite is a verb; resist its use as a substitute for *invitation*

iPad beware tendency to use this trade name as a generic term for tablets; same goes for iPhone and smartphones, and for iPods and MP3 players

Iran not Persia, except in historical context. The language is *Farsi*, not Iranian or Persian

Ireland the two parts should be called the Republic of Ireland or the Irish Republic (avoid Eire except in direct quotes or historical context) and Northern Ireland, or less formally Ulster. Do not use the phrase the Six Counties. The historic four provinces are Connacht (prefer to Connaught), Leinster, Munster and Ulster

Irish do not put accents on Irish words unless you are confident of getting them right

Iron Curtain

ironic, ironically beware of misuse. It means using or displaying irony, or in the nature of irony; it does not mean strange, paradoxical or incongruous

irony very difficult to bring off in a newspaper. There will always be readers ready to take literally even the most preposterous statement. Beware

irredeemable means not able to be redeemed, saved or reformed; do not confuse with *irremediable*, which means not able to be remedied, incurable, or irreparable

-ise, -isation avoid the z construction in almost all cases, eg apologise, organise, emphasise, televise. But note *capsize, synthesizer*

Islam is the religion of Muslims. *Islamic* is interchangeable with *Muslim* as the adjective, but normally use Islamic with religion and fundamentalism. *Islamist* (noun, adj) refers to support or advocacy of Islamic fundamentalism; beware of using when Islamic is all that is meant. Note *Shia Muslim(s), Sunni Muslim(s)*

Islamic State can be referred to as either Islamic State (no article) or *Isis* thereafter. You will need Isis for quotes and in headlines. Generally avoid writing IS, except in a quote, and never do it in a headline, as it looks odd. If a person is quoted as saying *Isil* there is no longer any need to replace it with [Isis] in square brackets, but restrict Isil to direct quotes. *Daesh* (without apostrophes) should likewise be used in direct quotes only (where it may for now mostly still need something like "ie Islamic State/Isis" in brackets by way of explanation). Abu Bakr al-Baghdadi is the leader of Islamic State, Baghdadi at second mention

Islamic terms note our preferred spellings of *fatwa*; *hadith* (the body of tradition and legend about Muhammad and his followers, used as a basis of Sharia); *haj*; *halal* ("lawful", eg ritually slaughtered meat); *Kabba* (the most sacred pilgrim shrine in Mecca); *kafir* (non-Muslim, "unbeliever", "infidel"); *umma* (the community of Muslims). The five daily prayer times, in sequence, are *fajr*, *duhr*, *asr*, *maghrib* and *isha* (use italics). See **Eid al-Adha**, **Eid al-Fitr**

islands use of the preposition "in" rather than "on" will depend on size: in for bigger islands, on for smaller

isotope hyphenate the element name and the atomic mass number, eg polonium-210, uranium-232, uranium-238 etc. (The atomic mass of a given element's isotopes varies because, while the number of protons is the same, the number of neutrons varies)

Israeli is a citizen of Israel; *Israelite* refers to Ancient Israel. Please bear in mind that *Jew* is not an appropriate alternative; many of Israel's citizens are not Jewish

it beware of multiple *it*s referring to different subjects; nothing is more confusing

Italian names note that surnames with Di or D' are generally capped at all mentions, eg D'Ancona, Di Canio

italics avoid in headlines and be as restrained as possible in their use in text. Do not use italics in captions. In text certain areas always take italics:

1. All works of art; thus, for titles and subtitles of books, poems, short stories, newspapers, magazines, pamphlets, chapter headings, programmes on radio and television, films, plays, computer games, musical works including operas, songs, hymns, album titles etc (see **musical vocabulary**), paintings, drawings, sculptures, titles of exhibitions.

2. Uncommon, non-anglicised foreign words go in italics, but roman is to be preferred if at all possible (eg in extremis, hors d'oeuvre, angst, de rigueur).

3. Names of ships, aircraft, locomotives, spacecraft etc.

4. Take care in presenting algebraic expressions: individual

terms should be in italics, and be sure that superscripts, including squares, and subscripts are properly rendered, ie with any figures in roman, eg $E=mc^2$ (superscript figure 2 in roman). See **algebra**

5. A word may be italicised for emphasis, but be extremely sparing with this device: let good writing show the reader where the emphasis is

It girl thus *It bag, It boy, It pet* etc; these coinages have rather gone out of fashion, which is no bad thing

its/it's the apostrophe version is an abbreviation for "it is" or (if you must) "it has"; there is no apostrophe in the possessive form

Ivory Coast not the; English for Côte d'Ivoire. Note the noun and adjective *Ivorian*

Jj

jack-knife use hyphen for noun and verb

Jacuzzi is a trade name, so cap; the company objects to use of the name as a noun, so write *Jacuzzi* only if certain of attribution, *whirlpool bath* or *spa bath* if in doubt

jail, jailer (not gaol, gaoler) remember that an offender aged 15 cannot be "jailed"; he or she is sentenced to detention in a young offender institution

jail sentences note that totting up the total number of years to which a number of defendants have been jailed is meaningless. Give the sentences of named individuals. If room does not allow, list the sentences of principal offenders and report that so many other people were jailed or whatever

jargon like journalese and slang, to be avoided. Do not use the strange, made-up language that is bandied about between professionals, particularly in business and in the public sector, if there are perfectly good familiar words that can be used instead. When absolutely unavoidable in writing about specialised fields, unfamiliar terms require considered explanations for our readers

Jeep is a trade name, so should be capped; use only if strictly applicable, otherwise *cross-country vehicle, small military truck, SUV* etc

Jehovah's Witness(es)

jejune means shallow, insipid, lacking in intellectual substance. It is widely used to mean puerile, juvenile, naive; this rests on a false etymology (and a common misspelling, jejeune) and is to be discouraged

jellaba a loose cloak with a hood; prefer this spelling to variants beginning with d or ending in h

jellybean one word

Jerusalem lower case for east/west Jerusalem. Jerusalem must not be used as a metonym or variant for Israel. It is not internationally recognised as the Israeli capital, and its status is one of the central controversies in the Middle East. Although the Knesset, the Israeli parliament, sits in Jerusalem, most embassies are in Tel Aviv. Jerusalem is known in Arabic as al-Quds

jet lag two words

jetliner avoid; say *airliner* or simply *jet*

jet ski two words as noun, but to *jet-ski* (verb, hyphen)

jet stream two words as adjective and noun; but *jet-stream* (hyphen) adjectivally

jeune maman in some contexts, best translated as new mother, rather than young mother. Note also *jeunes mariés*, meaning newlyweds

jeweller, jewellery

jibe use this spelling in all senses; ie prefer to gibe, gybe as appropriate

Jiffy bag cap, trade name

jihad holy war (roman, lower case)

jobseeker's allowance

job titles almost all of these should be lower case, even at first mention. Common sense is required, and consistency should not be sought at the expense of clarity, but as a general rule do not use capital letters merely to reflect the dignity or importance of a job. So, the prime minister, the home secretary, the lord chancellor, the French ambassador, the permanent secretary at the Ministry of Defence, the chief constable of the West Midlands, the editor of *The Times*. Similarly chairman, director, managing director (of a company), general secretary (of a union), artistic director (of a theatre) etc are all lower case; so are presidents and chairmen of societies and institutions.

Exceptions are made for job titles that are used in front of a name. We write President Trump or President Putin when using their titles to name them; otherwise they are the president of the United States, the Russian president. Other titles may be joined to names in a similar way (senator, congressman, councillor, alderman, professor etc), but British usage is quite sparing in this respect, especially in the realm of national politics. We do not refer to Foreign Secretary Johnson but to Boris Johnson, the foreign secretary, and so on.

Titles that name an individual as well as describing a job or role are also excepted. Aristocratic titles are the obvious example. These are capped at first mention, ie treated as a name. So, the Prince of Wales and then the prince; the Duke of Devonshire, and then the duke. (Most aristocrats in any case, whether the Marquess of X, the Earl of Y or Viscount Z at first mention, are subsequently just Lord XYZ.) Of individuals whose names are also job descriptions, two — the Queen and the Pope — take a capital letter at all times, not just on first mention; there is no reason for this other than courtesy

John o' Groats

jokey prefer to joky

journalese the bogus jargon of journalists, particularly prevalent in headlines, where words creep in that nobody else would use. Resist. The language of *The Times* should be the language of its intelligent readers

joyrider no hyphen, but use as little as possible as the term gives offence to many readers. An alternative could be *young car thief*

JP (Justice of the Peace) remains, in some contexts, an acceptable alternative for a magistrate or a district judge in a magistrates' court. Thus, we no longer write Josephine Bloggs, JP, but rather Josephine Bloggs, a magistrate; but we could write "The JPs decided ..." as a variant to "The magistrates decided ..."

jubilee strictly a fiftieth anniversary, although Queen Victoria and Queen Elizabeth II both had a golden and a diamond one; so the word can be used as a periodic celebration, especially of royalty. Note the Queen's *Golden Jubilee* in 2002, and also note *Jubilee Line* (caps) on the London Underground

judges' names For all circuit judges and below (ie those in the Crown Court, in county courts, and district judges), always include their first name at first mention. Thus, write Judge Fred Potts at first mention, subsequently Judge Potts or simply the judge.

First names will not normally be necessary with High Court judges unless there are two or more with the same surname, where again it will be essential to differentiate.

The failure to identify a judge correctly can lead to complaints, corrections and even the payment of substantial damages.

In the High Court, Mr Justice X should be referred to this way throughout a story (or simply the judge), never as Judge X. Note the designation of Lady Justice Butler-Sloss when she was a judge, and likewise other women judges

judgment not judgement

jukebox no hyphen

jump-jet (hyphen), but *jumbo jet* (no hyphen)

junior abbreviate to Jr (not Jnr) in American-style names, eg John Eisendorf Jr

junta by definition, a military government, so do not write tautologies such as "ruling military junta"

just deserts things that are deserved. Not to be confused with just desserts, when only puddings are on the menu

juvenile courts were renamed *youth courts*

Kk

k avoid for 1,000 except in direct quotes, eg "He used to earn 200k"

kabbalah initial k and lower case for the spiritual movement based on ancient Jewish mystical tradition

kafir Arabic term for a non-Muslim or infidel; *kaffir*, South African term of racial abuse

Kafkaesque no need for a hyphen. Not an adjective to overuse, especially if you haven't read Kafka. More generally, a hyphen is rarely needed for words with the -esque suffix

Kellogg's Corn Flakes trade mark, but *cornflakes* (generic)

kerosene is American for what is known as *paraffin* in a domestic British setting; but note that kerosene is the commoner synonym globally for aviation fuel, jet fuel etc; also note that kerosene is the far more frequently used word for the heating/cooking fuel, eg in Africa

kettling no quotation marks needed as a word for the police tactic of containment

key overused adjective that often adds little; it is shorter than prime, essential, important, crucial, decisive etc, but woollier too. If you must use it, attach it firmly to a word: "this is a key factor", not "this factor is key"

Khan beware of Khan as a family name: in Central Asia it is usually a title given to officials or rulers

kibbutz plural *kibbutzim*

kibosh

kick-off (noun), but to *kick off* (phrasal verbs do not take a hyphen, whereas compound verbs and nouns do)

kick-start hyphenate noun and verb

kids now near-universal, it still seems worth resisting as an ugly and unpleasant way to refer to *children*; do not use in news stories except in direct quotes

killer can be used for *murderer* but do not use assassin as a synonym

kilobyte abbreviate to kB; note also *megabyte* (MB), *gigabyte* (GB), *terabyte* (TB)

kilogram not kilogramme

kilometres per hour correct abbreviation is km/h rather than kph

kilowatt-hour correct abbreviation is kWh. The cost of generating electricity at a power station is usually expressed in pence per kilowatt-hour (eg 10p/kWh). Do not confuse kilowatts and kilowatt-hours; the kilowatt is a measure of power, the kilowatt-hour a measure of energy (power is the rate at which energy is generated or used). See **energy, power**

King's College London apostrophe, no commas

King's Cross in London

King's Heath in Birmingham (*pace* the apostrophe-light city council)

King's Lynn in Norfolk

Kings Road in Chelsea (do not use apostrophe)

Kingston upon Hull (no hyphens) is the official name for Hull; normally just say Hull. Note that Humberside no longer exists as a local authority

kiwi the flightless bird. But note *Kiwi*, colloquialism for New Zealander; *kiwi fruit* lower case

kneejerk (reaction etc), no hyphen; but beware of overuse

knick-knacks prefer to nick-nacks. This reduplicative word is derived from knack, an obsolete 17th-century word for toy

knockout (noun), but to *knock out* (phrasal verbs do not take a hyphen)

knowhow one word as noun

knowledgeable one where we keep the middle e

Koh-i-noor diamond

Koran, the cap and roman, like the Bible. For references to passages in the Koran, write, eg 26: 181-3, the first number being the *sura* (chapter) and the number(s) after the colon the line(s) in that chapter

Korean names thus: Ban Ki-moon, Kim Jong-il, Roh Tae-woo, Park Geun-hye etc. At second mention, Mr Ban, President Kim, Mr Roh, President Park etc

Kosovo, Kosovan do not use Kosova, Kosovar

kowtow no hyphen

Kristallnacht roman, note cap

Ku Klux Klan no hyphens

Kurdistan A sensitive subject. In reportage take care not to write about "Kurdistan" as if it were an internationally recognised state. The formation of an entity called Kurdistan, potentially involving territory in Turkey, Iraq, Iran, Syria and the former Soviet Union, is a key political aim of strands of Kurdish separatism; in this context, the word "Kurdistan" is perfectly acceptable in direct quotes. Additionally, there is an autonomous region of Iraq called Kurdistan, which comprises the provinces of Sulaimaniyah, Arbil and Dahuk, and in that context reference to Kurdistan is quite acceptable; it may also be referred to as "the Kurdish region of Iraq". There is also a province in Iran officially called Kurdistan, but note that Kurds live in other Iranian provinces as well, and they may be referring to this wider area when talking about Iranian Kurdistan

L l

Labor Day, Department of Labor, Bureau of Labor Statistics (in US); use US spelling

Labor Party (in Australia) leave spelling as it is the party name

Labour Party (in UK) abbreviate in lists etc to Lab

lackadaisical

lads' mag plural *lads' mags*

lady, ladies tends to sound horribly genteel; generally prefer to write *woman, women*

Lady (title) most female life peers like to use *Baroness* rather than *Lady* to indicate that they have the title in their own right. If possible, check which is preferred, and use Baroness if unsure, then Lady at subsequent mentions, but both are correct. Beware a frequent solecism: a formulation such as Lady Joan Smith may correctly name the daughter of a duke, marquess or earl; not many of these figure in the news pages, however, and the person so described is more likely to be the wife of a baron or knight, or a life peer in her own right – in which case she should be Lady Smith; always check. See **titles**

Lagos is the biggest city in Nigeria; the country's capital is Abuja

laid-back hyphenate for the adjective

laissez faire do not use the laisser version

Lake District no need to include Lake when the name contains its equivalent; thus Windermere, Derwent Water, but Bassenthwaite Lake

La-La land noun; extra hyphen as adjective, eg La-La-land mentality, but *La La Land*, the film

lambast not lambaste

lamé accent for the name of the glittery fabric to distinguish it from lame

lamppost no hyphen

landmine no hyphen

landslide (political) best not overused

landslip (earth)

languor, languorous not -our

lapdancer, lapdancing (nouns), a *lapdancing* club; but *pole dancer, pole dancing* (nouns), and a *pole-dancing* club (adjectival, hyphenate)

Lapp but note *Lapland*

laptop (computer) no hyphen

largesse not largess

lasagne prefer the plural to lasagna

last, past it is argued that last is better not used as a synonym of *latest*; "the last few days" ought to mean the final few days, and "the past few days" the most recent few days. The distinction, such as it is, is perhaps not as widely observed as its enthusiasts might like, and it is possible to worry about it too much. Take care not to write eg "last June" in December if you really mean "June last year"

Last Post, the like Reveille, is sounded, not played (neither is italicised)

Latin be sparing in its use, apart from in the Law Report (and the Latin crossword). When Latin phrases are in common usage, use roman rather than italics, eg caveat emptor, quid pro quo, QED, ex parte injunction, habeas corpus. When a Latin phrase is not common enough to run in roman, consider not using it at all

Latin dancing cap Latin in this and all other contexts, whether the Latin language or history, Latin music, Latin temperament etc

Latin Mass should not be used as a synonym for the older *Tridentine rite*

Latino, Latina plurals *Latinos, Latinas*

latitude, longitude write 45° 32'N, 40° 17'W etc

La traviata note lower case t; all other Italian titles similarly, with caps only for the first word (here the definite article) and any proper names. So *Un ballo in maschera, I masnadieri, La battaglia di Legnano, La clemenza di Tito* etc. See **titles**

launch a book/film/housing development is *launched* (not launches)

launch pad two words

launderette not laundrette

lavatory prefer this to toilet. Reserve the use of loo for informal contexts

law cases italicise, eg *Regina v Turnbull, Rex v Dyson*

law lords, law officers lower case

lawmakers pompous US journalese for *politicians*. Avoid

lawnmower one word

Law Report in *The Times*, always initial caps and singular (not Reports); so the style for x-refs is **Law Report, page 42** etc

lay, lie a person lays a carpet (transitive verb), but lies on a carpet (intransitive). Never confuse. The past participle of lie is *lain* (as in, "he had lain there all morning")

layby noun

layoff (noun), *lay off* (verb) refer to the suspension of workers from employment with the intention of re-employing them at a later date, or the temporary suspension of work introduced by an employer as an economic measure, so should not be used as synonyms for permanent job losses

layout (noun), *lay out* (verb)

lay person, lay people both two words, in church or professional contexts

lay waste means to devastate or destroy, so it does not need a following "to". Goats can lay waste a field, not lay waste to a field

lbw rarely any need to spell out *leg before wicket*

leach removing from a substance by a percolating liquid; do not confuse with *leech*, the blood-sucking creature or a metaphor for taking the life out of somebody or something

leader of the Commons/House of Lords; leader of the opposition, lower case; also Labour leader (lower case), Tory leader (lower case) etc

lean, leap past tenses *leant, leapt* (not leaned, leaped)

Leaning Tower of Pisa initial caps

learnt (past tense and past participle of learn), *learned* (adjective, as in *scholarly*)

Lebanon not the Lebanon (except occasionally in historical context)

leech do not confuse with *leach*

left no need for cap in the political context when referring to a group of like-minded individuals, eg "The left added to Tony Blair's worries"; also lower case in "the party swung to the left". When the left is qualified, keep the adjective lower case, eg the hard left, the far left. Also, *the left wing, left-wing contenders, leftwingers*

leftist, left-leaning try to avoid these, and also rightist, right-leaning, which are particularly liked by news agencies, not least in the Americas, and opt for *left-wing, right-wing, left-of-centre, right-of-centre* etc

leg despite several attempts to rewrite the anatomy books, stick with *femur* for the thigh bone and the *tibia* and *fibula* in the shin

legal aid lower case and never hyphenate, even adjectivally in phrases such as legal aid cases

legal terms in general, use lower case for titles; thus, the recorder of Liverpool (thereafter the recorder), Chelmsford crown court, Horseferry Road magistrates' court; also "the court was told", "the judge said", "the magistrate ordered" etc.

The Bench is capped only when referring to the judges as a group; a bench of magistrates is always lower case.

For clarity always cap the Bar and the Inn

legendary avoid its clichéd use

legionella, listeria, salmonella are all bacteria, not viruses

legionnaires' disease

Legion of Honour or **Légion d'honneur** either form is acceptable, according to context

legroom one word; also *elbowroom, headroom*

leitmotif (lower case, roman), prefer to leitmotiv

Leonardo da Vinci at second mention, and/or for brevity, is always Leonardo, never da Vinci (*pace* Dan Brown; use *The Da Vinci Code* for the book and the film only)

leprosy patient in modern context, prefer to leper. Avoid defining people by condition or illness: a schizophrenic, a diabetic, a paraplegic

Leptis Magna a few historical points: in 200BC it and Carthage were Punic; Alexandria was Greek. 200AD was the zenith for Leptis Magna as a Roman city and its benefactor was Septimius (not Septimus) Severus

lèse-majesté (treason, or insult to a monarch) takes roman and accents

less in quantity, *fewer* in number

lesser opposite to *greater* (eg the lesser evil)

letch (after) prefer to *lech* for informal verb meaning to behave lecherously towards, lust after

letdown one word as noun; but *let down* (verb)

letter bomb hyphenate only in adjectival use

letterbox, postbox no hyphens

leukaemia

liaison, liaise the word *link* would often be better. The verb to liaise has forced its way into the language; use sparingly, however, and only in its correct sense: to establish co-operation, to act as a link with, not as a synonym of *meet* or *talk*

Liberal Democrat(s) Lib Dem, Lib Dems are fine in headlines and text. Do not shorten simply to Liberals. Abbreviate in lists etc to LD

Libor London interbank offered rate. At first mention in some contexts, eg outside the Business pages, it may be helpful to explain that Libor is the rate at which banks lend to each other

Libya most centres of population are coastal and sizeable, so take care not to describe somewhere as a town if it is a city

licence (noun), *license* (verb); but beware of *licensee* (noun), *licensed, licensing*

lie of the land, the not lay

life cycle

life form

lifeguard (on a beach); *Life Guardsman* (on a horse)

lifelong one word as adjective

liferaft one word, as *lifeboat, lifebelt* etc

lifesize(d) no hyphen

lift-off (spacecraft etc), as *take-off* (compound nouns, hyphenated) but without a hyphen when used as phrasal verbs: "The take-off should have been at 2pm"; "The plane did not take off until 4pm"

lightbulb one word

light-hearted

light year

like may be used sparingly as a less formal alternative to *such as* (eg "cities like Manchester are ambitious" instead of "cities such as Manchester ..."); may also be used, more sparingly still and only in informal contexts, instead of "as if" (eg "it looks like he's going to win", rather than "it looks as if he is going to win")

likeable

likely in the unlikely event that you might be tempted to use the Americanism "He will likely send out another email soon", please don't. Instead write "He is likely to send out another email soon"; or "Most likely he will send out ..."; "Very likely he will ..."

lily of the valley

linchpin not lynchpin

line lower case in eg Maginot line

line of fire militarily, in the flight path of a fired missile, or likely to be attacked. In practice now used interchangeably with *firing line* (which ought strictly to refer to those doing the firing, but rarely does). As the literal sense of firing line is so rarely required, there seems little reason to resist common usage here

liner strictly speaking liners nowadays are cargo vessels trading regularly between designated ports, eg container ships; there are no longer scheduled passenger crossings over fixed long-distance routes. There may be a case, therefore, for confining the term's use for passenger ships to historical contexts, eg the transatlantic liner *Queen Mary*, but its extension to the more leisurely cruising successors of those great ships (eg the *Queen Mary* 2) seems unlikely to cause confusion or undue distress

line-up (noun) but to *line up* (verb)

Lions (rugby) officially the touring rugby union team are known as the British Isles; alternatively, the Lions. At a pinch, they may be referred to as the British and Irish Lions. They are not the British Lions

Lipizzaner horses not Lippizaner

liquefy not liquify; but *liquidate*

liquorice not the American licorice

lira (singular), **lire** (plural) the former Italian currency. Also Turkish Lira

Lisbon treaty lower case treaty, likewise Amsterdam treaty, Maastricht treaty etc

lissom prefer to lissome (or lithesome); means supple in the limbs or body; lithe; agile; nimble

literally the OED may now recognise its informal use as no more than an adverb of emphasis; we do not. Phrases like "he literally exploded with anger" are literally nonsensical; avoid

little 'un, big 'un apostrophe shows absence of the o producing the w sound

livery halls (in the City of London) do not take the definite article (eg Drapers' Hall, not the Drapers' Hall)

Livorno rather than Leghorn, alas, despite usual style on anglicising foreign names

Llanfairpwllgwyngyllgogerychwyrndrobwllllantysiliogogogoch Anglesey, which translates as "St Mary's Church in the hollow of the white hazel near the rapid whirlpool of Llantysilio of the red cave". It may be helpful in a tight corner to know that the name is often abbreviated to Llanfairpwll or Llanfair PG

Lloyds the bank, and *Lloyds Banking Group*; but *Lloyd's of London* (insurance)

Lloyd Webber all family members (father William and sons Andrew and Julian) have no hyphen except in reference to Andrew as *Lord Lloyd-Webber*

LLP (limited liability partnership) as for Ltd or plc, there is not normally a need to add LLP at the end of a company's name

loan is a noun (ie never say "I loaned him £20" etc); the verb is *lend/lent*

loathe (verb) the adjective is *loath* (not loth)

local adjective that often adds little

local government lower case councils even when full title, eg Watford borough council, Newtown district council; all council committees in lower case; lower case for all officials (including eg Sadiq Khan, the mayor of London); lower case for lesser council officials such as borough surveyor, town clerk; for clarity cap the seat of local government if we are sure of its title (eg Leeds City Hall, Birmingham Council House — not to be confused with Birmingham Town Hall — Lambeth Town Hall etc)

lochs in Scotland, *loughs* in Ireland

lockout (in industrial disputes etc), one word; but *to lock out*

locomotive names are italicised, as with ship or aircraft names, eg *Flying Scotsman, Mallard*. Do not use "the" unless certain it is part of the name, eg *The Queen's Own Hussars*. Beware of confusing locomotives with trains (for names of the latter use quotes); the "Aberdonian" or the "Cathedrals Express" (both named trains) might be pulled by the *Flying Scotsman* (a locomotive). Get this wrong, and you'll get letters — lots of them — from men who know

lodestar, lodestone prefer to load-

logjam one word

London cap the *East End* and the *West End* of London, but lower case *north London, south London, east London, west London, central London, inner London*; also lower case *southeast London,* *southwest London* etc. The local council for the City of London is the Court of Common Council, whose members are common councilmen; cap *borough* in titles of particular boroughs, eg London Borough of Bromley

London clubs we are expected to get the names correct. Most now have websites, so check. Note particularly the Athenaeum; Boodle's; Brooks's; Buck's; Pratt's; White's, the Beefsteak, the Garrick, the Royal Over-Seas League; the Savile; the Travellers; the Oxford and Cambridge; the Carlton. (If adding "club" to give full name – rarely necessary – treat like school, hospital etc and make u/c)

Londonderry but Derry city council; and Derry when in direct quotes or in a specifically republican context

London Stock Exchange may be abbreviated to LSE, but use sparingly and only in context, especially in headlines, because of confusion with the London School of Economics; ideally restrict to business pages. If not naming in full, prefer the stock exchange or the exchange to the initials wherever possible

London Underground

London Zoo

longstanding do not use hyphen

long-term restore the hyphen (as adjective) if only because it often appears alongside short-term, which needs one anyway

lookout noun, no hyphen

lord advocate do not add "for Scotland"

lord chancellor

lord chief justice

Lord Haw-Haw hyphenated. William Joyce, the Second World War Nazi propagandist

lord justice of appeal

lord-lieutenant should be hyphenated, according to the Association of Lord-Lieutenants (note this plural, not lords-lieutenant); use lower case

lord mayor lower case as in lord mayor of London, Birmingham etc

Lord's cricket ground

Lords (parliamentary) takes singular verb, eg the Lords is sitting

lords justices both words take the plural

lorry prefer lorry to truck, but the American *truck* has become ubiquitous and cannot be banned, especially from foreign stories

lossmaker, lossmaking no need for hyphen

lothario no need to cap except when referring to the character in *The Fair Penitent* (1703) by Nicholas Rowe, which mostly we won't be

loveable takes the middle e, as *likeable*

lowbrow as *highbrow*

lower prefer *lour*, as in a louring sky

Lower House and Upper House (of parliament)

lowest common denominator mathematically, this can be a big number (the lowest common multiple of the denominators of several vulgar fractions). The use of the term in a derogatory sense to mean the level of the least discriminating audience is in common usage and is quite acceptable (if a bit of a cliché)

low-key

loyalist lower case in all contexts including Northern Ireland

LSE short for the London School of Economics; also — sparingly, in context and ideally only in Business pages — for the London Stock Exchange

Ltd can usually be dropped from company names (as can plc, LLP)

lullaby not -bye

lumbar as in the lower back (eg lumbar puncture); *lumber* as in junk furniture, lumberjacks, or (verbally) moving clumsily about etc

Lurex initial cap

Luton airport (lower case a), and resist pressure to insert "international"

Lycra cap, trade name

lying in state noun, no hyphens; nor the verb, *to lie in state*

Lyons not Lyon, is the English name for the French city

-lyse the style is analyse, paralyse etc (not -ize)

Mm

Maastricht treaty (lower case treaty) or *Treaty of Maastricht* in full for the treaty on European integration, which led to the creation of the euro; signed in February 1992, it came into force in November 1993

Mac, **Mc** always check spelling of these prefixes, eg in *Who's Who*. In alphabetical lists, treat Mc as Mac. Note that when typesetting in caps, the c (and if in the name, the a) may need to be set in a small cap or even lower case, eg FRANK McAVENNIE

McCann, Madeleine regarding her age, use a form of words (to cover any eventuality) to the effect that she disappeared shortly before her fourth birthday

Macedonia the correct (and politically sensitive) title of the Balkan republic is the *former Yugoslav Republic of Macedonia* (in full); reserve Macedonia (on its own) for the modern Greek region and the ancient kingdom

Machiavelli(an)

machinegun but *sub-machinegun*

mackintosh (raincoat)

macroeconomic, microeconomic no hyphen

mad cow disease

madrassa Islamic school. No h, two esses. Plural *madrassas*

maestros (plural of *maestro*) not maestri

mafia always lower case. The Sicilian mafia, the Russian mafia, the mafia in the US. Caps, however, for Cosa Nostra (when used, to refer to the Sicilian mafia), the Camorra (the Neapolitan mafia) and 'NDrangheta (the mafia of Calabria); with an initial cap these can stay in roman rather than itals. For clarity also use cap in US references to the Mob

Mafikeng the new name (since 1980) of Mafeking. Spell according to historical context

Magdalen College, **Oxford** but *Magdalene College, Cambridge*

"magic circle" lower case and quotes first mention, for top law firms in the City; but cap *Magic Circle* for the magicians' organisation

Maginot line French fortifications against Germany before the Second World War

magistrates' courts the Metropolitan magistrate, the West London magistrate etc may if necessary be capped for clarity, but usually magistrates and their courts take lower case. The name of the court is lower case, as in Bow Street magistrates' court. An acceptable alternative for a magistrate or district judge is JP (justice of the peace) in some contexts. When the accused is appearing before the bench, he appears before the magistrates (plural) unless a stipendiary magistrate, now called a district judge (magistrates' courts) presides

Magna Carta not *the* Magna Carta, imposed on King John at Runnymede in June 1215; if you write that it was signed, as children's book illustrations like to suggest, you will be reminded by angry readers that it was sealed

maharajah prefer to maharaja; likewise, *rajah*

mailshot

major try to avoid as a lazy alternative for eg *big, chief, important* or *main*; often better deleted anyway

Majorca, **Minorca** use the anglicised forms

majority of prefer *most of*

majority verdicts are always guilty; there is no such thing as a majority acquittal

makeover one word as noun

make-up (cosmetics or typography) not makeup, but no hyphen in the phrasal verb *to make up*

Mall, The (cap T) the road in London. In Washington DC, the national park is *the* (lower case) *Mall*, more fully *the National Mall*

Mammon initial cap

Man cap in the context of humankind, the species. Also cap for clarity in names such as Essex Man, Mondeo Man, Neanderthal Man, White Van Man etc

management buyout spell out first time, although MBO (plural MBOs) is acceptable on Business pages

management-speak do not succumb, for example, to describing an organisation as meaninglessly as one press release did: "interested in non-face-to-face, high-volume, low-unit-cost solutions that would require the front-loaded investment the voluntary sector cannot acquire"

man and wife the traditional phrase in the marriage service of the Book of Common Prayer; husband and wife, or indeed wife and husband, may be preferable options if a direct quotation or reference is not required

Mandarin is a spoken form of Chinese, as is *Cantonese*. It is incorrect to refer to their common written form as, say, Mandarin or Cantonese: it is simply Chinese

mangos preferred plural

Manichean embodying or relating to the radically dualistic world view of the third-century gnostic religious movement; now used more generally (eg in the context of politics) to suggest a tendency to see life in stark terms of good and evil, light and dark, black and white, etc

manifestos not -oes

manmade no hyphen

manoeuvre, manoeuvring, manoeuvrable

mantelpiece not mantlepiece

manuscript(s) write out when part of a sentence, but abbreviate to MSS when quotation from catalogue, or in headline if context is clear

Maori noun, adjective; prefer *Maori* also as the plural

Mao Zedong not Mao Tse-tung, except perhaps in direct quotation in historical Pinyin context

marathon avoid in clichéd sense of a long time, as in "a marathon session". London Marathon, New York Marathon, Boston Marathon etc, all upper case

march past noun; two words in military context

Mardi Gras for the Shrove Tuesday festival, but note the self-styled *Mardi Gra bomber*

Marines cap in both Royal Marines and US Marines; also, for clarity, *a Marine*

marketplace one word

Marks & Spencer use the ampersand rather than *and* in text; can abbreviate to M&S in headlines; the formal legal title is Marks and Spencer plc, but we need use this form only rarely

marquess not marquis, except in foreign titles (and sometimes pub names)

Marrakesh not Marrakech

married couple's allowance

Marseilles prefer the anglicised version to Marseille; also call the football club Marseilles (not Olympique de Marseille)

martial law rule by the military, eg under a junta, in the absence of civil law; do not confuse with *military law*, eg that exercised at a court martial

Martini is a trade name, so cap in specific references to the brand of vermouth, made by Martini & Rossi; the *martini*

cocktail was not invented by the company and may be lower case

Marxist, Marxism capped

Mary Celeste not *Marie Celeste*

Masai prefer to Maasai

Mason-Dixon line state boundary between Maryland and Pennsylvania, regarded as the dividing line between the North and the South in America, especially between the free and the slave states before the Civil War

Mass cap in its religious context, also *Holy Mass, Requiem Mass* etc

massive use to convey great mass, solidity, bulk; do not waste as a vague synonym of *big*

masterclass (musical etc) no hyphen

master of foxhounds lower case

Master of the Queen's Music one of those few, rather ceremonial job titles that look unnatural lower case; the current incumbent is Judith Weir, the first woman to hold the post

Master of the Rolls president of the civil division of the Court of Appeal, another rare job title that resists our general preference for lower case

materialise avoid as a synonym of *appear, come about* or *happen*

materiel (military hardware) no need for the accent

matinee no accent, as *premiere, debut, decor* etc

matins lower case, only one t

matt not mat, as in matt paint, matt black etc

Mauretania the liner; Mauritania, the country

may/might do not confuse. Use "might" in sentences referring to past possibilities that did not happen, eg "If that had happened ten days ago, my whole life might have been different." A clear distinction is evident in the following example: "He might have been captured by the Iraqis [but he wasn't]," compared with, "He may have been captured by the Iraqis [it is possible but we don't know]". To write, eg "If the tree had not fallen on him, he may have survived" is absurd

Maya one of the Indian people of Central America; *Mayas*, plural; and *Mayan*, adjective

mayday as in SOS, lower case; but *May Day* (holiday)

mayor lower case, including the mayor of London

MCC short for Marylebone Cricket Club, owner of Lord's cricket ground and guardian of the laws of the game. Do not say *the* MCC (although lots of perfectly respectable people do)

me perfectly good word often wrongly avoided by the ignorant, who think it sounds insufficiently genteel. Do not use horrors such as "between you and I", or "he gave it to my wife and I". An easy way to avoid such mistakes is often to try out the sentence with the other party removed: no one would be tempted to write "he gave it to I"; the presence of a wife should make no difference to the grammar

mealtimes write *breakfast time, lunchtime, teatime, dinner time, supper time* (but use hyphens in compounds when adjectival)

meaningful useful word to convey "having meaning"; in other contexts (a meaningful relationship, a meaningful glance etc), you might do better to try *significant* or *full of meaning*

means test (noun) but *means-test* (verb) and *means-tested* (adjective)

means to an end is singular, eg "It is a means to an end"; but "his means *are* modest"

meatloaf the minced meat dish; *Meat Loaf* the substantial rock musician

mecca lower case in eg "a mecca for tourists"; obviously cap in actual refs to the Saudi city

Medal of Honor use the American spelling for the award and the game

media plural as in *mass media,* so do not write, eg "a media that is full of rumour". Note *mediums* (spiritualists)

medical terms never use these metaphorically or as terms of abuse (*geriatric, paralytic, schizophrenic*). In words ending in -tomy (appendectomy, hysterectomy etc), the word "operation" is tautologous and should not be used

medications give the generic name (lower case, parentheses) as well as the brand name, eg Casodex (bicalutamide) for those new or not familiar. Omit in reference to well-known medications, eg Valium, Viagra

medieval not mediaeval

Mediterranean

meet avoid the tautologous Americanism "meet with"; we may meet with criticism, or with a fate worse than death, but not with people

mega- be very sparing with this as a colloquial prefix meaning *big*

megawatts the capacity of a power station is measured in megawatts; the output is measured in megawatt-hours. Often confused, to the annoyance of readers who understand these things. The correct abbreviation of megawatt is MW (not mW, which means *milliwatt*)

mêlée

member of parliament lower case, similarly *member,* but MP almost always preferable. Plural MPs (never MP's)

mementoes not -os

memoirs not memoires

memorandum plural *memorandums* (not -a)

meningitis distinguish whether bacterial or viral; the headline cases are usually bacterial

mental never use pejoratively

Messerschmitt not -schmidt. Note that aircraft types are styled, eg Me-109, Me-262

Messiah cap in the religious context, eg in Judaism the awaited redeemer of the Jews, in Christianity in reference to Jesus Christ. But lower case in a more general sense, eg "Many managers at Newcastle have been hailed as messiahs"

metaphors should not be horribly mixed, or absurdly elaborate, or so familiar that they have become clichés. Beware the virgin field pregnant with possibilities

mete out (not meet out), in context of punishment

Method acting use cap M for clarity for the thespian school which demands complete immersion in a role

métier accent

Met Office formerly the Meteorological Office

metres as in distance, poetry etc; *meters*, as in gas, electricity or parking etc

metric *The Times* should keep abreast of the trend in the UK to move gradually towards all-metric use, but given the wide age range and geographical distribution of our readers, some continuing use of imperial measurements is necessary. The main aim is to avoid confusing the reader, so try not to mix the two systems in a single article. In general we should prefer the metric, with imperial conversions in brackets at first mention of specific figures. Whenever converting try to keep a sense of proportion: it is nonsense to express, for instance, an estimated 15ft as an excessively detailed 4.57m. If the first figure is no more than an estimate the conversion may safely be rounded to a similarly approximate 4.5m.

The following are the principal exceptions to the foregoing:

1. Temperatures nowadays will rarely need converting to Fahrenheit, so say that the temperature on the south coast hit the low 30s (no longer the 90s); where specific, just

16C, 28C etc. Give Fahrenheit only where there is good reason, such as in a historical context.

2. Distances globally. Use miles and in foreign stories convert (at first mention) to kilometres in brackets only where someone in the story is quoted using kilometres. For speeds, use only miles per hour (mph) and in foreign stories convert to kilometres per hour (km/h) in brackets only if someone is quoted using km/h. For areas of land use acres, and convert to square metres (not hectares, which few readers can visualise). In a technical or scientific context (as opposed to motoring, public transport or walking), kilometres first are acceptable, eg "North Korea's latest ballistic missile has a range of 10,000 km (6,200 miles)."

3. Personal measurements in height and weight. Continue to say she was 5ft 7in and weighed 9st 10lb.

4. Altitude and depth. An exception to metric should be aircraft altitude, where a pilot will announce that "we are now flying at 33,000ft"; metric conversion to 10,058m may be used in brackets here. But now specify mountain heights in metric first, eg "Ben Nevis is the highest peak in Britain at 1,345m (4,411ft)."

5. Volume. The main exceptions to metric should be pints of beer and cider, while milk (confusingly) is still sold in pint bottles as well as litre containers. With petrol and fuel sold in litres rather than gallons, use metric, eg 75p a litre (no longer any need to convert), but because car manufacturers still do so, give fuel consumption in miles per gallon.

The overwhelming preference is for sporting, foreign, engineering and scientific stories to be metric; similarly foodstuffs and liquids in cookery contexts, recipes etc should be metric, although small amounts can be given in tablespoons (tbsp) and teaspoons (tsp).

The most common metric abbreviations are mm (millimetre), cm (centimetre), m (metre) and km (kilometre); mg (milligram), g (gram), kg (kilogram); sq m (square metre), sq km (square kilometre), cu m (cubic metre); ml (millilitre), cl (centilitre), l (litre); W (watt), kW (kilowatt). Never add a final s to any of these abbreviations, eg 48km (not 48kms)

Metro in Paris, does not seem to need the accent

Metropolitan Police subsequently may be abbreviated sparingly to the Met

metrosexual fashionable heterosexual urban male who devotes much time and attention to his appearance; note that the term was coined by Mark Simpson, a British journalist, not by Marian Salzman, an American writer

MI5 is the *Security Service*; the *Secret Intelligence Service* is MI6

miaow the catty sound; note also *miaow-miaow* as the street name for mephedrone, which is a Class B drug

Michelangelo

mickey, take the

microchip

microgram do not abbreviate

microlight prefer to microlite

mid-air hyphenate, noun or adjective

midday, **midweek** no hyphens and avoid such terms as 12am, 12pm and 12 noon

Middle Ages, the cap

middle class hyphenate as adjective attached to noun, but not otherwise. He comes from a middle-class family; he is middle class; he is a product of the middle class

Middle-earth note hyphen and upper case, lower case

Middle East comprises Bahrain, Cyprus, Egypt, Iran, Iraq, Israel, Jordan, Kuwait, Lebanon, Oman, Qatar, Saudi Arabia, Sudan, Syria, Turkey, United Arab Emirates, Yemen. In a general sense it also takes in the countries of the Maghreb: Algeria, Libya, Mauritania, Morocco, Tunisia, as well as Western Sahara. Never abbreviate to the Americanism Mideast; *Middle Eastern*, adj, seems also to need caps for clarity

Middle England cap, in political context

Middlesex is no longer a county but people who insist, eg some correspondents to the Letters page, should be allowed to go on living there if they choose

Mideast unacceptable as abbreviation of *Middle East*

midlife crisis but do not overuse this cliché

midnight not 12 midnight

midsummer, midwinter

midterm

Midwest (US)

MiG the former Soviet aircraft

mike not mic, as abbreviation for *microphone*

mileage

military law not to be confused with *martial law*

military ranks Refer eg to Major-General Geoffrey Blimp, Lieutenant-Colonel Godfrey Blank (with caps) at first mention, thereafter General Blimp (or the general, lower case when not attached to the name), Colonel Blank (or the colonel); similarly, Rear-Admiral Horatio Salt, thereafter Admiral Salt (or the admiral). Use hyphens in compounds such as major-general, lieutenant-colonel etc (where two ranks are joined), but not with second lieutenant, lance corporal, air commodore etc. Do not abbreviate ranks except in lists

militate against or in favour of; never confuse with *mitigate*

Milky Way, the cap for clarity

millennium common usage says that the millennium ended on December 31, 1999, although technically it should have been

December 31, 2000, as a very few determined readers never tire of pointing out. We accept the former. Note the *Millennium Dome* (and *Dome* subsequently, now the *O₂ arena*), *Millennium Fund, Millennium Commission, Millennium Exhibition* (cap). Also *Millennium Eve* (as *New Year's Eve*). The London Eye was known as the *Millennium Wheel*. Note also the *Millennium Bridge* over the Thames. It all seems a long time ago. The plural of millennium is *millennia* (unlike *memorandums* etc; see **referendum**). Note also *millenarian* (only one middle n) meaning of, or related to, the millennium and usually used in relation to religious cults

millionaire a person whose personal assets are worth at least a million of the standard monetary units of his or her country. House price rises and historical inflation mean that millionaires, while not exactly paupers, are neither as rare nor as rich as they once were; their place in the popular imagination has largely been taken by billionaires

millions write out millions from one to ten, thereafter 11 million etc. Abbreviate to m only for headlines. Also for currencies, spell out in text, eg £15 million, and abbreviate to £15m in headlines

Miltonian prefer to Miltonic for the adjective relating to John Milton and, by extension, sublime and majestic writing

mindset

minimal do not use as a synonym of *small*; it means smallest, or the least possible in size, duration etc

minimalism, minimalist artistic movement, lower case

miniskirt no hyphen; also *minicab*

ministers (political) lower case. Thus, the trade minister, a trade minister, a Treasury minister, a Home Office minister etc. The same applies to ministers in overseas governments: give name and full title first time, thereafter name or just "the minister"

minus see **plus, minus**

minuscule not miniscule, however widespread this misspelling may now be. Originally a medieval script. Use sparingly; it is heavily overworked as a synonym of *very small* or *unimportant*

mis-hit and **mis-sell** with hyphens, but generally no hyphen in such compounds unless clarity seems to require one

Miss, Ms the latter is fully acceptable when a woman (married or unmarried) wants to be called thus, or when it is not known for certain if she is Mrs or Miss. Ms is increasingly common in American and UK contexts, with Miss now unusual among younger generations. Beware cultural and historical absurdity, however; an unmarried Victorian schoolmistress or Edwardian fellow of Somerville would not have been Ms then and should not be Ms now

missile a missile is a guided weapon. Do not use interchangeably with *rocket*. A missile may be a rocket, but a rocket becomes a missile only when it has (or is intended to have) a warhead for a payload

misspell no need for hyphen

mitigate means to make milder, moderating (as in mitigating circumstances in a law case); not to be confused with *militate*

mockumentary a parody of a documentary, eg *This is Spinal Tap*

MoD acceptable abbreviation for *Ministry of Defence* at subsequent mentions (but vary with *the ministry*) and especially in headlines

modelling double l

Mogul (not Mughal) for the empire and art

Mohammed continue to prefer *Muhammad* unless the individual concerned has indicated a preference for Mohammed or some other form of the name

Moldova no longer Moldavia

Molotov cocktail do not use this euphemism. Write *petrol bomb*

monarch lower case, for the British monarch; lower case also for the *monarchy*; but clarity often requires a cap for the *Sovereign*, the *Crown*; the *Queen* always has a cap in refs to the specific individual

monetise not moneytise

money when giving historical figures for prices, incomes or wealth, do not attempt meaningless conversions of old money to new; it is unhelpful to tell readers that a shilling "equals" 5p (its value on decimalisation in 1971); either establish a genuine equivalent at today's values or, better and easier, give some indication of what a shilling might have bought at the time

money laundering two words as noun; but hyphenate adjective, a money-laundering gang

moneys (plural of *money*) but money will usually serve. Also, *moneyed*, not monied

Mongol, Mongolian for the race. Never refer to a Down's syndrome sufferer as a mongol

Monsignor (Mgr abbreviated) is not an appointment but a dignity and form of address for Roman Catholic priests who hold certain honours or offices. In some countries and languages archbishops or bishops are also so addressed; this is not usual in English. Pope Francis has announced that he will no longer confer the title, but those who already have it should continue to be so addressed

Montenegrin is the adjective from Montenegro (not Montenegran)

moon there seems no reason to cap (except if it seems to help clarity or consistency in a strictly astronomical context such as the Night Sky column). There will rarely be any doubt as to what is meant. The Apollo 11 astronauts left behind a plaque to mark their visit. It was written in capital letters, but Nasa's own website transcribes it as follows: "Here men from the planet Earth first set foot upon the moon. July 1969

A.D. We came in peace for all mankind"; that seems authority enough for lower case when writing about, eg the first man to walk on the moon. Also lower case phases, eg full moon, new moon

moose plural *moose*, name of the large North American deer that in Europe and Asia is known as the *elk*, plural *elks*

more than prefer to over with numbers, eg "more than 2,500 people attended the rally", not "over 2,500 ..."; "their pay went up more than £300 a week", rather than "over £300 a week". Common sense is needed; with ages, for instance, "he is over 50" sounds right where "he is more than 50" clearly does not

Mormon a member of the *Church of Jesus Christ of Latter-day Saints* (note hyphen and lower-case -day). Also note the Book of Mormon (roman)

morris dancing/dancers

Morse code

mortar do not use by itself when the meaning is *mortar bomb*; the mortar is the launcher from which the shell is fired. But *mortar attack* is perfectly correct

mortuary not the American morgue

mosquitoes not -os as plural

most favoured nation status

MoT certificate, test; but the Department for Transport (not Ministry of ...)

Mother Nature initial caps

mother of five etc, no hyphens

"mother of Parliaments, England is the"

Mother's Day or **Mothering Sunday** not Mothers'

mother ship two words

mother-to-be hyphens, but say a *mother of two*, a *father of three* (no hyphens)

motocross not motorcross

motorcycle, motorcyclist, motorbike etc

motoring terms the following terms should be standardised throughout the paper thus: *carburettor, wheelspin, four-wheel drive* (preferred abbreviation is 4x4 rather than 4WD), but a *four-wheel-drive vehicle* (two hyphens when adjectival), *power steering, anti-lock brakes, 3-litre car, 1.9 diesel* (hyphenated when adjectival), *four-door, hatchback, four-star petrol, E-type Jaguar, Mercedes-Benz E-class* etc, *airbag, seatbelt, numberplate, sports car.*

For the foreseeable future, continue to give fuel consumption figures in miles per gallon

motor neurone disease with final e (as now almost universally used, eg by the NHS and the Motor Neurone Disease Association)

motorway junctions styled Junction 6 (cap, numeral) of the M40, etc

Mount spell out in names, Mount Kenya, Mount Fuji, not Mt

moustached having a moustache; cf *mustachioed*, often with a comic overtone, having a moustache, especially when bushy or elaborately shaped, eg a handlebar

mousy prefer to mousey

mouthwatering one word

moveable keep middle e

movies although an Americanism, is now so common as to be an acceptable synonym of *films*; but use *films* whenever possible

, MP, QC, commas each side when used after name

much no need to hyphenate when used as a qualifier, eg a much treasured gift

mugging strictly means theft by violence in the open air

Muhammad use this spelling for the Prophet. Use it also as the default spelling of the name, but respect variants according to individuals' preference; if in doubt, use Muhammad

mujahidin lower case, the fighters in a jihad or holy war. The singular is *mujahid*

multi incline towards making *multi* compounds one word wherever possible, whether used as a noun or as an adjective, eg multimillionaire, multinational, multilateral, multimedia, multiracial, multispeed, multistorey, multitrack (and note *multispeed, multitrack Europe*). Hyphenate when the compound appears too hideous, such as *multi-ethnic*

multimillion-pound (multimillion-dollar) deal etc

Mumbai prefer now to Bombay

Munchausen syndrome no umlaut, one h

Munster (Ireland); **Münster** (Germany)

muntjac

musical vocabulary

1. song titles (classical or pop), album titles, operas (including arias), take italics.

2. symphonies thus: Symphony No 3 (roman, cap); but where symphonies have numbers and popular alternative titles (Eroica, Pastoral) the titles, when used, are in italics, eg the *Eroica* Symphony.

3. concertos, roman caps, eg First Violin Concerto

music hall no hyphen as noun; *music-hall* hyphenate adjectivally, eg a music-hall act

Muslim not Moslem or Mohamedan

Mussorgsky, Modest prefer to Moussorgsky

mustachioed elaborately, even amusingly, moustached

Muzak cap, proprietary

Myanmar continue to call the country Burma, despite the preference of its rulers

mynah bird; prefer to mina, myna

myself needlessly and unappealingly used instead of *me* by people who know that there is something grammatically wrong with, eg "he gave it to my wife and I", but who suppose that "he gave it to my wife and me" is insufficiently genteel to be correct

Nn

9/11 is acceptable, but it may be helpful on occasion to use the full date elsewhere for clarification, eg "the events of September 11, 2001". Reference to the *9/11 commission* (strictly, the National Commission on Terrorist Attacks upon the United States) is also acceptable

Naafi the Navy, Army and Air Force Institutes; commonly used as the name for the canteen for service personnel run by the Naafi

Nabataean (rather than Nabatean) for the ancient Arab trading people and their language

naive, **naivety** no diaeresis

names as a general rule, people are entitled to be known as they wish to be known, provided that their identities are clear. Thus Cassius Clay became Muhammad Ali; but in such changes, give both names until the new one is widely known. Note *Lloyd's names* (lower case)

narcotrafficker one word; likewise, *narcoterrorist*

narrow boat two words

national avoid as a synonym of *citizen*, as in a French national etc

national anthem lower case always

national curriculum lower case

national grid lower case, generic, for pylons, wires etc; *National Grid*, cap for the power company

National Health Service *the NHS*, or *the health service* (NHS for headlines)

national insurance lower case, like other taxes, in general context, but cap for *National Insurance Fund*

nationalist lower case except when referring to name of a political party. Thus Scottish National Party (SNP) and Scottish Nationalists. But in other (eg Irish) contexts, lower case

National Lottery cap for clarity

national parks cap when part of the name (eg Snowdonia National Park, Kruger National Park etc)

National Service caps

National Theatre caps; generally omit Royal

National Trust operates in England, Wales and Northern Ireland. There is a separate National Trust for Scotland

nationwide no hyphen, but use sparingly as it borders on being a cliché; prefer *national* or *nationally*

Native American cap the N when referring to people historically and stereotypically referred to as Red Indian

Nature cap sparingly, only in the context of personifying the power that creates and regulates the world. Also *Mother Nature*

naught come to (not nought, which means the digit 0)

nave is a central space in a church; journalists who misspell the word are *knaves*

navy, naval the Royal Navy (thereafter the navy, lower case); otherwise, lower case: the merchant navy; the US navy, the Brazilian navy etc; *naval* is lower case except in titles such as Royal Naval Volunteer Reserve (RNVR) etc

navy ships classes are capped, but roman, not italic (eg a Leander Class frigate)

Nazi, Nazism cap

Neanderthal cap, and not -tal; note *Neanderthal Man* (caps)

nearby, near by the first is adjectival, eg "the nearby school was convenient"; the second is adverbial, eg "he sat on a bench near by"

near-demise, near-fatal hyphenate these and other constructions involving a noun or adjective with *near*

nearly one in three ... is prefer singular to the plural *are* in these constructions

neither takes a singular verb, eg "neither is ..."

neither ... nor when both subjects are singular, use a singular verb, eg "neither Bert nor Fred has any idea". If either subject is plural, use a plural verb, eg "neither the Johnsons nor the Smiths are coming"; "neither the Tories nor Labour know the answer". Do not use the construction "neither ... or ..." (must use *nor*)

nemesis lower case; any agency of retribution and vengeance

neoconservative, neocon no hyphen

neoprene lower case as it is a generic

neolithic lower case

Nepalese prefer to Nepali for both people and language of Nepal

nerve-racking not -wracking

Netherlands, the (no longer cap The). Do not use Holland as an alternative except in sporting or historical contexts

never means "at no point in the past or future"; there is a superstition (mercifully not widespread) that it may be used only if we can be absolutely sure that it is literally true, and that otherwise it must be replaced by *not*; this has never been the case. If you write "I never knew that" or "I'd never do that" or "Such a daft idea will never catch on", readers will never have the slightest trouble understanding what you mean

nevertheless one word, as *nonetheless*

new frequently redundant. Try the sentence without it and see if it really adds any meaning; always omit in "setting a *new* record". Try to avoid employing phrases such as "white is the new black"

New Age travellers no quotes

newborn as in babies, no hyphen

new-found hyphen

New Labour caps generally helpful for clarity when referring eg to party under Blair

newscaster prefer *newsreader*

newspapers and journals use italics for titles and make sure to use The in the title whenever appropriate and italicise The if part of the masthead.

When the publication's name is used adjectivally, omit The, eg "the *Times* reporter was attacked ..."

Always properly attribute material from another newspaper: never say "a report in another newspaper ..." but "a report in *The Guardian* ..." etc. The general phrases "media reports" or "press reports" are acceptable, however, when material has been widely disseminated

News UK The parent company of *The Times* was rebranded on June 26, 2013. Formerly known as News International (to which it should be referred in its correct historical context), it is a subsidiary of News Corporation

New Town cap for clarity in reference to a conurbation planned as a whole, eg postwar to accommodate overspill population, such as Basildon, Bracknell, Harlow and Stevenage. Plural *New Towns*

new year honours or **new year's honours list** (lower case); also **the Queen's birthday honours**

New Year's Day, **New Year's Eve**, but *the new year, new year's resolutions* and *Chinese new year*

New York streets use numbers in, eg 5th Avenue, 42nd Street etc

New Zealand never NZ, even in headlines

nightclub

nightmare an unpleasant dream; avoid its use as a lazy cliché for something that goes wrong

nighttime and *daytime* (both one word)

Nikkei average

nimby(ism) acronym for "not in my backyard", no initial cap

Nissan cars, but *Nissen hut*

nitroglycerin no terminal e needed; hence trinitroglycerin

No 1, No 2, No 45 etc for songs in a pop chart, bestselling books etc

No 10 or **10 Downing Street** not Number 10 or Downing St

no noun, plural *noes*

Nobel prize for literature, medicine etc; or *Nobel peace/literature prize*; *Nobel prizewinner, Nobel laureate* (lower case l), *Nobel prizewinning author* etc. Note that the Nobel prize for literature is awarded for a body of work, not an individual novel etc

Noël use the diaeresis in the synonym for Christmas

no-fly zone

no man's land

non try compounds as one word without a hyphen unless the result is baffling or hideous, which it often will be: *nonconformist*, but *non-event, non-appearance* etc

nonagenarian not nono-

noncommittal no hyphen

nonconformist lower case

non-cooperation

non-dom hyphen

none usually takes the singular verb, eg "none is available at present". However, a plural is perfectly permissible and often obviously right: "and then there were none"; "none of them are better singers than the Welsh"; "none of them have done their best" (where the inelegant alternative would be "none of them has done his or her best"); let sound and sense (and sound sense) decide

nonetheless one word

non-existent

nonfiction one word

no-no

non-profitmaking

nonsequitur roman

nonstop

noon (not 12 noon) and never say 12am or 12pm

no one two words, no hyphen; *nobody* is fine as an alternative

normalcy avoid; say *normality* instead

north, northeast, northern etc, almost always lower case

northerner, southerner lower case in most contexts; but *Southerner* (cap) in the United States

Northern Ireland thus

northern lights (aurora borealis) lower case; similarly aurora australis, the southern lights

northern powerhouse no need for caps unless helpful for clarity when writing about the Conservative government's ambitious (if so far somewhat elusive) scheme to boost economic growth in the north of England. References best kept to a minimum anyway, until we know what it means

nosey

notable no middle e

Note cap in the diplomatic sense

not only ... to be followed by *but* (and usually) *also*; often better to say simply *both ... and*

Noughties the decade 2000-09. This is not strictly speaking "the first decade of the 21st century" (2001-10); but the celebration of the new millennium at the end of 1999 and the start of 2000 (both years actually in the old millennium) has no doubt contributed to widespread misunderstanding and misusage of the phrase. Since the Christian era began with the year 1AD (not 0AD), it follows that the first year of any century ends in the figure -1 and its last year -00. There is little point in fussing over this, though you should be aware that some readers do. Use common sense

nouns as adjectives resist the urge to string them together without prepositions: "world oil supply situation", "drug traffic increase", "aircraft crash victims inquest" etc. This is tempting in headlines, and often useful, but the result can be ambiguous: "Miners dispute deal" etc

"no" vote, "yes" vote the general style for the two options in a referendum but, historically, the Yes campaign and No campaign in Scotland

no-win, no-fee legislation/agreement etc (no longer quoted)

nuclear terms should be used with precision. Take special care not to confuse *fission* and *fusion*

nul points for the British-invented cod French phrase applied to the Eurovision Song Contest when no points are scored. The phrase has no meaning for regular French-speakers, who would write and say *zéro points* or *zéro pointé*

number one, Number 10 use No 1, No 10 etc

numberplate on vehicles etc; one word

numbers write from one to ten in full, 11 upwards as numerals except when they are approximations, eg "about thirty people turned up". Exception is percentages, which always take figures (3 per cent, 5 per cent etc). Children's ages should now be written out up to ten, except when giving a range of ages in which one would normally be a figure (a child aged five, but children aged 5-14).

Try to keep consistency within a sentence: say "the number injured rose from eight to fourteen", and do not mix fractions and decimals. Note twenty-three etc with hypens.

At the start of a sentence, write all numbers in full.

For ordinals, and eg birthdays, as above, write out up to ten, then 11th, 15th, 21st, 33rd, 95th etc.

Note 42nd Street, 38th parallel etc

numeracy The figures in your story are as important as the words. If you say something is expected to cost £12 million, do you really mean £12 million a year? It makes a difference. If you are writing about a percentage increase, do you really mean percentage points? If VAT goes up from 18 per cent to 19 per cent, that is a one-point rise, not a 1 per cent rise. Do not cloud your meaning by mixing fractions, proportions and percentages all in the same paragraph (or story): "One in five parents is always too tired to read a bedtime story, while 27 per cent never miss a day and just over half manage to at least twice a week ..." Our first duty is to be accurate and easily understood in everything that we write

nut par In a running story, say about a strike, this will tell the reader what the dispute is about (the operation of train doors; a pay demand). In a follow-up to an event long ago, it will recall the starting point (local party accused of vote rigging). Don't leave it out

Oo

O for direct invocation but *oh* for general interjection; thus "O Jupiter" but "Oh dear"

oast house two words

oath of allegiance as sworn by new MPs; *the oath* at subsequent mentions

oblivious of (not "to") means forgetful of, unaware of. It does not mean ignorant or uncomprehending

obscenities, profanities, vulgarities almost always a sign of literary weakness, suggesting an inability to make a point forcefully without causing offence. "Four-letter words" and profanities should generally be avoided because they upset many readers. Columnists and other writers who resort to them too readily should be encouraged to think again. The first question to ask should not be "Does this need asterisks?" but "Does this need to be in the paper at all?" In direct quotes and when essential to the story there may be no alternative but to include these words. In such cases, it should be possible to distinguish degrees of offensiveness.

There is a commonsense distinction to be drawn between two sorts of words: those which are not in themselves offensive, but which are sometimes used with offensive intent; and those which in themselves, simply as words, will tend to offend whenever they are used.

Words of the first sort (bitch, bugger, bloody, prick etc) might all appear in the paper in some innocent context or other without causing alarm; the words themselves do not suddenly become too terrible to be written in full simply because they are being used as insults. (So, for instance, there is no reason not to spell out "he called her a bitch"; "she said he was a silly bugger"; " 'You're a useless prick,' the heckler yelled" etc).

Words of the second sort are as a rule to be asterisked at all times; f***, c***. There may be very rare exceptions — eg (almost exclusively) in quotations from works of literature — when the f-word might after serious thought and discussion be written in full; for the c-word, such exceptions will be rarer still.

Which category a word belongs in is of course a question of judgment and taste. (A lot of words — scatalogical terms, slang relating to masturbation etc — may be said to occupy a middle ground: vulgar colloquialisms of varying degrees of ugliness rather than outright obscenities, they are not always used with particularly offensive intent; if they must be used at all, they are generally better spelt out.) In most cases, however, the commonsense consensus is surprisingly clear, if the basic distinction is kept in mind.

Use asterisks thus, to a maximum of three: f***, f***ed, f***ing, f***wit; c***s etc (add final letters to indicate tenses/participles/plurals etc). These strings of asterisks look horrid; another reason to avoid such language in the first place if we can.

Be aware that other kinds of language may also offend. Racist terms (qv) belong with f*** and c*** in the second category described here, while casual blasphemy (the use of "Christ!" as an expletive, for instance) prompts far more complaints from readers than any of the words discussed above.

See **four-letter words, racist language, swearing**

Occam's razor (prefer to Ockham's) aka the principle of economy

occupied territories, the all lower case

octogenarian not octa-

octopuses (plural of *octopus*) not octopi

oedipal lower case, as pyrrhic, oriental

of avoid expressions such as "all of the people attending", "half of the children replied"; say simply "all the people", "half the children" etc

of all time do not use this meaningless phrase, as in "best golfer of all time", in any circumstances

offbeat (adj) no hyphen

officers (naval and military) do not call ratings or NCOs officers

off stage but *offstage* (no hyphen) as a modifier. Likewise *on stage, onstage*

oil-drilling, oil-fired, oil-slick, oil-tanker but *oildrum, oilfield, oilrig, oil platform*

oilseed rape no hyphen

OK generally prefer to *okay* if only because it is shorter, and probably more widely used (but there is no reason not to let, eg a columnist or a correspondent to the Letters page spell it out if they prefer; just avoid variations within a single article)

old think carefully before using old to describe almost anyone under about 80

Old Boy cap for clarity, for the former pupil of a school; likewise, *Old Girl* and *Old Chigwellian, Old Dunstablian, Old Etonian, Old Harrovian, Old Pauline, Old Salopian, Old Shirburnian, Old Wykehamist* etc. Try occasionally to resist the impulse to identify Old Etonians as such in any story where they occur. Always resist the impulse to identify as Old Etonians people who were not in fact at Eton

old city, old town no need to cap even for a well-established area, eg in Jerusalem. Similarly lower case in *old Havana*

old masters, old master paintings generally lower case; context will usually make the meaning perfectly clear, but upper case

(*Old Master*) may be resorted to if there is some real risk of confusion

Olympics can be used as a short form of *the Olympic Games*. Similarly, *the Games* (always capped, for clarity) can be used (same rule for Games in Commonwealth Games etc). Always cap Olympics and Olympic even when used adjectivally, eg an Olympic athlete. Note *International Olympic Committee* (no final "s" on Olympic)

ombudsman, ombudswoman keep lower case whether in general context, eg "he referred the matter to the ombudsman"; or for specifics, as in the local government ombudsman, the legal services ombudsman, and the unofficial title of parliamentary ombudsman (the parliamentary commissioner for administration). Do not confuse the parliamentary ombudsman with the parliamentary commissioner for standards, an entirely separate post

omega-3, omega-6 etc, lower case and hyphen, for fatty acids

on behalf of is a frequently misused phrase. It means *in the interest of* (a person etc) or *as representative of* (eg "acting on behalf of his client" is correct). It does not mean "on the part of" or simply "by": "the book betrays a lack of understanding on behalf of the author" is verbose and wrong

one use the singular verb in structures such as "one in three says that ...". Also use the singular in "Nearly one in three is ..." In first-person pieces, try to avoid the use of *one* as a synonym of *I*

one member, one vote no hyphens unless used adjectivally, as in a one-member, one-vote system

One Nation Tories, One Nation politicians etc (cap O and N)

one-time do not use as synonym of *former* as in "one-time chairman" etc

ongoing do not use this ugly adjective; say eg *continuing* or *in progress* if anything is necessary; often the word is redundant and can just be taken out

online one word (adjective and adverb)

only be aware that the positioning of this word can significantly affect the meaning of a sentence, and generally take care to place "only" before the word or phrase it qualifies: "she *only* touched the key, but did not press it"; "she touched *only* the key, not the switch"; "she touched the *only* key". Do not take this to extremes, however. If the effect of placing the word correctly is awkward, and if the intended meaning is clear, *only* should be left where it seems most naturally to fall

on stage two words, as in "She was wonderful on stage"; one word if it has to be used as a modifier: "The onstage arrangements are bizarre." Likewise, *off stage, offstage*

on to unlike *into*, two words generally better than one, as in "she moved on to better things", although "he collapsed onto the floor" is acceptable

opencast mining

open-heart surgery; *open-door* policy (if this overworked phrase has to be used); *open-plan* living room, office

openly gay there should rarely be any need for this phrase. *The Times* does not "out" gays so it is in almost every case redundant. Mention that someone is gay only if it is relevant to the story; to do otherwise is a breach of the Editors' Code

open skies (lower case, no longer quotes at first mention only, for adjective and noun), international airline bilateral access agreements; hyphenate adjectivally, eg *open-skies policy*

ophthalmologist, ophthalmic etc (not opthalmic); spell as properly pronounced, oph, not op

opposition in politics lower case as noun or adjective (like *government*) except in the rarely needed phrase *Her Majesty's Opposition*

Opus Dei the conservative organisation is a personal prelature of the Pope, and so should not be referred to as a sect

or need not be preceded by *either*, although it is strengthened thereby if two options are mentioned. Usually avoid a comma before it

oral must not be confused with *verbal*; it means pertaining to the mouth, often in the spoken context (eg the oral tradition, by word of mouth); verbal means pertaining to words (contrasted with, eg physical or choral). Take care

orangutan no need for hyphen

orders in council are approved, not signed, by the Queen

Ordnance Survey and *ordnance* in military contexts; but *ordinance* as in regulations

organic food never say that organic farmers use no chemicals; they frequently use a limited range

Orient, the wherever possible, say the East. The adjective is *oriental*, lower case. The east London football club is *Leyton Orient*, but was known as *Orient* from 1966 to 1987 and *Clapton Orient* from 1898 to 1939

orientate, orientation prefer this to *orient, oriented* etc

Orkney or *the Orkney Islands*, not the Orkneys (regarded as a solecism by those who mind about such things)

Oscars, the cap. Also, Academy awards. Note that as the word Oscar and the Oscar statuette are trademarks belonging to the Academy of Motion Picture Arts and Sciences we should not use the word in such phrases as "the annual beauty Oscars" to describe unrelated competitions of excellence; lower case names of specific awards: best actor, best supporting actress etc

Ouija (board) takes the cap as it is proprietary

-out suffixes in nouns, generally join up rather than hyphenate, as in fallout, knockout, printout, callout, dropout, bailout etc (but *to fall out* etc)

outback, the in Australia

outdoor (adjective); but *the outdoors*

outpatients, inpatients no hyphen

outside there is no obvious need for the more cumbersome "outside of"

Outward Bound must be used only when referring specifically to the work or courses of the Outward Bound Trust Ltd, and never in general use in phrases such as "outward bound-style activities". Use alternatives such as *outdoor pursuits, adventure training, outdoor adventure courses* etc. Outward Bound's lawyers pounce on every perceived infringement of its service mark

over in some cases *more than* may be preferable when followed by a number, eg "she waited more than four hours for the train" instead of "... over four hours ..."; "there were more than 60 victims" instead of "... over 60 ..." This is not a rule

over as prefix wherever the word does not look too ugly, dispense with the hyphen, even when this leads to a double "r" in the middle; thus, *overcapacity, overestimate, overreact, override, overrule, overuse, overvalue;* an obvious exception where the hyphen is essential is *over-age;* similarly, for words beginning with under

overall one word as adjective, but use sparingly

overestimate all too often foolishly confused with *underestimate:* note that the importance of writing "Its importance cannot be overestimated" cannot be overestimated

overly do not use as an alternative for *over* or *too*

owing to may sometimes be right when *due to* would be wrong; *because of* may well serve better than either

Oxbridge be sparing in using the term as a "catch-all" for Oxford and Cambridge universities

Oxford, University of colleges and halls are: All Souls College; Balliol College; Blackfriars; Brasenose College; Campion Hall; Christ Church; Corpus Christi College; Exeter College;

Green Templeton College (after merger of Green College and Templeton College in 2008); Harris Manchester College; Hertford College; Jesus College; Keble College; Kellogg College; Lady Margaret Hall; Linacre College; Lincoln College; Magdalen College; Mansfield College; Merton College; New College; Nuffield College; Oriel College; Pembroke College; The Queen's College; Regent's Park College; St Anne's College; St Antony's College; St Benet's Hall; St Catherine's College; St Cross College; St Edmund Hall; St Hilda's College; St Hugh's College; St John's College; St Peter's College; St Stephen's House; Somerville College; Trinity College; University College; Wadham College; Wolfson College; Worcester College; Wycliffe Hall

Pp

pace for clarity italicise the preposition meaning "with due deference to", but often better to find a less stuffy alternative

pacey

paedophile an adult sexually attracted to children, but *pederast*, a man who has sexual relations with boys; the distinction, now often blurred, may sometimes be worth making

page 1, **page 3**, **page 187** etc; a *page 3 girl*

paintings titles in italic

palace cap in full names, such as Blenheim Palace, thereafter the palace; the Palace (cap) is reserved as a useful shorthand for Buckingham Palace (and the vast royal operation based there)

palaeo- (not paleo-), so *palaeography* etc

palaeontology concerns the study of fossils and must not be confused with archaeology, which concerns human cultural remains

panama lower case for the hat, traditionally made in Ecuador but then taken to Panama for international distribution

panic do not overuse; it is not, for instance, a word to bring out every time stock markets fall; save it for a real crash

papacy lower case, like comparable institutions (eg the monarchy); the Pope gets a cap at all times in reference to the specific individual

paparazzi plural; singular is *paparazzo*

papyrus plural *papyruses*

paraffin prefer to the American kerosene

paragraph "a unit of thought, not of length" (Fowler)

paratroops prefer to paratroopers; a general term for troops dropped by parachute; a parachutist is a specialist in the activity. Note, The Parachute Regiment

parentheses see **punctuation**

Parker Bowles, Camilla no hyphen. With her marriage to the Prince of Wales, she became the Princess of Wales, but (for obvious reasons of tact) she does not use the title, choosing instead to be known as the Duchess of Cornwall. When in Scotland, and when the prince is identified as the Duke of Rothesay, she is officially the Duchess of Rothesay and may be referred to as such

parliament lower case even in British context (except when naming the building, the Houses of Parliament). Also lower case in overseas contexts even when the word forms part of the institution, eg the European parliament, Canadian parliament and in many Commonwealth countries. Also obviously lower case in non-anglophone parliaments; in those cases use a cap for the original name if giving: so the Spanish parliament (the Cortes), the Russian parliament (Duma), the Israeli parliament (Knesset), the Polish parliament (Sejm), the Irish parliament (the Dail), the German parliament (Bundestag) etc

Also, lower case *parliamentary*, even in parliamentary private secretary (abbreviated PPS), parliamentary Labour Party (PLP) and similarly, parliamentary ombudsman

parliamentary commissioner for standards (lower case) the post created in the light of the Nolan committee on standards in public life. He or she must not be referred to as the parliamentary ombudsman, who is the parliamentary commissioner for administration

Parsee prefer to Parsi

partially, partly *partially* is of degree, eg partially deaf; *partly* is of extension, eg partly under water

participles beware the dangling (disconnected or unrelated) participle, where the wrong subject ends up being modified: "Rushing for the train, his hat fell off"; "Speeding over the top of the hill, the town came into view"; "Born in Paris, his best known novel is ..." As Fowler says, these infelicitous constructions "seldom cause real ambiguity, but they jar and can distract the reader and are to be avoided"

part-time, part-timer hyphens

party (political) cap when integral to an official name in common usage, eg Scottish National Party, Conservative Party (but Tory party), Workers' Party, Freedom Party, People's Party, Communist Party etc. Subsequent mentions of *the party* should be lower case

partygoer one word, no hyphen

Pashtuns biggest ethnic group in Afghanistan. Prefer this designation to Pathans, by which they are also known. The language is *Pashto*

past use rather than last in such phrases as "the past two weeks". See **last**

past tense of verbs: almost always prefer the shorter form using final -t where appropriate; eg *spelt* not spelled, *dreamt* not dreamed (although never earnt for *earned*)

pâté regularly used as an English word, but retains accents (the second for pronunciation, the first because it would be odd to do one and not the other)

payout, payoff no hyphens

peacekeeping, peacemaking etc no hyphens

Pearl Harbor not Harbour

peccadillo plural *peccadillos*

pedal as in bicycle; *peddle* as in selling drugs or advocating ideas. Thus a *pedaller* is someone who pedals a bike; a *pedlar* is the (often shady) small trader; and a drug-pusher is a *peddler*

peers a peer or a peeress holds a title either by birth (a hereditary peerage) or conferred in recognition of public or political service or distinction (a life peerage). Some (but no longer all) peers sit in the House of Lords. There are five ranks of the peerage: duke, marquess, earl, viscount and baron or baroness. A female life peer is a peeress usually referred to as, eg Baroness Smith. After the first mention of, eg the Marquess of Paddington, Earl of Euston, Viscount Pimlico or Lord Holborn, call them Lord Paddington, Lord Euston etc. (A duke, however, remains at subsequent mentions the duke.) Not all lords and ladies are peers; some are styled Lord or Lady by courtesy: sons of dukes and marquesses; daughters of dukes, marquesses and earls; or wives of barons, baronets and knights.

The titles of peers, and of life peers in particular, should be checked in *Who's Who*. The full title, which should be given at first mention, is whatever appears in bold capitals in *Who's Who*. So, if in *Who's Who* a place name is given in bold capital letters with the surname (LORD BLACK OF CROSSHARBOUR) and without a comma, it is part of the title, which should be given in full at first mention; the place name may subsequently be dropped (so that we refer just to Lord Black, unless, unhappily, the other Lord Black — Lord Black of Brentwood — figures in the same story; in which case we would need to retain the full titles of both throughout to distinguish).

If in *Who's Who* the place name is not given in bold with the surname, but is separated from the name by a comma and printed in lighter type, it is NOT part of the title and should never be used. So Lord Mandelson is just Lord MANDELSON (bold caps in *Who's Who*), never Lord Mandelson of Foy, let alone Lord Mandelson of Foy in the County of Herefordshire and Hartlepool in the County of Durham. For peers who sit in the House of Lords, the parliamentary website has an updated list of peers, with their titles rendered correctly, and is another useful point of reference.

It may often be helpful to identify life peers who have been familiar figures in public life and whose titles are not based on their surnames, or whose common surnames might lead to confusion. Lord Deben, the former Conservative minister John Selwyn Gummer (NB never "the former John Selwyn Gummer"); Lord Black of Brentwood (Guy Black, the former director of the Press Complaints Commission) etc. If a first name is to be added, it must always be in brackets: Lord (Conrad) Black. See **Lady** and **titles**

pejorative not perjorative

pekinese lower case for the dog breed. See **dogs**

Peking only in phrases such as Peking duck or Peking Man. The city is now Beijing

peninsula never peninsular when used as a noun; *peninsular* is the adjective, as in the *Peninsular War*

pensioners take care with this word. Some readers take exception to "ambiguous" usage, so it should strictly be confined to people drawing their state pension. If in doubt, write *older people, the elderly* (but beware), or as a last resort *senior citizen*. See **elderly**, **aged**, **old** and **retiree**

peony not paeony

people use rather than persons wherever appropriate; exceptions would be "the law is no respecter of persons" or the ubiquitous *missing persons*. Take care with the apostrophe: remember that *people* is in effect a singular collective noun, so the normal use is apostrophe "s", eg "it is the people's wish"; *peoples* in the sense of races, however, is the plural of a singular *people* and so takes an "s" apostrophe, eg, "the African peoples' common heritage"

per try to avoid in phrases such as "six times per year"; "six times a year" is preferred

percentages should always take figures rather than be spelt out, eg 3 per cent, not three per cent. Usually use decimals rather than fractions (3.25 per cent rather than 3¼ per cent). Use % sign in headlines, never pc, and spell out per cent in text.

Take care in calculating percentages, a frequent pitfall for journalists. Note eg that if the price of an apple goes up from £1 to £1.50, this is a rise of 50 per cent; but if it subsequently falls back to £1, the fall will be 33 per cent.

Beware in particular of the distinction between percentage and percentage point. If the mortgage rate rises from 8 per cent to 10 per cent, it does not rise by 2 per cent, but by two percentage points. Similarly if a political party's support drops from 50 per cent to 40 per cent in an opinion poll, it has lost ten percentage points or 20 per cent of its support.

More generally do not use the terms "percentage" or "proportion" as synonyms of "part" or "many" if that is all they mean in a sentence; eg instead of "a large percentage of parents objected" say "many parents objected"

perihelion the point in a planet or comet's orbit when it is nearest the sun. See **aphelion**

permanent secretary lower case always

Persia use Iran for the modern state, and never Persian Gulf except in historical context

personally adverb that can almost always be removed

personnel prefer *people* or *employees* or *workers* wherever possible

Perspex is a trade name, so must cap

peshmerga ("those who face death"); roman, lower case, for the Kurdish fighters in Iraq

Peterhouse the Cambridge college, never takes College after the name. Neither does Christ Church, Oxford; nor do any Oxford or Cambridge colleges ending with Hall, eg Lady Margaret Hall. Nor do, eg Queen Mary and Royal Holloway at the University of London (though both used to). See **Cambridge, University of** and **Oxford, University of**

petfood no hyphen; similarly, *catfood, dogfood*

petrol bomb not Molotov cocktail

phalangist in Lebanon; *falangist* in Spain

pharaoh (not -oah), lower case generic, cap when naming a specific king; adjective *pharaonic* (lower case)

philistine lower case noun and adjective re boorishly uncultured etc; *Philistine* cap noun and adjective re Philistia and its inhabitants, eg Goliath

phone hacking two words as noun; hyphenate adjectivally, eg phone-hacking scandal

phoney not phony

phosphorus (noun) but *phosphorous, phosphoric* (adjectives); *phosphorescence*; also note *white phosphorus* and *white phosphorus bomb or shell* (a shell that contains white phosphorus)

photo-finish but *photocall* (one word); likewise, *photo opportunity, photoshoot*

photofit lower case, but Identikit, cap

photographer credits For all *Times* photographers the style is TIMES PHOTOGRAPHER JACK HILL. For freelancers commissioned by *The Times* it is JOE SNAPPER FOR THE TIMES. For agencies, eg ADAM GERRARD/SWNS

pidgin English not pigeon

Pill, the (contraceptive), but *morning-after pill* (lower case)

PIN (exceptionally keep caps for this acronym, for clarity, so not Pin), personal identification number. Do not write PIN number, a tautology. Note *chip and PIN*

pitbull one word

pitstop (motor racing) also *pitwall*

pizzazz

place name constructions two ugly devices to avoid are, eg "a Gosport, Hampshire, housewife", and "Manchester's Piccadilly station"; say instead "a housewife from Gosport, Hampshire", and "Piccadilly station, Manchester"

place names use the online Ordnance Survey gazetteer for place names in England, Wales and Scotland, and *The Times Comprehensive Atlas of the World* for the rest of the world. But there are exceptions; beware eg the revised Welsh county and Northern Ireland district names

plainclothes one word as an adjective but two as a noun: *plain clothes*

planes always prefer *aircraft* or *jets* (where applicable). Avoid airplanes

plant names first comes the name of the genus, for example *Malva*. Added to this is the species, for example *moschata*. Both of these should be written in italics, with the genus capped up and the species lower case, eg *Malva moschata*.

If a subspecies/variety/form is included, this is also in italics, eg *Malva sylvestris* subsp. *mauritanica* OR *Malva alcea* var. *fastigiata* OR *Malva moschata* f. *alba*.

When something is a cultivar or hybrid, ie it is manmade or a popular cross-breed, it may be identified with a catchy name, eg *Malva sylvestris* 'Primley Blue'. The latter is not italicised, but has single quotation marks. Just to confuse matters, this catchy name is sometimes referred to as the variety, which is not technically correct, but it is how some gardeners refer to popular hybrids.

Examples: *Calendula officianalis* 'Touch of Red', *Geranium cinereum* 'Ballerina', *Brachyscome iberidifolia* 'Summer Skies' with the genus capped up and the species lower case. For definitive detailed guidance consult the Royal Horticultural Society website

Plasticine trademark

Play-Doh proprietary

play down preferred to downplay

plays titles in italics

plc all lower case, can usually be dropped from company names

plimsoll the footwear; Plimsoll (cap) line, the load line on the hull of a ship

plurals make corporate bodies and institutions singular unless this looks odd. Thus "The National Trust is ...", but sports teams are plural, eg "Arsenal were worth their 8-0 lead". Whether singular or plural, always maintain consistency within a story. Treat nouns such as couple, family and public as plurals

plus, minus do not use as variants of *and* or *without*. NB, *pluses* and *minuses*

poetess avoid (say *poet*). See **feminine designations**

poet laureate lower case for a specific one and for the generic, as for chancellors, prime ministers etc; the plural is *poets laureate*, lower case

poetry or blank verse quotes spacing should be as follows around the slash to separate the lines:

The play's the thing/ Wherein I'll catch the conscience of the king

poinsettia the showy coloured parts of this Christmas plant are not flowers but bracts (modified leaves)

point-to-point

pole lower case for an end of the earth and, adjectivally, *polar*, but *the North Pole, the South Pole*; also *the magnetic North Pole, the geographical North Pole*

police in the United Kingdom, the underlying concept of the police is "citizens in uniform". Beware use of language from any quarter that seeks to establish the police as having quasi-military status. Thus, for example, do not refer to ancillary staff as "civilians", which would imply that police officers are not civilians

police forces lower case the word police whether or not it is part of the full name of the force. City of London police; Devon & Cornwall police etc. Note, however, five exceptions: *Metropolitan Police* (seems more logical and natural than *Metropolitan police*; may be abbreviated sparingly to *the Met* subsequently); *British Transport Police*; *Royal Military Police*; *Police Scotland* (the single service for all Scotland formed on April 1, 2013, by the merger of the eight regional forces); *Police Service of Northern Ireland* (formerly the Royal Ulster Constabulary).

Some forces have constabulary in their names instead of police, but they too may simply be referred to as eg Avon & Somerset police. If for some reason using constabulary, also always lower case (Durham constabulary etc), except in historical references to the Royal Ulster Constabulary (the RUC).

Police forces take plural verbs (West Midlands police "are investigating, have arrested" etc) — except for "the Met" (when abbreviated), which is singular

policemen do not use this word if we mean police officers, including women; likewise, *firefighters* rather than firemen

police ranks wherever possible outside lists, avoid the inelegant abbreviated forms such as Det Con, Det Chief Insp. Spell out, even if inconvenient sometimes. The use of WPC (Woman Police Constable) is allowed historically, eg WPC Yvonne Fletcher (murdered outside the Libyan Embassy in London in 1984); otherwise now use PC, eg PC Sharon Beshenivsky (shot dead in Bradford, 2005). More generally, use PC for all constables, with no need to spell out. PC is also acceptable in headlines. Cap police ranks when, and only when, attached to a name: Sergeant Dixon, Superintendent Knacker, Detective Chief Inspector Morse (as with army ranks, ecclesiastical titles etc); subsequently, and otherwise, lower case: the chief inspector, the superintendent. Treat chief constable as a job title rather than a rank: it is not usually used in front of the holder's name — we don't refer to Chief Constable Smith but to Mr Smith, the chief constable — and will therefore invariably be lower case: "the chief constable of Greater Manchester announced"; "the mayor said he would complain to the chief constable" etc. Inspector and all ranks above, eg chief inspector, superintendent, chief superintendent, assistant chief constable, deputy chief constable, chief constable are usually referred to as Mr/Mrs/Ms after first mention. Helpful also to make all detectives Mr etc at second mention to distinguish from uniformed police

Police Staff College at Bramshill, Hampshire; or simply *the police college* (lower case), Bramshill

policyholder, **policymaker** but *policy document*

Politburo usually cap

political correctness overblown euphemisms and clumsy circumlocutions annoy. That said, newspapers must beware of normative or emotive language, especially when referring to, eg women and race. Resist absurd neologisms, but never cause needless offence. See also **race, racist language**

politics treat as singular when talking of the form or process of government; plural when meaning a particular set of principles, ideas etc, eg "Politics is a popular subject at many universities"; "What are your politics?" (Fowler)

pollock prefer to pollack for the fish

polonium-210 hyphenate as for any isotope

Pom, **Pommy** cap the Antipodean slang for an English person. Plural *Pommies*

poncey

Pond cap as a sobriquet for the Atlantic

pop art (painting etc) generally lower case but may be capped if helpful for clarity or if making a precise art-historical point

the Pope not usually necessary to give his full name, eg Pope Benedict XVI, Pope John Paul II, unless several popes (lower case, generic) are mentioned in a story, but always cap when used specifically. Note *pontiff, papacy, pontificate* (the nice distinction between the last two words is worth preserving in the face of near-universal indifference: *papacy* for the office itself, *pontificate* for the tenure of a particular pope)

pop groups no need to cap the *the*: the Beatles, the Rolling Stones, the Who

pop, pop music, pop star always lower case

populist should not be confused with, or used as a synonym of, popular; it means supporting the interests of ordinary people, or pandering to mass public taste

Portakabin, Portaloo trade names: always use the capital. If in doubt use generic phrases such as *portable building, portable lavatory*

Porton Down is the location of two quite distinct research establishments, one public health and the other military. The former has not undertaken any human experiments with service personnel

possessives generally avoid the journalese of inelegant "geographic possessives" such as London's East End, Colorado's Breckenridge ski resort: prefer the East End of London, Breckenridge, the Colorado ski resort. Similarly, do not use the possessive in phrases such as BBC One's *Panorama* programme: write "the BBC One *Panorama* programme", or simply "*Panorama* on BBC One"

possibly like most qualifiers it can often be omitted with benefit

postage stamps write *first-class* and *second-class* for stamp denominations

postal addresses in news and features, prefer to say Bromley, southeast London (rather than Kent); and Kingston upon Thames, southwest London (rather than Surrey); Richmond upon Thames, southwest London etc. This leaves the old counties such as Middlesex to be used principally in their historical or sporting contexts. Correspondents to the *Times* letters page may generally be allowed to live where they think they do, eg Twickenham, Middx.

Also prefer to avoid the clumsy possessive form (unless the alternative is even clumsier): so instead of Manchester's Moss Side, London's East End, say Moss Side, Manchester, the East End of London. There is no need to use postcodes except when giving an address for information

postgraduate, **undergraduate** noun and adjective both one word

Post-it Notes proprietary, cap P and N

postmodern one word, lower case in all senses. See **artistic movements**

post mortem wherever possible write *post-mortem examination* in reports, certainly at first mention; repetition may be cumbersome, however, so *post mortem* is acceptable at subsequent mentions and in headlines; autopsy sounds (and still is) American, even if British pathologists sometimes use it, and everyone knows what it means; not banned, but use sparingly

postwar, **prewar** (adjectives, commonly referring to the Second World War); do not use adverbially, as in "there were a million unemployed prewar"

pound do not use the £ symbol by itself, even in headlines

PoW prisoner of war; plural *PoWs*

power measured in watts, megawatts etc, eg a 60W light bulb. Beware confusion, all too common, with consumption of energy, measured in watt-hours etc. How much energy something consumes depends on how long it is on. See **energy**

power stations take great care in expressing capacity and output correctly

PPE the university degree is philosophy, politics and economics (not politics, philosophy etc)

practical, practicable do not confuse. Practical means adapted to actual conditions or (of a person) able to make things function well; practicable means capable of being effected or accomplished

practice (noun), *practise* (verb) in British usage. It is an inexcusable practice for sub-editors to confuse the two; writers should practise getting it right

praesidium not presidium

Praetorian relating to the Praetorian Guard, or resembling it, especially with regard to corruption

praying mantis (not preying); the preferred plural is *praying mantises*

pre- often redundant yet increasingly attached for no good reason to the front of perfectly decent verbs: coinages such as pre-order, pre-book, pre-prepared, pre-installed etc are not to be encouraged

pre-budget report lower case

precede hence *preceded*

précis use accent

pre-Columbian before Columbus

predominantly some dictionaries acknowledge the variant predominately; *The Times* does not

prefixes such as e, super, mega, multi, eco, over, under, micro, mini rarely need a hyphen: *supersize; multifaceted* (but exceptions when two vowels fall together, eg *multi-ethnic*); *overrule, oversensitive, overuse* (exception is *over-age*); *underperforming, underreact* (exception *under-age*); *macroeconomic; microskirt; miniskirt* etc

pregnant avoid the infelicitous phrase "she fell pregnant". Write instead "she became pregnant"

premier do not use in text as a synonym of prime minister, although very occasionally its use in the headline of a foreign story (never British) may be permitted. Generally, confine the word to heads of government of, eg the Canadian provinces, Australian states and some British overseas territories; always lower case. Premiership is preferable to prime-ministership

premiere of a play, ballet etc (no accent)

Premier League the top division of English football, formerly known as the Premiership. In Sport, and perhaps in Business contexts, but rarely in News, it may be appropriate to refer to the sponsor at first mention, should another come along, as we used to with the Barclays Premier League. The organisation running it remains the FA Premier League

premise is an assumption in an argument; *premises* (property) take the plural verb, eg "the premises are well positioned"

Premium Bonds caps

prenuptial no hyphen; likewise the informal *prenup*

prepay, prepaid etc no hyphens

prepositional verbs there can be no general objection to these. Most are perfectly useful (and used all the time): *take off, get stuck in to, put up with, play down, play up, go through, go through with, measure up to, get on with, fall out with* etc. In some, however, the preposition is tautologous (consult with, meet with etc); these are hideous and to be shunned

pre-Raphaelite cap R for the name, lower case p

presently use in the sense of soon, not to mean currently, at present or now

president of any country, cap when used with the name, but otherwise lower case: eg "President Trump said that ... the president said that ..."; "Richard Nixon was the president until 1974." Write, eg President Poroshenko of Ukraine (simply President and surname and country) at first mention.

Also lower case when using president more generally, eg "Richard Nixon was the 37th president of the United States." Also lower case *presidency* (as in the French presidency of the EU), and note that presidents of companies or organisations will always take lower case, even with leading national organisations, academic institutions etc such as president of the Royal Society, president of the TUC etc. Note also *presidential* (lower case), thus *vice-presidential* (lower case, hyphen). See **prime minister**

press always lower case except in titles such as the Independent Press Standards Organisation

prestigious try to avoid this overworked and unappealing word and if necessary find an appropriate substitute such as *highly regarded, admired, eminent, esteemed, leading, noted, outstanding, powerful* etc. Often it is more or less redundant and can just be deleted anyway

pre-tax hyphenate

pretension but *pretentious*

prevaricate must not be confused with *procrastinate*. The first means to speak or act evasively; the second to defer action, to be dilatory

preventive not preventative

pricey prefer to pricy

prime meridian lower case

prime minister lower case always: "Theresa May's record as prime minister"; "the prime minister said that ... "; "Margaret Thatcher was the prime minister from 1979 to 1990." Also lower case when using prime minister more generally, eg "Being prime minister has affected many men's health"; "This is a prime minister with much still to prove." Avoid not only "prime minister Theresa May", but also eg Theresa May, the prime minister (*Times* readers will know who Mrs May is); say instead Theresa May at first mention, then the prime minister at next mention. Never use premier for the

British prime minister, and never use PM except sparingly in headlines; *prime minister's questions*, also lower case (but *PMQs*)

prime time noun; *primetime* adjective

primeval rather than primaeval

Prince generally prefer to avoid the familiar forms of Prince Charles and Prince Philip until they have been given their full designation of the Prince of Wales and the Duke of Edinburgh; prefer the prince and the duke at subsequent mentions. Note the Prince's Trust.

The Duke of Cambridge at first mention, thereafter simply the duke (or for variation Prince William, or William); Prince Harry at first mention, thereafter simply Harry (or for variation the prince, if not ambiguous)

principal (noun or adjective) means chief, main, important, head etc; eg the principal of a college, or the team's principal objective. It must never be confused with *principle*, which is a noun meaning concept, ideal, rule, moral etc; eg her Christian principles

principality, the lower case in Welsh, or any other, context

printout one word as noun, two as a verb, *to print out*

prior to avoid wherever possible; use *before*

prison service lower case; *director-general of the prison service* lower case; *chief inspector of prisons* lower case

private finance initiative (PFI), sometimes known as a *public-private partnership* (PPP); note no longer caps when spelt out

private sector, **public sector** do not use hyphens even when employed adjectivally, eg public sector pay (as high street shopping)

privy council and **privy counsellors** not councillors

prize lower case whenever possible: Nobel prize, Booker prize, Academy award etc

prizewinner one word; eg a Nobel prizewinner; also, a Nobel prizewinning novel

probation service lower case, as *prison service*

probe use only in a scientific, medical or space context. Never to be used as journalese for *inquiry*, even in headlines

problem be sparing with use of this dull and overworked word

procrastinate means to defer action, to be dilatory; do not confuse with *prevaricate*

procurator fiscal lower case. Crown prosecutor in Scotland

prodigal, the Prodigal Son take care, as the precise essence of prodigality is wastefulness or squandering (rather than going far away from home and coming back). Other words, such as *wayward* or *wandering*, may be more appropriate in some contexts

Professor cap when used with name, Professor Jones; otherwise lower case, professor of history, the professor etc; prefer not to shorten to Prof except in lists of names

profits especially in Business stories should always state the basis of the figure (pre-tax, operating etc)

program (computers); *programme* (the arts etc)

"pro-life" beware this contentious phrase for the anti-abortion lobby (especially in US context); use the phrase *anti-abortion* wherever possible, but when "pro-life" is unavoidable always quote it

Proms summer season of *promenade concerts* at the Albert Hall, attended by enthusiastic *Promenaders* (or *Prommers*) and culminating in the *Last Night of the Proms*

prone means lying face down; *supine*, face up

proof (legally) the *standard of proof* is the level of proof required of a party to discharge its *burden of proof*. In a criminal context, the burden is with the prosecution to prove the facts essential to its case and the standard of proof is beyond reasonable doubt; in a civil context, the burden rests with the party bringing the action and the standard of proof is on a balance of probabilities

proofread one word; also *proofreader, proofreading*

propeller not -or; *propellent*, prefer to propellant

prophecy noun, *prophesy* verb

pros and cons

protagonist means a supporter (of either side) in a debate or quarrel; it does not mean advocate or proponent

protégé if female, *protégée*; do not confuse with *prodigy*

Protestant cap, beware of using for all Christians who are not Roman Catholic

protester never -or

proven "not proven" is the Scottish legal verdict. In general use, prefer *proved* to proven; but proven and unproven may be used as a colloquial alternative

provided that ... not "providing that ...", but simply "provided" works in some cases

provinces, provincial take great care of these words in the context of "outside London". Many regard them as patronising; use *the regions* or *regional* wherever possible

prurient means having an unhealthy obsession with sex; it does not mean puritanical

psychotic describes a mental health condition; never use as a term of abuse

public one of the few collective nouns where the plural is preferred, eg "the public are concerned about their safety"

public school *independent school* is now a preferable term; say *public schoolboys, public schoolgirls*, if we have to use the phrase

Pulitzer prize lower case p for prize

pullout noun, one word; but *to pull out*, verb

punctuation No newspaper sentence should be confusing or open to double meaning. No paragraph should need to be read twice. A sentence other than an exclamation should have a subject and a verb. The best punctuation is the full point. Commas should usually be kept for punctuating lists and breaking up sentences to avoid confusion. They should not join sentences that are better separated by a full point. Semi-colons are generally best confined to separating lists of phrases. Colons have a specific use, throwing meaning forward. Dashes are a bad habit, often used to pursue a line of thought that the writer cannot be bothered to construct some other way. Brevity is all.

Some important reminders:

1. Keep commas where they should be logically in "broken" sentences. Thus, the comma goes outside in the following example: "The trouble is", he said, "that this is a contentious issue." Omit the comma before *if, unless, before, since, when* unless the rhythm or sense of the sentence demands it. Avoid the so-called Oxford comma; write "he ate bread, butter and jam" rather than "he ate bread, butter, and jam", EXCEPT where to do so creates nonsense or confusion. There is no need to put a comma between adjectives that form a kind of unit or where the last adjective is in closer relation to the noun than the preceding one(s), eg fine dry evenings, a good little boy. See **commas**

2. Dashes should not be used in place of commas. Too many dashes can be ugly and disruptive. See **dashes**

3. Note that punctuation marks go inside the inverted commas if they relate to the words quoted, outside if they relate to the main sentence, eg She is going to classes in "health and beauty". If the whole sentence is a quotation, the final point goes inside, eg "Beauty is truth, truth beauty."

4. Interrogation marks are never used with indirect questions or rhetorical questions, eg "She asked why he did not laugh."

5. Parentheses should be used sparingly; try to use commas instead. Use square brackets when writing words into a direct quote that were not said, but which explain context or meaning, eg "I condemn [this totalitarianism]" when a speaker has said "I condemn it".

6. With ellipses, use three points with full non-breaking space after last word, then thin-spacing between points, then full space before next word; for example, *not only ... but also*

puns an enjoyable device for headline writers. Don't overdo. Restrict their use to funny or light stories or features and if in doubt avoid; if irresistible they must at least be in good taste

Puritan do not use the word for the 16th/17th-century religious group as a contemporary adjective: write *puritanical*

putsch a military seizure of power, as in *coup*

pygmy, pygmies

Pyramids the three main Pyramids at Giza (including the Great Pyramid) should be capped for clarity. But there are many other pyramids (lower case) throughout Egypt

Pyrenees no need for accents unless referring specifically to the French *département*

pyrrhic (as with victory) lower case

Qq

qat rather than kat or khat, the hypnotic drug

, QC, MP, commas each side when used after name

QE2 ideally spell out *Queen Elizabeth 2* at first mention, thereafter *QE2* or simply *the ship*. Strictly speaking, she is not a liner but a cruise ship. See **liner**

qi prefer *chi* for the vital energy in oriental medicine, martial arts etc, believed to circulate around the body in currents

quality press papers like *The Times*. While *quality* generally needs a qualifier (good-, poor-, high-, low- etc), this has never been a rule: quality grocers and quality chop houses have been with us for many years

quango (short for quasi-autonomous non-governmental organisation), no need to spell out or to quote

quantum leap avoid this cliché wherever possible

quasi- normally hyphenate, as in quasi-judicial, quasi-stellar

Quebecker a native or inhabitant of the province of Quebec; *Québécois*, likewise but especially French-speaking

Queen, the retains her capital letter at all specific references; note *the Queen's Speech* (to parliament), caps for clarity, but *the Queen's birthday honours*. NB the Queen is not "introduced" to people; people are introduced, or (more correctly) presented, to the Queen. See **job titles**, **royal family**

Queen Elizabeth the Queen Mother (no commas) was in her lifetime referred to at first mention thus in *The Times*; on her death she became at first mention *the late Queen Elizabeth the Queen Mother;* subsequently *the Queen Mother* or *the late Queen Mother.* So long after her death, there seems no reason not to use the shorter, more familiar form throughout when reference to her needs to be made

Queensberry Marquess of, and *Queensberry rules*

Queens' College, Cambridge but *The Queen's College, Oxford; Queen's University Belfast* but in formal contexts *The Queen's University of Belfast* (and either form can be shortened to *Queen's Belfast*). See **Cambridge, University of** and **Oxford, University of**

queueing with middle e

question useful concrete word implying the need for an answer; resist overuse as a synonym of *problem, issue* etc

"question mark hangs over" an especially poor (going on bizarre) metaphor. "There are questions about" is straightforward and more acceptable

question time, prime minister's questions (lower case), also *questions* (lower case) *to the prime minister, foreign secretary* etc

quicker do not use as an adverb — always say *more quickly* (or prefer *faster, sooner,* according to sense). Quicker should be confined to adjectival comparison, eg "he started at a quicker pace"; adverbial use of *quick* itself is best restricted to direct quotations of spoken exclamations such as "Come quick!"

quid pro quo not italic

quiz show as chat show, game show, talk show etc; no hyphen, even in the adjectival sense, eg chat show host

quotation marks (inverted commas) remember, single quotes in headlines, straps and standfirsts; double quotes in captions. The only other use for single inverted commas is quotations within quotations. Avoid inverted commas in sentences where they are clearly unnecessary, eg He described the attack as "outrageous". Quotation marks are not to be used for works of art.

When copy starts with a drop cap (as in some features) and the opening words are a quotation, the quotation must be opened as well as closed, ie there must be a large single quote mark alongside the initial drop cap, as well as closing quotes in the text; it may be preferable to rewrite the intro to avoid this

quotes direct quotes should be corrected only to remove the solecisms and other errors that occur in speech but look silly in print. Make sure that literary or biblical quotations are absolutely accurate. Always take care that quotes are correctly rendered and properly attributed; never present a quote as having been given directly to *The Times* if it was not. Unattributed quotes (eg from anonymous "sources") should be kept to a minimum, and used only when confidentiality is vital. Unattributed derogatory quotes should not be relied on as the sole basis for criticism of individuals or institutions; they need supporting evidence, and those criticised should have an opportunity to respond before publication.

Normally introduce direct speech with a colon, particularly in news reports; but in features, columns and less formal writing, where direct speech appears mid-sentence and where colons might disrupt the flow, a degree of flexibility must be allowed; the opening and closing quotation marks are often enough to make clear what is going on — if not, a comma may help; use common sense

qwerty lower case for the arrangement of the standard English language keyboard

Rr

race reference to a person's race, colour or ethnicity may be made only when genuinely relevant to the story; pejorative or prejudicial references breach the Editors' Code. The word race itself is often better replaced by *people, nation, group* etc

racecourse, racehorse, racetrack

Rachmaninov, Sergei not Rachmaninoff

racist language as with other offensive language, avoid. As a general rule, if necessary in direct quotes, use asterisks: y**; n***er etc, even when quoting the deliberate use of racist language by those who are usually its targets (eg rap musicians, Tottenham Hotspur fans). On occasion, eg in historical contexts or when quoting from works of literature etc, room for editorial discretion may exist; such occasions will be rare, and require careful thought; if in doubt, use asterisks. See **obscenities**

racked by doubts, pain etc; not wracked

racket for tennis, not racquet. The game is also *rackets*

racoon prefer this shorter spelling to raccoon

radio compounds are generally one word in the wireless context (eg radiotelephone) or when they concern rays (eg radioactive, radioisotope, radiotherapy). Broadcasting frequencies are measured in megahertz (MHz) and kilohertz (kHz). But note *radio telescope*

radio ham this term should strictly be applied only to licensed amateur radio operators, who are offended when it is used to refer to unlicensed "eavesdroppers" spying on private phone calls etc. Take care

RAF the Royal Air Force. Cap if spelling out

RAF crews went on *operations* (or *ops*) in the Second World War; Americans went on *missions*. Do not mix up

railways write *east coast main line, west coast main line, Channel tunnel rail link*

railway station do not use the Americanism train station except, eg in direct quotes, preferably from North Americans

rain, rein, reign beware!

rainforest one word

raison d'être roman

rajah takes the final -h, as does *maharajah*

rand the South African unit of currency. Plural *rands*. Write, eg 12.1 billion rands at first mention; subsequently R2.3 billion etc

R&B if a distinction is needed, use *R&B* for the contemporary dance genre influenced by hip-hop and *R'n'B* for the vintage rhythm and blues from which it ultimately derives

ranging from overworked and often unnecessary phrase. There must be a scale in which the elements might be ranged: "ranging from 15 to 25 years" is correct, "a crowd ranging from priests to golfers" is not

ranks in the armed services, cap only when attached to a name, eg General Jones. Prefer not to abbreviate in news stories (Adm, Sgt etc are acceptable in Court page lists of appointments etc).

Times style is to hyphenate those ranks consisting of a compound of two individual rank designations, eg:

for the navy, lieutenant-commander, commandant-general, surgeon-captain; also any rank with vice or rear, eg vice-admiral, rear-admiral; also hyphenate commander-in-chief for the army, major-general, lieutenant-general, lieutenant-colonel, sergeant-major etc. (Note that there have been no brigadier-generals in the British Army since 1921, although they exist still in eg the American and French)

for the RAF, air vice-marshal is the only hyphenated rank; ie no hyphen in squadron leader, wing commander, leading aircraftman, air chief marshal etc

Do not hyphenate compounds (apart from naval ranks with vice and rear) that are not made up of two individual rank designations. So, no hyphen for able seaman, staff sergeant, lance corporal, warrant officer etc

rarefied, rarefy not rarified

rateable

rating agency prefer to ratings agency

rave acceptable in context as a musical event. See **gig**

raze means demolish, destroy, tear down completely, level; there is rarely much to be gained by adding "to the ground", which in any case risks turning a vivid verb into a dull cliché

razzmatazz

re- whenever possible, run the prefix on to the word it qualifies, eg readmission, remake, rework, etc; but there are two main classes of exceptions:

1. where the word after re- begins with an e, eg re-election, re-emerge, re-examine, re-enter etc

2. where there could be serious ambiguity in compounds, such as re-creation (recreation), re-cover (recover), re-dress (redress), re-form (pop groups) v reform (delinquent)

reach out appalling, cloying corporate jargon for *contact*; do not use

real estate acceptable as a synonym for (real) property in a North American context, but write property wherever possible. Technically, the "real" means immoveable property, eg land and tenements, to distinguish it from personal property

realpolitik roman, lower case

reason "the reason why he did this" is a tautology; prefer "the reason that he did this", or rewrite to avoid (eg "he did this because")

rebut means to argue to the contrary, producing evidence; *to refute* is to win such an argument. Neither should be used as a synonym of *reject, deny* or *counter*, all good, straightforward words. Nor should they be used for *dispute* or *respond to*

receive "receiving an injury" is to be discouraged, but not banned. Prefer to say *sustained* or *suffered*; and never say someone received a broken leg etc — prefer suffered a broken leg or, better still, broke a leg

record never say "set a new record", "was an all-time record" etc, where both the qualifiers are tautologous

rector like vicar, lower case

recrudescence do not confuse with *resurgence* or *revival*. It means worsening, in the sense of reopening wounds or recurring diseases

redbrick universities and buildings

red planet informal name for Mars. No need for cap unless context allows some possibility of confusion without

reductio ad absurdum (note, not reduction, absurdam or italics), proving a premise is false by showing its logical consequence to be contradictory or absurd

referendum plural referendums, as with *conundrums, stadiums, forums* and most words ending in -um. But note *millennia, strata*

Reformation, the retain cap only for the historical schism in western Christianity

refusenik

refute take care with this word; see **rebut**

regalia plural. Prefer *insignia*, eg for an MBE appointment, to regalia, which are originally and strictly emblems of royalty

Regent's Canal and **Regent's Park** take an apostrophe s, but Regent Street

regimen should be restricted to medical contexts: a prescribed course of exercise, way of life, diet etc

register office not registry office

register of members' interests lower case

registrar (University of Oxford); but *registrary* (University of Cambridge); both lower case

registrar-general

regular not the same as frequent

relatively a word that rarely adds anything useful

religious right in American politics. Mostly this will work lower case, so try it that way first. If the meaning is not clear, cap

Remembrance Sunday preferred to day

Renaissance, the cap the historical transformation in western culture that began in the 14th century, but lower case all general use of *renaissance* as synonym of revival or rebirth

reorganise

repellant noun; *repellent* adjective

repetition not always a bad thing. Fear of repetition too often leads reporters to try their hand at elegant variation, which is usually worse. Eager not to overuse a key word in a story, they resort to a strange and jarring synonym. Thus the otter becomes "the popular fish-eating mammal", head teachers become "school leaders", a killer whale becomes "the cetacean"; more worryingly, "pupils" in the north are compared with "students" in the south, leaving readers unsure whether we are comparing like with like. At worst a factual error is quite needlessly introduced; at least one idiotic reference to Istanbul as "the Turkish capital" would have been avoided had the writer just repeated the city's name.

You want to avoid repeating the same key noun, so make full

use of pronouns. Elegant variation is not the answer. Not only is it better to repeat the right word than to use a weird, unsuitable and possibly wrong alternative, but repetition may sometimes be just what is required: what's sauce for the goose is sauce for the gander; there's no business like showbusiness; the king is dead, long live the king ...

One mention of yesterday or last night in your story is usually enough. You are working at speed and it is easy to repeat this inadvertently. Don't. Another common failing is to repeat the intro in the second par, rephrasing it slightly and adding only minimal extra information. Don't

replacements in rugby union, not substitutes

report lower case in titles of official documents such as Taylor report

reportedly avoid this slack word, which suggests that the writer is unsure of the source of the material and less than confident of the facts

Republic of Ireland or Irish Republic. Ireland is acceptable, particularly in a sporting context

republican lower case except when in an official name, such as the Republican Party in the US or the Republicans party (lower case p) in France

rerun

research shows that ... in many cases it does nothing of the kind. Often it is not research but a (more or less serious) survey or poll. These can make perfectly good stories, but they rarely have the methodological rigour that research implies. If a new survey suggests or a new poll claims, then that is what we should say. None of these phrases inspires much enthusiasm in the reader, in any case. See also **expert**

resolution cap for clarity in context of a specific UN one, eg Resolution 688

responsible people bear responsibility, things do not. Storms are not responsible for damage; they cause it. Avoid the phrase "the rebels claimed responsibility for the bombing"; say instead "the rebels admitted carrying out the bombing"

result in avoid this lazy phrase and find an alternative, such as *cause, bring, create, evoke, lead to* etc

retiree ghastly word. Try to find an alternative, such as *retired person*. See **elderly**, **aged**, **old** and **pensioners**

Reveille like *the Last Post*, it is sounded, not played

Revenue & Customs became the new name (April 2005) for the combined Inland Revenue and Customs and Excise bodies. At first mention refer to HM Revenue & Customs (HMRC) and subsequently HMRC

reverend at first mention the style is "the Rev Tom Jones", then Mr Jones; a parson and his wife are "the Rev Tom and Mrs Jones". Never say "the Rev Jones" or "Rev Jones"; outside the world of Reverend Bacon, the Harlem demagogue in Tom Wolfe's *Bonfire of the Vanities*, these are solecisms on a par with calling Sir Bobby Charlton "Sir Charlton". Never assume that anyone called "the Rev" is "a vicar" or even an Anglican priest

review takes lower case in names of government programmes, such as strategic defence review, comprehensive spending review etc

rhinoceroses for the plural

Richter scale measures the energy released by an earthquake. It runs from 0 to 8; say "the earthquake measured 6 on the Richter scale". The *Richter scale* and *magnitude* measurements are not completely interchangeable, so use the scale that is filed in an individual story

riffle, riffling as in flicking through papers or clothes on a rail; *rifling* only in the sense of ransacking

the right aim not to cap in the political context when referring to a group of like-minded individuals, eg "the right added to

Theresa May's problems over Brexit"; "the party swung to the right". When the right is qualified, keep the adjective lower case too, eg the far right, the religious right. Be guided by common sense; if there ever seems to be a risk of serious confusion or ambiguity, resort to a cap, but it should rarely be necessary. Also, *the right wing, right-wing contenders, rightwingers*

rightist, **right-leaning** try to avoid these, and also leftist, left-leaning, which are particularly liked by news agencies, not least in the Americas, and opt for *left-wing, right-wing, left-of-centre, right-of-centre* etc

right-to-buy hyphenate whether noun or adjective in relation to the policy first introduced by Margaret Thatcher allowing tenants to buy council-owned properties

rigmarole not rigamarole

ringfence no hyphen

riot act lower case, eg "read the riot act", unless specifically referring in a legal/historical context to the passing of the Riot Act (1714)

riots as good a place as any for a couple of thoughts. First, a riot is defined in the context of law and order as "a violent disturbance of the peace by a crowd". Second, a reminder to beware claims about any event, including outbreaks of public disorder, being "unprecedented". For example, in London in the anti-Catholic Gordon Riots of June 1780, there were 700 people killed over five days; in Manchester on August 16, 1819, at the Peterloo Massacre, it is thought that there were up to 18 deaths and 700 people seriously injured

rip off (verb), **rip-off** (noun or adjective); avoid this cliché except in quotes such as "rip-off Britain"

riverbank one word

River cap as a shorthand for the River Thames, eg "All he wanted was a cab going south of the River"

rivers cap in context of River Thames, the Hudson River, the Mississippi River (or simply the Thames, the Mississippi etc if adjudged well known to all our readership). See **estuary**

roadblock, roadbuilding, roadbuilder etc

"road map" quoted at first mention and in headlines for the two-state Middle East peace formula

road rage no need to quote, even at first mention

roads it is as tautologous to write "the M5 motorway" as "the A435 road", but it seems pompous to worry unduly over this, as the usage is widespread. It is in any case correct to say "the M40 London to Birmingham motorway". There is no need to define the M25 as London's orbital motorway, but generally try to define/locate a road geographically unless context is clear

Robert the Bruce (prefer to Robert Bruce); subsequent mentions, *the Bruce*

rock a *stone* is a small lump of rock that can be thrown by someone, eg hypothetically, by an alleged protester at the police. In British English, a rock is too big to be thrown effectively in that way; however, chiefly in North American and Australian English, a stone that can be thrown is called a rock. As we aspire to British English, please do not refer to a rock when we mean a stone

rock'n'roll

Rohypnol must not be referred to as the "date rape drug" but must be capped

Rollerblade is a trade name, so must be capped. The American company's lawyers insist that even Rollerblading takes the cap; use *in-line skates/skating* instead

rollerskate, rollercoaster

roll-on, roll-off (as in ferries), abbreviated to *ro-ro*

rollover (as in the National Lottery), no hyphen

Rolls-Royce note hyphen; Rolls-Royce objects to use of its exclusive marque in a descriptive sense, eg online advertising service spoken of as "The Rolls-Royce of Car Locators"

Roman numerals usually no full points; thus, Edward VIII, Article XVI, Part II, Psalm xxiii. But in official documents, to designate sub-sections, use the points, eg i., ii., iv. etc

Romanov prefer to Romanoff for the surname of the Russian imperial family

rom-com hyphenate. Acceptable shorthand for romantic comedy, especially in cinematic context

roofs absolutely not rooves

rooms say *living room, drawing room, laundry room* (no hyphens except when adjectival, eg living-room carpet), but *bathroom, bedroom, tearoom*

ropey prefer to ropy

rottweiler lower case. See **dogs**

rouble not ruble

Rough Guide a trademark, rigorously protected by the publisher. So generic phrases such as "a rough guide to ..." must be avoided

row be sparing in the use of this word, especially in headlines. Alternatives are *rift, split, clash* etc, and *dispute* in text. However, row is not banned

royal, royalty lower case for royalty and for the royal family; royal is usually lower case when used adjectivally, as in royal couple, royal baby, royal approval, royal visit, the royal wave, royal wedding; a cap may sometimes help clarity in eg royal assent, royal collection, royal household, royal yacht, but try them all lower case first (except when naming the Royal Yacht *Britannia* etc)

Royal Academy cap, then the academy (lower case) or the RA; a Royal Academician (cap) or an RA, but an academician (lower case). Note the Summer Exhibition (cap, roman)

royal charter no need to cap

royal commissions should be capped when the full title is given, eg the Royal Commission on Environmental Pollution, but otherwise lower case: the royal commission. NB Royal Commission on Reform of the House of Lords

royal family lower case, British and overseas; with names of the British royal family, generally give fully at first mention, eg the Duke of Edinburgh, thereafter the duke (lower case) or occasionally Prince Philip; the Duke of Cambridge at first mention, thereafter simply the duke (or for variation Prince William, or William); Prince Harry at first mention, thereafter simply Harry (or for variation the prince, if not ambiguous). In England and Wales, prefer the Prince of Wales and the Duchess of Cornwall (the prince and the duchess at subsequent mention, although Prince Charles is also acceptable). In Scotland, the usage the Duke and Duchess of Rothesay is permissible. The duchess is technically the Princess of Wales, but does not use the title; nor do we. In royalty context, the cap after first mention should be confined to the Queen.

Take care with the naming of deposed and former royalty. For example, write "the former King Constantine of Greece" and then Constantine subsequently.

Note, "for Queen and country", "for King and country", cap as the monarch being served is always specific

Royal Marines use military rather than naval ranks, but are the amphibious troops of the Royal Navy. Carelessly referring to them as "soldiers" or as part of the army will annoy

Royal Shakespeare Company (thereafter the RSC) and Royal Opera House (ROH), or informally Covent Garden; the Albert Hall and the Festival Hall are acceptable with or without their Royals; the National Theatre is better without Royal

Royal Standard is only for the Sovereign. Other members of the royal family have a personal standard

royal train lower case

royal wedding usually lower case

rubbish do not use as a verb

Rudolph not Rudolf, the red-nosed reindeer

run-down (adjective), as in decaying or exhausted; *rundown* (noun) as in briefing; to *run down* (verb)

running-mate hyphen

run up (verb), *run-up* (noun); "In the run-up to" is a cliché, beware of "in the run-up to last week's climbdown" and similarly absurd combinations

rush hour (noun), but *rush-hour* (adjective, hyphen, as in rush-hour traffic)

rushed to hospital avoid this cliché. Say simply *taken to* or *driven to*; similarly, say a victim was *flown to hospital* rather than "airlifted to ..."; generally avoid the American hospitalise

Russia take care not to designate parts of the former Soviet Union as Russia when they no longer are, even if Russia might wish they were — eg Ukraine, Georgia. The same applies to the people (although there are millions of ethnic Russians throughout the former Soviet Union). So always specify the republic concerned and do not use Russian in the inclusive sense except in the phrase *Russian vodka*. Use *Soviet* and *the Soviet Union* only in their historical contexts — and avoid USSR except in the titles of popular songs

Russian names generally use "i" as first name ending, but "y" for surnames, eg Arkadi Volsky, Gennadi Yavlinsky; and use "ks" rather than "x" in the middle, eg Aleksei, Aleksi, Aleksandr (except for historical figures, eg Alexander the Great). We should use the -ya rather than -ia in Natalya and Tatyana (not Natalia, Tatiana). But note that the styles of Garry Kasparov and Anatoly Karpov are sufficiently westernised to be spelt thus

Ss

saccharin (noun), *saccharine* (adjective)

sack beware of using in the context of losing a job if not absolutely confident of the circumstances; it is almost certainly defamatory to say that someone was sacked when they resigned

sacrebleu one word (lower case, italics) for the French exclamation

sacrilegious from *sacrilege*; not sacreligious

Sadler's Wells

said prefer the construction "Mr Brown said" rather than "said Mr Brown"

Sainsbury the formal style is J Sainsbury (no point), especially in business stories, but Sainsbury's is preferable in general news stories

St Catharine's College, Cambridge, but *St Catherine's College*, Oxford

saké Japanese rice wine. Use accent to avoid confusion with *sake*

saleroom one word

salutary not salutory

sanatorium (not sanitorium), plural *sanatoriums*

sarcophagus plural *-gi*

sarin the nerve gas, lower case

Sars the viral respiratory complaint is *severe acute respiratory syndrome* (lower case); spell out in copy at first mention if deemed necessary

sat is the past tense and the past participle of "to sit". Except in (rare) deliberate use of regional dialect, never write that somebody "was sat" in his car, her living room etc; write "was seated" or "was sitting"

Satan cap; but *satanism, satanist, satanic* etc, lower case

sat-nav lower case and hyphen for acceptable abbreviation for *satellite navigation system*

Saudi must not be used as short form for the country, Saudi Arabia; the people may, however, be referred to as *Saudis*

sautéed prefer this variant for fried quickly in a little hot fat

saveable use the variant with the middle e

scarify take care; its meaning is to cut into, to cut skin from; its colloquial meaning of to terrify should be avoided wherever possible

scars do not heal (even metaphorically); wounds heal, scars remain

schadenfreude (lower case, roman) means the malicious enjoyment of another's misfortunes. Do not misuse

schizophrenic never use as a term of abuse and avoid as a metaphor

schmaltz prefer with the t

schools cap when the full name is given, and after checking that it is a school and not a college or academy (if in doubt, consult the school's website); nowadays use the classifications of independent, state, grant-maintained, comprehensive, grammar, secondary modern (rarely) etc, rather than public, private etc (except in historical context)

schoolchildren one word, similarly *schoolgirl, schoolboy, schooldays, schoolmaster, schoolmistress* and *schoolteacher* (rarely; just *teacher* will usually do); but *school-leaver*

science *The Times* has a reputation for reporting science accurately and responsibly. That reputation should not be jeopardised by sloppy reporting or by credulous repetition of pseudo-scientific nonsense, whatever the source. The paper employs excellent specialist correspondents in science (and in medicine); non-specialists should consult them if in any doubt about the reliability of information supplied or if unsure about the use of scientific terminology or facts

scientific measures write out first time with abbreviations in parentheses, shorten thereafter. The abbreviation takes no point and no "s" in the plural, eg 14km, not 14kms. Some basic international units and their abbreviations are: metre (m); gram (g); litre (l); ampere (A); volt (V); watt (W); note also kilowatt-hour (kWh). Only abbreviate mile to m in mph and mpg; and gallon to g in mpg (otherwise gal). Beware of using m for million or for miles in any scientific context when it might be taken for metres

scientific names when employing the Latin terminology, we must use the internationally accepted convention of initial cap on the first (generic) word, then lower case for the second (specific); eg *Homo sapiens, Branta canadensis* (Canada goose) etc. All should be italicised

Scilly, Isles of prefer to Scilly Isles

Scotch upper case for whisky, broth, mist, egg, terrier etc. Scotch (upper case) is not to be used generally as a substitute for the adjectives *Scottish* and *Scots*. Note *Scots pine*

scot-free without harm, loss or penalty; derived from the 13th-century scot, meaning a tax

Scottish National Party (SNP) cap Nationalists in the Scottish party context, but lower case nationalists in the wider sense

Scottish place names never say, eg Motherwell, Scotland; instead say Motherwell, North Lanarkshire. The same principle about counties applies to Wales and Northern Ireland; give the county unless the town or city is big enough or well enough known for the county to be unnecessary

scrapheap one word

scratchcard one word, as *smartcard, swipecard*

Scripture(s) cap as in Holy Scripture, but *scriptural* (lower case)

scriptwriter

sculptures should have their names in italic. With photographs of sculptures always give the sculptor's name

seabird, seahorse, seagull, seasick, seawater no hyphens; but note also *sea bed, sea lion, sea shanty, sea snake, sea urchin* etc

seance no accent

seasonal relating to, occurring at a particular time of the year; note *unseasonable* meaning not suitable, appropriate to the season — definitely not unseasonal. Note also *seasonal affective disorder* (lower case), abbreviated to SAD

seasons always lower case when unattached, ie spring, summer, autumn, winter; but Winter Olympics etc. Note also *summertime, wintertime, springtime*, but *British Summer Time* (BST), and *Greenwich Mean Time* (GMT). Write, eg "in the spring of 2009", not "in spring 2009"

seatbelt

second as an adverb, prefer to secondly; thus write "first ... second ... third ... " etc

secondhand no hyphen

Second World War not World War II/Two etc

Secret Intelligence Service (SIS or MI6) takes cap; its head is its chief

Secret Service in the US protects the president and vice-president. As a colloquial phrase in the UK it must be lower case, but prefer (to avoid confusion) to use Secret Intelligence Service (MI6 or SIS)

secretary-general of the United Nations, Nato

Security Service (MI5) takes cap; but lower case for *the security services* in non-specific use

see people see things; so do collective entities made up of people (companies, teams, clubs, organisations etc). Dates, developments, situations, incidents, objects, concepts etc can't "see" anything at all. So, the BBC can see its audience figures fall; the working classes can see bread prices rise; Manchester United can see their prospects of victory dwindling. Tuesday, however, cannot see a fall in the BBC's audience figures; higher bread prices cannot see an increase in starvation; Manchester United's poor season cannot see an outbreak of panic in the boardroom

select committees and parliamentary committees are lower case even when full title is given, eg the (Commons) foreign affairs select committee, the Treasury select committee; thereafter, *the select committee* or *the committee*

self- hyphen in general for *self-* compounds such as *self-employed, self-interest, self-service* etc

sell-off, sell-out as nouns, but see **buyout**

Sellotape is a trade name; otherwise, write *sticky tape* or *adhesive tape*

Senate (US) Senator Joe Bloggs, then the senator; alternatively, Mr Bloggs, the Massachusetts senator. Note lower case in phrases such as the first-term senator. Also note cap in titles of the Senate majority leader, the House minority leader etc

senior abbreviate to Sr (not Snr) in American-style names, eg Henry Ramstein Sr. Avoid the cliché "senior executive" when you mean *executive* — nine times out of ten the adjective is redundant (like "major")

sensational generally best avoided; readers can mostly judge for themselves the significance of revelations, claims, allegations etc

serious case review lower case for this and other generic social work procedures

serjeant the archaic spelling still used in The Rifles for the rank that the rest of the British Army renders as *sergeant*

serjeant at arms the House of Commons official should be fine lower case

serve in a warship (but *on* a merchant ship), and serve in (not on) a submarine, even though subs are boats, not ships. Important to make this distinction; readers complain every time we get it wrong. See also **boat**, **ships**

services, the lower case; the *armed services* or the *armed forces* (lower case); lower case *serviceman, servicewoman*

setback noun; but *to set back*, verb

set piece two words

sett as with badgers

settlement by definition, not possible in a contested divorce, in which case there will be a decision, order or judgment

set to eg "the Bank of England is set to raise interest rates"; journalese for "will" or "will probably" (particularly when we're not sure which); often just *to* would suffice

set-up try to find a synonym such as *arrangement, organisation, structure, system* etc

sewage is the waste matter that is carried in sewers; a system of sewers is *sewerage*

sex change avoid this inaccurate and potentially offensive shorthand for the process of *gender reassignment* by surgical and other medical procedures. Note that from a legal perspective, people in the process of gender reassignment should be called by whatever name and honorific they prefer, and that the appropriate personal pronouns reflecting that change should also be used. The Gender Recognition Act 2004 makes it an offence to identify a person who has been granted a gender recognition certificate by their previous name or gender. The Editors' Code covers gender identity in its clause on discrimination: it is one of the things to which pejorative or prejudicial reference may not be made, and details of which must be avoided unless genuinely relevant to a story. Note that *transgender* and *transgendered* (adjectives, never nouns) are terms used by people with this condition and by the medical profession in preference to the older term transsexual

sexism without destroying idiom, we should acknowledge changing usage and avoid giving needless offence; we should beware, in particular, of casual sexism, using language of women that we would not use of men

sex offenders register lower case, no apostrophe

shadow use of the titles may be applied to the main opposition party and the Liberal Democrats, for example, the shadow chancellor, the Liberal Democrats' shadow chancellor. Lower case in all cases, ie shadow cabinet, shadow environment secretary, shadow chief whip, a shadow spokesman

shake-out, shake-up as nouns

Shakespeare titles as *Henry IV (Part One)* to avoid use of two sets of Roman numerals. And NB *Shakespearean* (not -ian)

shall, should good practice is that *shall* and *should* go with the first person singular and plural (I shall, we shall), *will* and *would* with the others (he will, they will). *Shall* with second and third persons singular and plural has a slightly more emphatic meaning than *will* ("they shall not pass", "you shall go to the ball")

shambles strictly, if archaically, a butcher's slaughterhouse, and by extension a scene of carnage; by all means deploy it in that sense if an opportunity should arise, at the risk of being misunderstood; generally, however, there seems no reason to follow previous (quite recent) editions of this guide in trying to discourage its more familiar use to describe a state of chaos or disorder

Shangri-La

shanks's pony lower case

shantytown one word

share a joke self-evident local paper cliché banned in captions on photographs showing people laughing; likewise, "in happier times", for photographs showing grinning people now divorced, gravely ill or dead etc

Sharia means Islamic law; "Sharia law" is a tautology, if not a particularly offensive one

sheikh not shaikh

shemozzle a noisy confusion; uproar

Shetland or the Shetland Islands, not the Shetlands

Shia not Shiite or any such variation; write Shia Muslims, in contrast to Sunni Muslims

shiitake prefer to the single i variant

Shipping Forecast the BBC programme. Write the areas thus: Southeast Iceland, Faeroes, Fair Isle, Viking, North Utsire, South Utsire, Fisher, Forties, Cromarty, Forth, Tyne, Dogger, German Bight, Humber, Thames, Dover, Wight, Portland, Plymouth, Biscay, Trafalgar, FitzRoy, Sole, Fastnet, Lundy, Irish Sea, Shannon, Rockall, Malin, Hebrides, Bailey

ships do not italicise the HMS when giving names, eg HMS *Sheffield*. Ships are generally treated as feminine; thus *she* and *her* rather than it and its; if they are Royal Navy vessels, they are served *in*, not *on*. See also **boat**

ship's company all the officers and men

ships' tonnage These are deep waters for the unwary. Your first question should be: do we really need to give the tonnage for the ship we are writing about? In most cases it will be nothing but a big, impressive figure. If you have a photograph of a giant cruise ship, or cargo ship, is that not enough to give the reader a good idea of the scale? If you decide to give the relevant tonnage you must be 100 per cent certain that it is accurate. The figures most commonly given are net registered tonnage and gross registered tonnage. These are measurements of volume, not weight, and the correct spelling is *ton*, each ton being 100 cubic feet. The gross tonnage is the total volume of all the enclosed spaces on board; the net tonnage is the volume of all the enclosed spaces available for passengers and/or cargo — ie the gross tonnage minus the space allotted for the crew, machinery and fuel. Ship owners will often give the gross tonnage because it is a bigger figure and they like to boast. The actual weight of a ship is called *lightweight tonnage* and is rarely given in a news story. If you are writing about gross or net tonnage, never say that the ship "weighs" so many thousand tons. That is wrong. But it is possible to say, using the gross tonnage: "the QM2 is a 150,000-ton ship" or "the 150,000-ton QM2". Do this if you really need to, but check with *Lloyd's Register*

shock as an adjective is journalese, and to be treated with caution. Shock victories, defeats, results, revelations etc are mostly clichés and often just empty hyperbole. No need to ban the usage altogether. "Shock" meaning "highly unexpected" has more force than eg "surprising" while avoiding the suggestion of disapprobation that "shocking" tends to convey; on the whole, however, readers should be left to decide for themselves whether something is a shock

shock waves two words, but use sparingly as a metaphor as it is a cliché

shoo-in (not shoe-in), if you have to use this American phrase

shoot-out hyphenate the noun, as in penalty shoot-out; but avoid in the sense of gunfight

shopaholic and *workaholic*, but *chocoholic*

shopkeeper, shopowner, shopfront, shoplift etc; but *shop assistant* and *shop steward*

shortcut one word

shortlist one word as noun or verb

shortselling, shortseller no hyphens

short sentences and **short words** are often better than long ones

showbusiness one word (except in the title of the Irving Berlin song from *Annie Get Your Gun*, where it's two); *showbiz* is an acceptable abbreviation in quotes and informal context

showcase try to avoid using as a verb. Prefer, eg *display* or *exhibit*

showjumping one word except when it appears in a title such as the British Show Jumping Association, or is part of the name of an event that uses it as two words; similarly, *showjumper*

shrink, **shrank** (past tense), **shrunk** or **shrunken** (past participle)

shtoom as in *to keep shtoom*, or remain silent

shut down (verb), two words (the factory was shut down); one word as a noun (a factory shutdown); hyphenate as an adjective (a shut-down factory)

Siamese cats, twins; for Siam use Thailand except in historical context (adjective Thai). Note that Siamese twins is the non-technical name for *conjoined twins*; the latter term is now widely preferred

[sic] generally avoid; if it were not [sic], why would we be publishing it like that?

sickbed one word, as *deathbed*

side-effects

Silicon Valley, **silicon chips** but *silicone implants* (for breasts etc)

silk barristers take silk and become silks (all lower case)

sin-bin use hyphen

singalong

Singh when used as a surname, eg Manmohan Singh, write Dr Singh subsequently. When a middle name, eg Manohar Singh Gill, write Mr Gill subsequently

sink, **sank** the past participle is *sunk*, the adjective *sunken*

siphon not syphon

sitcom no hyphen; permissible abbreviation for *situation comedy*

situation dismal word, to be avoided wherever possible; such inelegant and lazy phrases as crisis situation, ongoing situation and no-win situation are banned unless a direct quote positively demands them

sizeable

skulduggery with one l

Sky In writing about Sky, we should generally, and almost always in Business stories, declare our commercial interest. Add eg "The chairman of News Corp — the owner of *The Times* — is also the co-chairman of 21st Century Fox, a leading shareholder in Sky"

Slavic do not use; *Slav* is the noun and adjective for the people; use *Slavonic* relating to the languages

slay is a biblical word; US newspapers are fond of it, especially in headlines, for kill or murder; do not emulate

slither to slide cf *sliver*, a thin piece; do not confuse

slimline one word

Slovak for the people and language, *Slovakian* for the national adjective

slow motion render the informal (and faintly antique) abbreviation, whether noun or adjective, as *slow-mo*

smart aleck not Alec

smartcard one word, as *scratchcard, swipecard*

smartphone

smelt not smelled

smidgin

smokescreen one word

smoky also the Great Smoky Mountains

smorgasbord avoid its clichéd metaphorical use

snarl-up do not use as a synonym of *traffic jam, confusion* etc

snowball, snowbound, snowdrift, snowfall, snowman etc

soap opera normally use rather than just soap, although the latter may have its place in less formal pieces, as in diary items or reviews

sobriquet prefer to soubriquet

so-called normally there is no need to write the following noun etc in quote marks, as context will make it clear, eg "The so-called disaster has turned into something of a triumph"

soccer is an alternative for football to be avoided except in direct quotes, or in the American context

social chapter lower case, as it is an informal title for a separate protocol attaching to the Maastricht treaty

socialism, socialist cap only in names of specific political parties

softie prefer to softy

soirée use acute accent

solar system lower case. In order from the sun, its planets are Mercury, Venus, Earth, Mars, Jupiter, Saturn, Uranus, Neptune. Pluto, formerly classified as a planet, has been downgraded to a dwarf planet by the International Astronomical Union

solicitor-advocate hyphen

solicitor-general hyphen, as *attorney-general*; similarly *solicitor-general for Scotland*

soothe to make calm, hence *soothing*; cf *sooth*: truth, reality, true, real, hence *soothsayer*

Sophie's Choice In the novel and film of that name, a mother is forced on arrival at Auschwitz to choose which of her two children is to be immediately killed. Resist the temptation to use it as a crass, lazy, inappropriate and clichéd headline on any feature about a woman called Sophie with some lifestyle decision to make

sorcerer not -or

south southern etc; NB southeast, southwest (one word for adjective and noun)

southerner lower case, as *northerner*, in most contexts, including the United Kingdom; but *Southerner* (cap) in the United States when referring to the Confederacy

Southern Ocean cap

south of France

South, Southern cap in US contexts when referring to the

Confederacy; otherwise lower case

Sovereign, the cap not essential but may be helpful for clarity

Soviet Union never refer to "the Soviets" for the people or the government, even in the historical context. The phrase is an Americanism often with disparaging overtones; a soviet is a committee, not a person. Refer instead to *the Soviet people* or *the Soviet government* in historical context

soya bean two words (not soybean)

Spam the foodstuff is an American invention. See **trade names**

Spanish surnames conventionally, someone called Juan García López would be Juan García at first mention and subsequently, using the patronym only (López being the matronym) eg: *Severiano Ballesteros (Sota); José María Olazábal (Manterola); Mariano Rajoy (Brey);* and *Rafael Benítez (Maudes)*. But there are exceptions: some use only the matronym, particularly if their patronym is a common name (the footballer *David Silva*'s full surname is *Jiménez Silva*). Others use both at all times, sometimes with a hyphen. This is perhaps more common in public life. The Spanish poet *Federico García Lorca* is always known as *García Lorca* at second mention, the Colombian author *Gabriel García Márquez* is always *García Márquez* subsequently; again, García is a relatively common name. No alternative but to check; if completely stumped, give both surnames, which will at least not be wrong

spastic never use figuratively or as a term of abuse

Speaker, the seems to need a cap for clarity in parliamentary context; *deputy speaker* is lower case, however; there is no risk of linguistic confusion, and there are several of them anyway

Speakers' Corner in Hyde Park (not Speaker's)

Special Branch cap for clarity

special forces in the UK or US, generically lower case. But cap, eg 5th Special Forces Group in US for specific units

spelt not spelled; note *misspelt*

Spider-Man the agile comic-book superhero is written, oddly, thus

spiders are not insects, although like insects they are *arthropods*

spiky not spikey

spilt not spilled

spin, spun do not use span as past tense

spin doctor two words

Spinning, Spinner trade names for stationary bicycle exercise

spiritualism, spiritualist

split infinitives are generally to be avoided, if only because they irritate many readers. They are by no means banned. The split infinitive has been variously in and out of favour with English grammarians over many centuries. What matters is that, on occasion, avoiding the split infinitive can lead to an unnatural or ambiguous construction. In such cases, it is better to split

spoilt not spoiled; but *despoiled*

spokesman, spokeswoman avoid where possible, eg "the ministry said" rather than "a ministry spokesman said". *Official* is a useful alternative. Use *spokeswoman* if appropriate, but spokesman if in any doubt. Never use spokesperson. See **chairman**

spongeing prefer to sponging

sportsmen, sportswomen omit the Mr, Mrs, Miss, Ms etc unless they are in news reports in a significantly non-sporting context (eg court hearings)

sports writing notoriously vulnerable to cliché and jargon. Apart from direct quotes, avoid the kind of language used by players and television commentators

spot one word for *blackspot, hotspot, troublespot* etc; but *spot check, spot market* etc

sprang prefer to sprung as the past tense of the verb to spring, eg "she sprang into action"; *sprung* is the past participle, and has no alternative, eg "the wind has sprung up"

spring-clean hyphenate noun and verb

squads in police context, usually lower case, but *Flying Squad* better capped for clarity

stadium plural *stadiums*. See **-um**

stagey now seems the more natural and less ugly adjective from stage, meaning excessively theatrical, unrealistic, unconvincingly dramatic etc

stakeholder meaning "someone with an interest" is silly corporate jargon, widespread in business and the public sector but not to be used unblushingly in *The Times*

stanch (verb), as "to stanch a flow of blood"; *staunch* is an adjective meaning loyal or firm

stand-off noun, hyphen; but *standby* (noun, no hyphen)

stand-up prefer to spell out *stand-up comedian/comic, stand-up act*

stargazers, stargazing

Stars and Stripes cap for clarity in reference to the flag

state lower case in political context, whether for the state as a wide concept, or the welfare state, the nanny state or used adjectivally, such as state benefits; *the state opening of parliament*. Lower case also in US contexts: Washington state, New York state, the state legislature; cap only in names eg US State Department, the State University of New York (SUNY) etc

state of the union address

stationary (not moving), *stationery* (writing materials)

stationmaster one word; but *station manager*

stations lower case in Euston station, Waterloo station, Birmingham New Street station; but where possible, simply Euston, Waterloo etc

statistic(s) do not use as a fancy word for figure(s) or number(s)

status quo roman; likewise, status quo ante

statute book

stealth bomber

steamroller one word

steelworks, steelworker etc

stem cell thus for the noun, but hyphenate adjectivally, eg the stem-cell procedure

stepchild, stepfather, stepmother, stepson, stepdaughter but *step-family, step-parents*

sterling lower case the currency; not worth a capital

stetson lower case even though a trademark

stock exchange lower case, whether London, New York or anywhere else; note lower case for the *stock market*

stony not stoney

storyteller, storytelling

straight be very sparing in the use of this word to mean heterosexual

straightaway

straight-faced but *straightforward*

strait and narrow (not straight) the phrase comes from the Authorised Version (King James Version) of the New Testament, Matthew vii, 13-14: "Enter ye in at the strait gate: for wide is the gate, and broad is the way, that leadeth to destruction, and many there be which go in thereat: Because strait is the gate, and narrow is the way, which leadeth unto life, and few there be that find it." Strait is a synonym for narrow. In the Greek, there are two different words

straitjacket

strait-laced

stratum plural *strata*

stress-free hyphen

stricture means adverse criticism or censure, not constraint. Take care

stripy prefer to stripey

strive note the past tense "he *strove* to get things right", and the past participle *striven*

stylebook one word, as with *guidebook, textbook* etc; but *style guide*

student now commonly and rather tiresomely used to refer to schoolchildren. There may be little point in resisting this, as the usage is almost universal within the education system; but there is certainly no reason to encourage it. *Pupil* remains a perfectly good word for those engaged more in learning than in studying

sub- like *multi-*, the hyphen here is often a question of what looks better. A random sample gives us subdivision, sublet, subnormal, subplot, subsection, substandard, subtext, subtitle, subcontract(or); in contrast, sub-committee, sub-editor, to sub-let, sub-postmaster, sub-post office etc

sub-continent, the lower case, for India, Pakistan and Bangladesh

subjects (academic) use lower case for most subjects studied at school or university, eg "she was reading modern history with philosophy"; but where a proper name is involved, the cap is retained, eg "he got a first in English literature and German after he dropped Latin in his second year"; and always cap Classics and the abbreviated PPE (short for philosophy, politics and economics)

sub-machinegun

submarine always a boat, not a ship

subpoena, subpoenas, subpoenaing, subpoenaed

sub-Saharan Africa

subtropical one word

such as do not always substitute for *like*; the effect may sometimes be unnatural and needlessly ponderous

Sudan not *the* Sudan, except occasionally in historical context. Note *South Sudan* (cap)

sudoku

suffragan lower case

suffragette lower case, double f, double t; *Emmeline Pankhurst*; her daughters *Dame Christabel Pankhurst* and *Sylvia Pankhurst*

suicide be sensitive in reporting suicide; avoid sensationalism, oversimplification and speculation about motive; in particular beware, in giving details of method, of the risk of encouraging imitation; excessive detail of method will breach the Editors' Code

suicide bomb, bomber, bombing two words

suing not sueing

Summer Exhibition cap, roman, for the Royal Academy event

summit avoid calling every high-level meeting a summit. Restrict its use to meetings of heads of government

summon the verb is *to summon*, the noun *a summons* (plural *summonses*). A person is summoned to appear before a tribunal etc; but a person in receipt of a specific summons can be said to have been *summonsed*

sun rarely any need to cap, (except rarely if it helps clarity or consistency in specific astronomical context such as Night Sky column etc when surrounded by lots of capped planet names etc), so usually lower case; *solar system*, also lower case

sunbathing, sunburn, sunglasses, sunlounger, sunstroke, suntan etc but *sun-care* (products etc)

super- as a prefix, use a hyphen only if the compound looks hideous

superbug note that someone can be a carrier of/colonised by, say, MRSA (methicillin-resistant *Staphylococcus aureus*) and suffer no ill effects because they are not infected

supercasino one word

superhighway (as in information superhighway); similarly, *superconductor*

superinjunction one word; likewise *hyperinjunction*. Injunctions always prevent publication of something. A superinjunction prevents publication even of the basic information that the particular order exists. Only a few superinjunctions are granted each year so the likelihood is that most orders granted are simply privacy injunctions. A hyperinjunction is a superinjunction that additionally seeks to gag parliament (eg the Trafigura injunction) but it seems unlikely that there will be any more of them

superlatives beware of calling any person, event or thing the first, the biggest, the best, the last etc without firm evidence that this is correct. Also, never say first-ever, best-ever etc

supernova plural *supernovas*

supersonic (of speeds); for waves, use *ultrasonic*

supervisor not superviser

supine means lying face up; face down is *prone*

Supreme Court cap for US and also now for UK

swap not swop; do not use unless a mutual exchange is involved and never for organ transplants

swathe prefer to swath in all senses

swearing avoid wherever possible. If there is no alternative (eg in direct quotes essential to the story), use asterisks — f***, f***ing, c*** etc. Many readers are much less tolerant of this kind of language than some regular *Times* columnists would like to believe. See **four-letter words, obscenities**

swatting (flies), *swotting* (study)

swingeing best avoided; unthinking use with "cuts" is a cliché

swipecard as *scratchcard, smartcard*

Symphony Hall, Birmingham does not take "the"

sync prefer to synch, as in the phrase "out of sync"

synod lower case on its own, but *General Synod* (cap)

synthesizer (musical), but *synthesise* (chemical etc)

Tt

3D no hyphen

-t in nearly all cases, where there is a choice of past tense between a final *-t* or *-ed*, use *-t*, as in *burnt, spelt* etc. But never earnt

tabloidese we do not put hobbies, geographical origin, political allegiance, sports positions or job descriptions in front of a person's name as if they were titles: stamp collector Stevie Smith, Yorkshireman Bob Bradley, Labour voter Fred Roberts, barmaid Bet Lynch, Rovers striker Roy Race; no one, outside the columns of popular papers, actually says such things. You can write *the* actor Tom Cruise or *the* Labour MP John Smith (with "the" and no commas) for someone who is famous as such. That is plain English

t'ai chi note apostrophe

take-off (noun), but *take off* (verb)

takeover (noun), but *to take over* (verb); *takeover code* but *Takeover Panel*

Taliban refer to *the* Taliban (or the Taliban authorities etc), and use the plural verb ("are" rather than "is" etc)

talk show as *chat show, game show, quiz show* etc

tally-ho hyphenate; plural *tally-hos*

Tannoy is a trade name; use eg *loudspeaker* or *PA system* as generic alternatives

taoiseach lower case; "the Irish taoiseach" is redundant because no other country has one; prefer in any case to write "the Irish prime minister"

target beware lazy use of this word as a verb; eg a campaign is *aimed at* or *directed at* children (rather than targeting children). Try to restrict its use to military (hostile acts) contexts. Note *targeted* (not targetted)

Tarmac is a trade name, but confine the cap version to the civil engineering company. Common usage allows the road surface or airport runway to be written as tarmac; *tarmacadam* is not a trade name

Tartars now seems old-fashioned; prefer *Tatars*

Taser cap (trademark) for the stun gun, but as a verb *to taser*

Tatars prefer now to Tartars

teabag, teacup, teapot, teacake, teaspoon, tearoom, teatime one word; but *tea biscuit, tea break, tea cloth, tea cosy, tea dance, tea garden, tea kettle, tea lady, tea leaf, tea light, tea maker, tea party, tea towel, tea trolley*

team-mate note hyphen

teams normally plural, eg "West Ham United are on outstanding form." But sports clubs usually take the singular, especially in news stories, eg "Manchester City Football Club was fined heavily for crowd disturbances"

teamwork one word, no hyphen

tear gas two words

Tea Party cap the US right-wing movement (which is not a political party)

Technicolor is a trade name. It should be used only in the context of the making of colour motion pictures and not as a descriptive adjective or synonym for *multicoloured*

Teddy boy cap T for adherents or imitators of the 1950s subculture

teen avoid use as substitute for the adjective *teenage*

Tel Aviv do not use as a metonym or variant for Israel. Most embassies are in Tel Aviv, in recognition of the disputed status of Jerusalem (where the Israeli parliament sits). Neither city should be referred to as the country's capital. This a highly vexed question; take great care

telephone numbers with three groups of figures, no need to hyphenate the first two (eg 0151 234 8464; 020 7782 5000; 030 312 31113). For other national numbers write as two groups of numbers (eg 01483 123456). Similarly, for numbers with, eg 0800, 0845, 0870 codes, and for mobile numbers, write as two groups of unhyphenated numbers, thus: 0870 1234567, 07721 123456

television TV is acceptable in headlines and text

television and radio programmes are italicised

telltale one word

temazepam is a non-proprietary sedative, so lower case

temperatures nowadays will rarely need converting to Fahrenheit, so say that the temperature on the south coast hit the low 30s (no longer the 90s); where specific, just 16C, 28C etc. Give Fahrenheit only where there is good reason, such as in a historical context. Conversions, where appropriate, should be in brackets: 19C (66F). In any case, remember that a rise in temperature of 3C does not equate to 37F (the direct equivalent of 3C), but rather to an increase of 5.4F, and you will never need to convert that. Prefer "minus" to a minus sign in text. Do not refer to temperatures as hot or cold; they are high or low

ten-minute rule (bill) etc

tennis Centre Court at Wimbledon cap; likewise No 1 Court, No 14 Court etc

tepee use this variant for the Native American tent

Territorial Army now known as the Army Reserve

terror there was no good reason to follow George W Bush in abandoning the perfectly good and specific words *terrorism* or *terrorist* (adj) in favour of a "war on terror". But follow him the world did. Terror suspect, terror attack, terror group, terror trial etc are all in common use; in headlines, where space is tight, they have the advantage of concision; but the more precise terms should not be abandoned

terrorist take care with this word and the associated *terrorism*. Use only to describe those who seek to achieve their political aims through illegitimate acts intended to provoke widespread fear in a civilian population (or in a particular community). Beyond this, there is neither a generally accepted definition of terrorism nor a universal agreement on which groups are terrorists and which are not; be aware, especially in news reports, that through our use of language we can seem to be taking sides. Other words — *radicals, militants, paramilitaries, guerrillas, separatists* etc — may sometimes be less loaded, but their use will depend on context

Test match should apply only to international cricket (five-day games) and rugby union; for other sports use the term *international* (*match*)

tête-à-tête for the plural, prefer *tête-à-têtes*

that do not be shy of this word after said, denied, claimed etc; eg "he denied that the evidence was confusing" is more elegant than "he denied the evidence was confusing".

The word "that" is generally better than "which" in a defining (or restricting) clause, eg "the train that I take stops at Slough". As a general rule, prefer *which* for descriptive clauses (ie ones that add information) and place it between commas, eg "the night train, which used to carry newspapers, stops at Crewe". Be aware, however, that usage (at least in British English) is quite flexible here, and that more damage is probably done to decent prose in the name of this "rule" than of almost any other; if in doubt, and if the meaning is clear, leave well alone

theatre attach *Theatre* (cap) at first mention to names where it is part of the title, eg the Criterion Theatre (thereafter the Criterion or simply the theatre). Some of the main London exceptions are the Old Vic, Young Vic, Palladium, Coliseum, Apollo Victoria, Donmar Warehouse, Hackney Empire; and outside London, many such as the Birmingham Hippodrome, Oxford Playhouse, West Yorkshire Playhouse etc

theatregoer see **-goer**

the then then is not an adjective, so prefer to avoid expressions such as "the then prime minister" or (worse) "the then Mr Callaghan"; say "Mr Callaghan, then prime minister", "Mr Callaghan, who was prime minister at the time" and "Lord Callaghan of Cardiff (then Mr Callaghan)"

thinly veiled cliché that without any real loss of meaning can usually just be deleted from phrases such as "thinly veiled warning" etc

The Times almost always use italics for the name of the newspaper, except in headlines. But Times Newspapers Ltd (roman), publisher of *The Times* and *The Sunday Times*, is the operating company of Times Newspapers Holdings. The parent company of *The Times* is News UK.

In text, say "the *Times* political correspondent", "the *Times* wine correspondent" etc, if you need an alternative to "political editor of *The Times*", "wine correspondent of *The Times*" etc; these forms are easier to read and less ugly than "*The Times*'s correspondent" etc. Also The Times art critic etc is an acceptable style in headlines to avoid a mass of italics and apostrophes. Always say "the editor of *The Times*", "the deputy editor of *The Times*" etc. It is permissible to say "a *Times* reader", "*Times* readers", but prefer "readers of *The Times*". Similarly, adjectival uses such as "a *Times* article", "a *Times* offer" are acceptable. Keep phrases such as "told *The Times*" to a minimum: *said* is usually preferable.

Also note Times Law Report (without The), the Times Crossword etc. Again, some flexibility — to avoid a proliferation of italics — can be used in puff material etc.

For sections of the paper, whether historic or current, avoid italics: eg Times2 (closed up), *The Times* Magazine etc.

Write *The Times* Christmas Charity Appeal, *The Times* Christmas Appeal or *The Times* Charity Appeal (cap); also Christmas Appeal, Charity Appeal.

Note *The Times Literary Supplement*, which is owned by News UK; other UK publications with "Times" in their mastheads, such as *Times Higher Education*, are not owned by News UK.

Times+ (roman) is the agreed marketing device, so do not write Times Plus.

Cap Times Archive for the online resource, and for the invaluable corporate repository of material relating to the paper's history; Times archives (lower case) in reference to generic source material, eg at the end of fact boxes.

"*The Times* climbed into a taxi ... was bought a beer ... ducked to avoid the incoming missiles" etc. It is probably a while since any *Times* reporter was tempted to adopt this coy impersonal substitute for "we" or "I"; let's keep it that way

Thermos must take the initial cap; it is a trade name that must always be observed

The Sunday Times Rich List "calculates" people's worth

think tank no hyphen

third (adverb), prefer to thirdly

third world no need for cap unless confusion seems likely without (same for *first world*); prefer terms such as *developing world* anyway

Thought for the Day no need to italicise this and similar slots in radio or TV programmes

throne cap sparingly, only in terms of the institution, eg "he deferred to the wisdom of the Throne"; in other contexts, as with the chair itself, use lower case, eg "The Queen came to the throne in 1952"

thunderbolts are mythological and do not exist; lightning bolts and thunderclaps do exist and can also be used metaphorically

"tiger" economies of southeast Asia and the Pacific; use quotes for first mention, subsequently without quotes, and always lower case

time bomb, time frame but *timeline, timescale, timeshare*

Time Lord cap in the context of *Doctor Who*

times never write, eg 6pm last night, 9am tomorrow morning; say six o'clock last night, 11 o'clock tomorrow morning or (if the context allows) 6pm, or 9am tomorrow. Use a point in expressing continental time — 01.55, 14.00 etc

Tinseltown (as in Hollywood) one word

titles The most common solecism is the misplaced use of first names with titles. It is wrong to write, eg Lord Peter Mandelson when we should write Lord Mandelson, or Lady Helen Brown etc when we should say simply Lady Brown. "Lord Peter Mandelson" improbably suggests that the Labour life peer is the younger son of a duke or a marquess; "Lady Helen Brown" would be correct for the wife of, eg Sir John Brown ONLY if she were also the daughter of a duke, marquess or earl.

Other examples of what readers still expect *The Times* to get right are covered at some length below.

Titles of nobility in descending order of precedence are as follows: *duke, marquess* (not marquis, except in foreign contexts, occasional Scottish titles and the names of pubs), *earl, viscount* and *baron*. At first mention, give the formal title (as in *Who's Who*), eg the Marquess of Paddington, the Earl of Waterloo, but then Lord Paddington, Lord Waterloo etc. This does not apply to *barons*, who are always *Lord* except in the formal announcement of new baronies. *Dukes* are always dukes and do not become Lord (eg the Duke of Rutland; at second mention "the duke").

Baronesses in their own right or life peeresses are generally

Baroness at first mention. Subsequently Lady (eg Baroness Thatcher, then Lady Thatcher).

The wife of a duke is a *duchess* (and is always, eg the Duchess of X, later the duchess). The wife of a marquess is a *marchioness*, of an earl a *countess*, of a viscount a *viscountess*; use Lady at second and subsequent mentions for these. Widows or former wives of peers who have not remarried use their Christian name before these titles, eg Margaret Duchess of Argyll (no commas) or Mary Lady Jones. A widow may also be known as the Dowager Duchess of Y, or the Dowager Lady Z.

All these titles, including royalty, take cap only at first mention, when the full name is given, then lower case (the Duke of Argyll, or of Edinburgh, thereafter the duke).

Some titles include a place name, eg Lord Callaghan of Cardiff, while others do not. Follow *Who's Who*: if the place name appears in bold caps there and is not separated from the name by a comma, it is part of the title and should be included at first mention (it may subsequently be dropped, unless this would cause confusion). Always check with *Debrett's* or *Who's Who* if in the slightest doubt; for peers who are members of the House of Lords, the UK parliament website gives titles in the correct form.

Baronets and knights are known as Sir John Smith, thereafter Sir John. Again, to repeat this essential point, no wife of a baronet or knight takes her Christian name in her title unless she is the daughter of a duke, a marquess or an earl. If a baronet has had more than one wife, the former wife is eg Mary Lady Smith (no commas, the style also assumed by a baronet's widow) while the current one is Lady Smith — the same forms apply to the wives of a baron. If a knight has had more than one wife, the former wife puts her Christian name in brackets, eg Lady (Alice) Brown, to distinguish her from the present wife, Lady Brown. Also, if there are two baronets or knights with the same name, their wives (when mentioned apart from their husbands), put his Christian name in brackets, eg Lady (Stephen) Brown, Lady (Andrew) Brown. Baronets may be distinguished from knights by writing the suffix Bt after the name: Sir John Smith, Bt. In practice we tend to do this only on the Court Page or in obituaries.

Dames of an order of chivalry take the same style as knights, eg Dame Felicity Brown, thereafter Dame Felicity. A dame who is married may prefer to use her own style, eg Dame Margaret Arrowroot, wife of Lord Arrowroot of Nice; personal preferences should be respected.

Children of peers. The eldest sons of a duke, marquess or earl use the father's second title as a courtesy title (eg the Duke of Bedford's son is the Marquess of Tavistock). These people are not peers, even in headlines. Younger sons of dukes and marquesses use their first names and the family surname, eg Lord John Worthington; subsequent mention, Lord John, never Lord Worthington; his wife is Lady John Worthington, never Lady Worthington (and not Lady Carol Worthington unless she is also the daughter of a duke or marquess whose title takes precedence over that of her husband's family and she has chosen to style herself so — a complication mercifully quite rare).

Again, a woman is Lady Olive York etc only if she is the daughter of a duke, marquess or earl; in subsequent mentions she is Lady Olive, never Lady York. Younger sons of earls and all children of viscounts and barons have the style the Hon, but it is unnecessary to use this except in Court Page copy; normally, they are simply Mr, Miss, Ms etc (none is a peer).

Baronets, knights and dames take the appropriate title as soon as the honour is announced. Peers have to submit their choice of title for approval, so they must wait until the formal public announcement (usually in *The London Gazette*) and then their formal introduction in the chamber of the upper house

titles of books, films, discs, programmes, albums, stories, poems, songs etc. In English titles avoid an initial cap for every word (eg do not write *The Hound Of The Baskervilles*). As a rule of thumb, use lower case for prepositions, conjunctions, definite and indefinite articles, eg *Don't Cry for Me, Argentina*; *Hit Me with Your Rhythm Stick*; *Rikki Don't Lose that Number*; *The Hound of the Baskervilles*; for French titles capitalisation is complicated (and the French can't seem to agree on how to do it). Traditionally it involved capping the first word and the first significant noun, as well as (sometimes) any qualifying adjective, and (perhaps) any subsequent noun that might be linked to the first in a familiar phrase. The simpler and more consistent approach, now quite widely adopted in France, is to treat titles as in Italian and capitalise only the first word, which may well be an article or a preposition. So, *Le rouge et le noir*, *À la recherche du temps perdu*, *De la guerre*, *L'éducation sentimentale*, *Splendeurs et misères des courtisanes*, *La cousine Bette* (any proper names are also capitalised, of course), and so on

tmesis interpolation of a word or group of words between the parts of a compound word, eg absof***inglutely

together with avoid; prefer simply *with*; also beware such tautology as *blend together*, *meet together*, *link together* etc

toilet prefer the word *lavatory*. Reserve the use of loo for informal contexts

toll used with *of* or *on*, depending on context: "The war took its toll of the inhabitants," "Years of pumping iron have taken their toll on his body"

Tomb of the Unknown Warrior in Westminster Abbey (not Unknown Soldier)

tons, tonnes prefer to use *tonnes* in most contexts, although in historical passages *tons* would be more appropriate; and note "tons of help" metaphorically

too does not need a comma preceding it, for example at the end of a clause or sentence

too-wit too-woo render thus how an owl sounds

Top Ten, Top 20, Top 40 etc caps for official or semi-official musical or other lists; but lower case for more generic uses

tormentor prefer to tormenter

tornado plural *tornados* (storms); also *Tornado, Tornados* (aircraft)

torpedo but plural *torpedoes*

Tory, Tories acceptable alternative for Conservative(s), especially after first mention. *Tory party* is permissible

totalisator, tote take lower case, no quotes; the Tote refers to the organisation

Tourette syndrome

towards not toward

tracheostomy, tracheotomy note no letter a in the middle. The -ostomy is the surgical formation of an opening into the trachea after an (emergency) incision, which is the -otomy

trademark one word

trade names many names of products, services and organisations in common use are proprietary. They should not be used as generics and must be given a capital letter. There is a risk of legal action for failure to do so. Biro, Outward Bound and Portaloo are among those whose use is policed by their owners with particular zeal. Be especially careful about drugs; try if possible to use non-proprietary words such as aspirin, sleeping pills etc

trade unions (plural), not trades unions; but Trades Union Congress

transatlantic, transcontinental but *cross-Channel*

transpire means to come to light or to leak out. Do not use as a pompous alternative of *to happen* or *occur*

transsexual no hyphen; but now prefer *transgender*

trauma, traumatic avoid in the clichéd sense of deeply upsetting, distressing etc; it ought really to be confined to its medical meaning of severe shock after an accident or stressful event

Travellers as with Gypsies, cap when referring to what is now a legally recognised and protected ethnic group; lower case if simply describing an elective itinerant lifestyle; so *Irish Travellers*, but *New Age travellers*

Treasury cap the government department (but not the titles of those who work there), eg financial secretary to the Treasury

treaty lower case in Amsterdam treaty, Maastricht treaty etc, but note Treaty of Amsterdam etc

triads no need to cap in Chinese gangster context

tribunals industrial tribunals are now called *employment tribunals*. Note that *immigration adjudicators* and *immigration appeal tribunals* deliver *determinations*. See also **industrial tribunals**

Tricolour cap for the French flag, lower case in more general context

trillion originally American for a thousand billion (or a million million, 1,000,000,000,000), and now accepted in British usage with that meaning, superseding the earlier British definition of a trillion as 1 followed by 18 zeros. In headings, abbreviate to trn, eg £1trn, $1trn

trinitroglycerin no terminal e needed

triple crown in rugby union; an honour contested annually by the home nations (England, Ireland, Scotland and Wales) who compete in the larger Six Nations Championship. If any one of these teams beats the other three they win the triple crown

tripos lower case for the final honours degree examinations in all subjects, eg the history tripos, at the University of Cambridge

Trojan horse but the computer virus is a *trojan*, lower case

Trooping the Colour (not of the Colour); similarly, *sounding reveille, beating retreat*

tropical storm cap as part of title, eg Tropical Storm Linda; similarly, Hurricane Andrew

Tropics, the cap; note also the *Tropic of Capricorn/Cancer*, but *tropical, subtropical* (lower case)

Troubles, the cap in Irish context

trumpeters, buglers cavalry regiments have trumpeters, infantry regiments have buglers. They are not interchangeable

try to the verb *try* should be followed by *to* before the next verb, not by *and*, eg "I will try to cross the road", not "I will try and cross the road"

tsar not czar. Likewise, *tsarevich, tsaritsa* (not czarina); caps with the name (Tsar Alexander II), otherwise lower case. There is no reason that government-appointed co-ordinators should not be spelt the same way: drugs tsar, mental health tsar etc, although these terms are in any case best not overused

T-shirt

Tube cap, acceptable in context on its own for the London Tube, or London Underground. Also cap the various lines, such as Central Line, Metropolitan Line, Victoria Line etc

tuberculosis prefer *tuberculous* as the adjective for the disease, rather than tubercular

TUC the Trades Union Congress. Note, first mention, general council of the TUC, thereafter general council; general secretary of the TUC and general secretaries of individual unions are lower case

tumbrel prefer to tumbril

turbo-jet, turbo-prop

Turin Shroud cap, then the shroud at second and subsequent mentions (lower case)

Turkestan prefer to Turkistan

Turkey the capital is Ankara, not Istanbul

turn down prefer *reject* or *refuse* (except of beds)

Turner prize and note *Turner prizewinner, Turner prizewinning artist* etc

turnlines should be styled, eg "Continued on page 2, col 7" or "Continued from page 1"

turn-off, turn-on (nouns), but no hyphens in *turnout, turnaround, turnabout*

Tutankhamun if the name has to be broken across two lines, it may be hyphenated as Tut-ankhamun or Tutankh-amun

twat not, as one former prime minister seemed to think, a harmless variant of *twit*, but quite a rude word

twentysomething, thirtysomething, fortysomething etc; thus, if you must use

Twenty20 the limited-overs cricket format; can be abbreviated to T20

twin towers (of the former World Trade Center in New York, destroyed in the 9/11 attacks in 2001); the *northern tower* and the *southern tower* (all lower case)

Twitter cap the name of the site; lower case *tweet* for the verb to post on it; *tweet* (noun) for a posting

twofold, threefold, fourfold, tenfold etc. Beware of confusing, say, a threefold increase with a 300 per cent increase (if it goes up by 300 per cent it is a fourfold increase — do the maths)

two minutes' silence

two thirds, three quarters etc, but a two-thirds share (hyphenate adjectival use). See **fractions**

tyrannosaurus roman, lower case when used as the common name of the dinosaur ("he was attacked by a tyrannosaurus"). But for the scientific name write *Tyrannosaurus rex* (italics), and *T. rex* at subsequent mentions. (The pop group led a long time ago by Marc Bolan chose to style itself first Tyrannosaurus Rex and then T.Rex; resist any urge to correct)

Tyrol not Tirol

Uu

U no full point after Burmese title, eg U Nu, U Thant

UAE acceptable at first mention for the United Arab Emirates. The seven emirates in order from west to east are Abu Dhabi, Dubai, Sharjah, Ajman, Umm al-Quwain, Ras al-Khaimah and Fujairah. The UAE has a president

uber, ur German prefixes, meaning super and original respectively; generally no hyphen, no umlaut and lower case in hideous constructions such as uberbabe. Use sparingly. The minicab operation Uber has no umlaut

ubiquitous means being everywhere; so treat like *unique*, and do not attempt to qualify or suggest nonsensical gradations (more ubiquitous, most ubiquitous etc)

Uefa not UEFA, European football's governing body

Uighur prefer to Uyghur. Do not refer to this predominantly Muslim ethnic group, who live in East Turkestan, as Chinese

UK acceptable abbreviation for United Kingdom in text and headlines but use sparingly and be careful that it is strictly applicable

United Kingdom comprises Great Britain and Northern Ireland; strictly, Britain or Great Britain is made up of England, Wales, Scotland and islands governed from the mainland (ie not the Isle of Man or the Channel Islands), but Britain is now widely used as another name for the United Kingdom or Great Britain, and pragmatically we accept this usage; the

British Isles is the United Kingdom and the Republic of Ireland, Isle of Man and Channel Islands

Ukip cap then lower case as any acronym; the UK Independence Party if ever spelt out, but usually no need

Ukraine omit *the*. Note *the Orange Revolution*

Ulster permissible, especially in headlines, but use *Northern Ireland* or *the province* when possible

ultimatums not ultimata. See **-um**

ultraviolet one word

Uluru traditional and now preferred name for Ayers Rock

-um for plurals of words ending in -um prefer to add an s, thus *stadiums*, not stadia; *gymnasiums*, not gymnasia. But note *millennia, strata*

unchristian lower case

uncoordinated but co-ordinate

under-age hyphen

underestimate often confused with overestimate: note that the importance of writing "its importance cannot be overestimated" cannot be overestimated

Underground London

under-secretary hyphen, lower case

under the hammer avoid this cliché for auctions, especially when it produces unintentionally comic effect about apparent vandalism: "Gandhi's iconic spectacles to go under the hammer"

under way always two words

Union cap for the union of England and Wales from 1543; that of the English and Scottish crowns (1603-1707); the union of England and Scotland from 1707; the political union of Great Britain and Ireland (1801-1920); and the union of Great Britain and Northern Ireland from 1920. Also cap as a synonym of the United States; and the northern states during the American Civil War (also cap Confederacy)

Unionist cap in the Northern Ireland political context

Union Jack is fine and arguments to the contrary may be ignored. The Flag Institute ("the UK's National Flag Charity") says this: "It is often stated that the Union Flag should only be described as the Union Jack when flown in the bows of a warship, but this is a relatively recent idea. From early in its life the Admiralty itself frequently referred to the flag as the Union Jack, whatever its use, and in 1902 an Admiralty Circular announced that Their Lordships had decided that either name could be used officially. Such use was given parliamentary approval in 1908 when it was stated that 'the Union Jack should be regarded as the National flag'."

unique means only one, having no like or equal. Do not use except in this absolute specific sense, and do not accept gradations, as in "almost unique", for which words such as *rare* or *remarkable* suffice. Phrases such as "very unique" are nonsense and are banned

unitary authorities since the abolition of Avon, Humberside and Cleveland, and the wholesale reorganisation of Welsh and Scottish local government from 1996 to 1998, we should take especial care about how we locate towns in these areas

United Nations or the UN; usually no need to spell out even at first mention. Also note, the UN secretary-general, UN security council, UN general assembly, all lower case; UN derivatives such as Unesco, Unifil, Unprofor etc are written thus where the word can be voiced (see **initials**); the UN high commissioner for refugees (never commission) is the organisation, as well as a person, but we may as well treat as a job title, which is what it sounds like, so lower case; abbreviate to UNHCR after first mention

United States (of America) is always followed by a singular verb. Common usage allows abbreviation to US in text as well as headlines, but do not ignore the word America

universal and absolute claims beware of making assertions about what "everybody" thinks or does or is talking about. Be careful, too, in stating that anyone is the first or the last or the only person to do a particular thing, or that anything is the biggest, fastest, oldest of its kind. Readers like nothing better than to prove such statements wrong

universe lower case in all contexts, including astronomical

units Downing Street policy unit (lower case), social exclusion unit etc

University College London no comma; similarly, *University College Dublin*

university posts all lower case, eg the vice-chancellor of the University of Sheffield, the chancellor of ..., pro-vice-chancellor, master, professor, reader in chemistry, fellow etc

unlikeable, unloveable with the middle e

unmistakable not one of those with the middle e

unparalleled

unprecedented never done or known before; use it to mean what it means, not as an empty hyperbolic alternative to eg *striking, unusual* or *big*

unshakeable e

until as a shorter variant, prefer *till* to 'til

"Untouchables" (in Indian caste system), cap and in quotes at first mention; also (and now more often) known as *Dalits*

unveil take care with this word, which means to remove a covering from something, or (by extension) to disclose. It should not be used in phrases such as unveiling a ship, or unveiling a flag

up avoid unnecessary use after verbs, as in meet up, rest up, end up

upbeat, upgrade, upfront, upmarket

upcoming prefer eg forthcoming, coming soon, imminent etc

upon take care with use of *up, upon, up on* and *on;* eg "The cat jumped *on* the floor, *upon* the mouse, *up on* the table, then *up* the tree"

upper house, lower house

useable prefer to usable

USSR avoid wherever possible; say Soviet Union instead (and now only in historical context)

U-turn is an overworked phrase, especially in the political context. Be sparing in its use, particularly when only a minor change of policy direction is involved; a partial U-turn is no U-turn at all; cap U if you must use it at all

Vv

vacuum in common use as a verb

vagaries means aimless wanderings or eccentric ideas, not vicissitudes or changes (as in weather)

Valentine's Day normally omit the St, and keep cap for *Valentine card* etc

Valium proprietary name of diazepam, so cap

valley cap in full name of recognised places, such as the Thames Valley, the Wye Valley etc

Van cap in Dutch names when surname alone is given, as in Van Gogh, but lower case when used in full, eg Vincent van Gogh. Note Ludwig van Beethoven (not von), although the composer was German

Varsity match acceptable colloquialism for the Oxford-Cambridge rugby match

Vaseline proprietary, so cap

VAT keep caps for clarity, even though often treated as an acronym

VE Day May 8, 1945, no need for hyphen; likewise VJ Day, August 15, 1945

Velcro cap, proprietary

veld not veldt

veranda no final h

verbal means pertaining to words, *oral* means pertaining to the mouth. Do not confuse. Sadly, corrupted phrases such as "verbal abuse" and "verbal warning" have permeated journalism to the point of our having to accept them, but try to restrict such use and find an alternative

verbosity watch out for, and eliminate, wordy phrases such as "on the part of" (use *by*), "a large number of" (*many*), "numerous occasions" (*often*), "this day and age" (does not even demand an alternative)

verbs a dull or poorly chosen verb will drag a sentence down. For telling a story, active is often better than passive, transitive than intransitive; headlines, in particular, are almost always better with a well-chosen active verb. Adverbs may distract the reader, and so weaken rather than strengthen the verb they modify; a different active verb may do a better job

verdict do not use for civil hearings, verdicts come at the end of criminal trials

verger generally (and if in doubt) thus for the church official; some cathedrals, eg St Paul's and Winchester, prefer *virger*, in acknowledgment of the *virga* or rod of office, which symbolises the role

vermilion prefer to vermillion

versus abbreviation is v (lower case, no point)

very rarely a helpful word, and usually redundant ("constant use merely inflates the language without strengthening the meaning", according to the 1959 edition of this guide)

vet(s) at first mention, write *veteran(s)*, *veterinary surgeon(s)*, *veterinary scientist(s)* etc as appropriate; vet(s) is allowed in headings for veterinary surgeons or scientists

vetoes plural noun and third-person singular

viable do not use as a synonym of *feasible* or *practicable*; it means capable of independent existence

vicar take care to use this word accurately, because it is not a generic for parson, clergyman etc. Always check that the cleric in question actually is a vicar and not, for instance, a rector or a perpetual curate, let alone a nonconformist minister or a Catholic priest. Vicar (and rector) should absolutely not be applied to other categories of Anglican cleric, eg bishops, priests-in-charge, deans, canons, non-stipendiaries etc. Clergy of other denominations should be referred to as priests, ministers etc as appropriate. Lower case always except in names of literary figures and titles of books/poems/television programmes (the Vicar of Bray, Wakefield, Dibley etc)

vicar-general

vice always hyphenate in its deputy context (vice-chairman, vice-president of a company etc) but not in its depravity context, eg vice squad. Do not confine the meaning of vice to sex; it is the opposite of virtue and has a correspondingly wide range of meaning

vice-chancellor of a university

vice versa roman, no hyphen

Victoria and Albert (Museum) use the ampersand only in the abbreviated V&A, which now appears to be the museum's preferred way of marketing itself, perhaps because Victoria and Albert are felt to sound a bit behind the times; there is no reason that this preference should particularly bind the rest of us

vintage car is one made between 1919 and 1930; a *veteran car* is one made before 1919

vis-à-vis roman, hyphens, with accent

viscountcy describes the rank

viz abbreviation for *videlicet*; prefer *namely, that is*, or simply *ie*

VJ Day August 15, 1945, no need for hyphen. See **VE Day**

Vodafone not Vodaphone

vogue words new words, or old words with new and peculiar meanings, come along all the time and need no encouragement from us; they soon become tired and meaningless. Or else they pass into general use. The hazards (and limits) of prescription are soberingly demonstrated by the 1970 edition of this guide, which lists the following as vogue words "to be avoided wherever possible": *abrasive, ambience, backlash, blueprint, catalyst, charisma(tic), confrontation, consensus, dichotomy, escalate, facelift, grass-roots, gritty, massive, persona, preemptive, symbiosis, trauma(tic)*; all may be words to approach with circumspection, and some are worth eschewing even now; most, however, remain as irritatingly in vogue as they were half a century ago. See **Canute**

voiceover one word

volcanoes plural of *volcano*. Note also prefer *volcanology, volcanologist* to vulcan- spellings

volte-face roman, hyphen; plural remains *volte-face*

von (German) is usually lower case in the middle of a name, and capped only at the beginning of a sentence. See **Van**

vote "yes" vote, "no" vote

VP never use as abbreviation of vice-president of the US or other state (or vice-president of a company)

wacky not whacky

WAGs wives and girlfriends (especially of sports teams); singular WAG (acronym but upper case needed, exceptionally, for clarity)

Wahhabi (Muslim sect), not Wahabi

Wales lower case *north Wales, south Wales, mid Wales, west Wales*

walked free from court avoid this lazy cliché

walkout

war cabinet no need for caps unless helpful for clarity in historical refs

war crimes tribunal lower case even when using the full title, *the international criminal tribunal for the former Yugoslavia*. It sits at the Hague and has a president and a chief prosecutor. Be specific in dealing with war crimes: they relate only to the treatment of prisoners in the custody of a military force

war game(s) two words

war zone two words

warn may be used transitively or intransitively. A caveat is not to create an epidemic of "he warned" etc if we only mean "he said". We are at liberty, however, to avoid the cumbersome "gave warning that", or the strange "he cautioned". For variety, do use transitive constructions as appropriate, eg: "The chancellor warned MPs that ..."

war on terror caps seem obtrusive and unnecessary now

warrant officers in the British Army, regimental sergeant-major and company sergeant-major are warrant officer ranks (between the NCOs and commissioned officers)

wars cap the First World War, Second World War, the hypothetical Third World War (or World War Three), Cold War, Korean War, the Vietnam War, the Six Day War (no hyphen), the Gulf War etc; prefer the Falklands conflict because war was never formally declared; if the phrase has to be used, write Falklands war (lower case); similarly, the Iraq war

warships take care with the following distinction: to serve *in* a warship, but *on* a merchant ship; a naval officer is *appointed* to serve *in* HMS *Sheffield*, and not posted to serve

Washington DC no comma if you need to distinguish from Washington state (which mostly you will not). Do not generally use abbreviations in this way to refer to US states (or districts, or counties): write out Richmond, Virginia, not Richmond VA etc

washout one word

Wasp acronym for White Anglo-Saxon Protestant; adjective *Waspy*

waste usually better to write *waste* than wastage, which means the process of loss or its amount or rate

watt unit of power, eg a 60W lightbulb. See **energy, power**

weapons no hyphens for AK47 (although we prefer Kalashnikov), M16, M79 etc

wear write *menswear, women's wear, children's wear, sportswear*

weather stations try always to include the county or other location if not widely known

weather stories (about floods, hurricanes, snow, record sunshine etc in the UK) should always take a cross-reference to the weather forecast. Style is: "Forecast, page 69" or "Weather Eye, page 69"

website one word. Unlike, say, computer games, do not routinely italicise websites in normal copy. Italics or other type changes may be appropriate for display purposes in some contexts, eg listings pages

week, weekend the week ends on Saturday night. Common sense will dictate whether to say last week, this week, next week etc. Beware of references to "at the weekend" in Monday papers: always make clear whether you mean the weekend just past or next Saturday and Sunday, although the tense of the verb may be enough to indicate this. The phrase "this weekend" should refer only to the coming weekend, but if it is likely to cause any ambiguity then do not use it. "On the weekend" remains an Americanism

weigh anchor means to raise a vessel's anchor, not to drop it

weights and measures abbreviations context will determine when to shorten kilometres, grams, feet, inches, stone, pounds, ounces etc. "He was 6ft 7in" (not ins, and no space between number and abbreviation); but "she stood two feet from the kerb". Similarly, "she weighed 8st 12lb" (not lbs); but "he was several pounds overweight"

welfare state lower case

welfare to work programme (lower case, no hyphens)

well or **well-** with adjective: no hyphen needed if the construction is after the noun, but write a hyphen if before the noun. Thus, "the island is well regulated", but "it is a well-regulated island"

wellwisher do not hyphenate. Beware of misuse: people who line the street to watch a funeral procession are not wellwishers

Welsh assembly likewise *Northern Ireland assembly*; *Scottish parliament*. The leader of the assembly is called the *first minister* (no longer the first secretary)

Welsh secretary or the *secretary of state for Wales*

Welsh valleys for the (former) mining valleys of South Wales

west, western etc usually lower case, but cap *the West* for clarity in its geopolitical sense (similarly *East*); always *western leaders, western Europe* etc (unless capital is helpful in a specific historical Cold War context); the *Wild West* (but the films are *westerns*, lower case)

West Country, the upper case, for clarity

wharf prefer *wharfs* as plural

whence means "from where". Never write "from whence"

whereabouts is singular, eg "his whereabouts is not known". Prefer "nobody knows where he is"

which in an ideal world, a relative clause with *which* would give additional information, while one with *that* would define and restrict. In practice there is a degree of fluidity (or muddle); it is possible to be overzealous in tidying this up

while not whilst

whingeing with middle e

whips lower case *chief whip, whips' office,* a *government whip*

whisky from Scotland, *Scotch* as alternative; but *whiskey* from Ireland and America; prefer *whisky* (but not *Scotch*) in more general or non-specific use, eg Japanese whisky, whisky sauce, etc

whistleblower but *whistle-stop* (hyphenated), as in whistle-stop tour

White Cliffs of Dover caps

White House chief of staff

white paper as with *green paper*, lower case

white phosphorus, white phosphorus bomb for adjective and noun, and its adjectival use

whizz double z in all senses and compounds

who, whom which of these to use is determined solely by its function in the relative clause. Remember that *whom* has to be the object of the verb in the relative clause. Thus, "she is the woman whom the police wish to interview" (ie the police wish to interview her, not she); the other most common use of whom is after a preposition such as by, with or from, eg "the person from whom he bought a ticket".

Beware of traps, however: "Who do you think did it?" is correct (not whom, because who is the subject of "did it", not the object of "do you think"); and "Give it to whoever wants it" is correct (not whomever) because whoever is the subject of the verb "wants".

Beware too of constructions such as "he squirted ammonia at a van driver who [correct] he believed had cut him up" (where "he believed" is simply an interjection; "who" is not the object of "he believed" but the subject of the subordinate clause, "who ... had cut him up")

whodunnit not whodunit

WH Smith no full points

why often superfluous after *reason*, eg "the reason he did it was ...", not "the reason why he did it was ..."; "there are good reasons why this is the case" is a long way of saying "there are good reasons for this"

-wide no hyphen in compounds such as *countrywide, nationwide, worldwide*, but needed in *Europe-wide*

wifi lower case, one word, no hyphen

wind with strong winds, give a description as well as force number in numerals (add "on the Beaufort scale" where appropriate. The scale grades wind speeds from 0 to 12; Americans use the scale to 17). Write, eg force 4 (lower case, numeral), up to force 7; thereafter, gale force 8, severe gale force 9, storm force 10, violent storm force 11 and hurricane force 12. But the vernacular "force 11 winds" is acceptable

wind farm two words

wines definitely not an area where consistency should trump common sense, but generally prefer lower case when a familiar proper name is being used in a generic way, ie to describe a well-known style or type of wine rather than to name an individual bottle or denote a precise geographical origin: a first-growth bordeaux, red burgundy, vintage champagne, good ordinary claret, decent chablis, fruity beaujolais, white rioja etc. Cap when proper names are used more specifically, eg to identify individual wines ("Of the several excellent chablis bottlings by the enterprising young winemaker Patrick Piuze, the Chablis 'Terroirs de Courgis' is one of the best." "If you like mature rioja, it is worth looking out for older vintages of Rioja Reserva Vina Ardanza from La Rioja Alta"); to attach a geographical designation to a grape variety also grown elsewhere (an Alsace pinot blanc, a Mosel riesling, a Hunter Valley chardonnay, a New Zealand pinot noir; grapes all lower case); to refer to specific villages/ vineyards and to smaller or less familiar appellations or those which simply look odd without a cap ("When it comes to red burgundy, Fixin, Marsannay and Rully are much cheaper than Chambolle-Musigny or Gevrey-Chambertin"); to refer to the wine-growing region rather than the wine itself ("If you are looking for the best-value classic French wine, it comes neither from Bordeaux nor Burgundy but from the Rhône"; "he preferred to buy his champagne only in Champagne")

wintry prefer to wintery (or indeed winterly)

Wirral (not Wirrall); permissible to refer to *the* Wirral, or the Wirral peninsula

wisteria now prefer to wistaria as the variant for the common name, after epic, unfathomable controversy in 2009 at *The Times*. The internationally agreed scientific name for the genus is *Wisteria*, hence, for example, Chinese wisteria is *Wisteria chinensis*. The plant was named by Thomas Nuttall, an English botanist, in honour of Caspar Wistar, an American anatomist and physician (1761-1818) and friend of Thomas Jefferson, but bizarrely he decided to spell the genus *Wisteria*.

Wistar's family came from Germany with the surname Wüster: one branch, so to speak, decided to change it to Wister rather than Wistar, which may have confused Nuttall (for more detail, see a passage and footnote from *The Perennial Philadelphians*, by Nathaniel Burt). Incidentally, the Wistar Institute in Philadelphia, the first American independent biomedical research facility, also commemorates Caspar Wistar

witch-hunt but *witchcraft* and *witchdoctor*

witnesses in British courts, witnesses go into the witness box and give evidence; they do not take the stand and testify

women doctors, women teachers etc adopt the plural through common usage; but beware of gratuitously using "woman" or "women" as an adjective in this way; always ask what it is adding and why it is there

Woolf reforms several important changes have been made in civil litigation rules and terminology since April 1999. Three of the commonest are: plaintiffs became *claimants*; a writ became a *claim form*; and *notices of application* are served in the place of summonses

Woolsack in parliament, initial cap

word hyphenate in c-word, s-word, f-word etc. See **four-letter words, obscenities, swearing**

wordiness should be resisted. Do not use a long phrase if a shorter one says the same thing

workaholic as *shopaholic*, but note *chocoholic*

workers *farmworkers*, *metalworkers* and *roadworkers* each one word, but two for *car workers*, *care workers*, *oil workers*, *office workers* etc

workforce, workshop, work-to-rule

world avoid, wherever possible, phrases such as the fashion world, the theatre world, the cricket world etc

World Cup, World Cup final

worldwide one word for general adjective

World War One/Two/I/II/1/2 etc avoid. Use only First World War, Second World War. *World War Three* acceptable in metaphorical sense

wrack means seaweed or wreckage and must not be used as a synonym of torture; thus, "racked by doubts" etc

wreaked (not wrought) havoc, heavy damage, vengeance etc

Wrens use only in historical context. Women sailors are now fully integrated into the Royal Navy and the WRNS no longer exists as a separate entity. If necessary to specify, refer to a woman captain etc

writes with written-in bylines, prefer the construction *Ann Bloggs writes* to *writes Ann Bloggs*. Use the singular with eg "(Our foreign staff writes)". Normal style is to use the brackets on news and sports pages, the italics on features

wrongdoer, **wrongdoing** but *wrong-footed*, *wrong-headed*

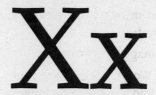

Xx

Xbox

Xerox a trade name so must cap

The X Factor, The X Files no hyphen

Xhosa (not Khosa), plural *Xhosas*, the Bantu tribe

Xmas should not be used in *The Times* unless part of a special title or in a direct quote etc

x-ray fully acceptable abbreviation of *x-ray examination*. It can also be used as a verb, to x-ray someone. Note, however, *Camp X-Ray* at Guantanamo Bay, Cuba (later replaced by *Camp Delta*)

Yy

Yahweh vocalisation of the Tetragrammaton, YWWH, the Hebrew name of God

Yale lock trade name so must cap

yard the metre and the yard are sufficiently similar that conversions such as 500m (547 yards) are generally unnecessary. Conversions between metres and feet are often far more useful

years note that two and a half years is spelt out

yellow cake lower case, no quotes for semi-refined uranium ore

Yemen not *the* Yemen

"yes" vote, "no" vote but Yes campaign, No campaign

yoghurt prefer with the h

yoke (oxen), *yolk* (egg)

Yorkshire specify the location for smaller towns and villages, eg Thirsk, North Yorkshire, but not for eg Bradford or Leeds (West Yorkshire)

Yorkshire pudding, Yorkshire terrier

young offender institution lower case, as in Feltham young offender institution

Young Turks cap

youth courts not juvenile courts, which no longer exist

yuan the Chinese currency; prefer to *renminbi*. Renminbi — "the people's currency" — is the official name of the currency introduced by the Communist regime in 1949. A yuan is a unit of the renminbi. A parallel distinction might be between *sterling*, the currency, and *pound*, the unit in which sterling is denominated. Yuan, like pound, will be right in almost all contexts: it is the unit for indicating eg prices (something costs 1,000 yuan, not 1,000 renminbi) but it will also serve as a synonym for renminbi in discussing eg "the strength of the yuan against the dollar"

Yugoslav (meaning southern Slav) is the adjective from Yugoslavia (not Yugoslavian)

yuletide lower case, but hard to think of a good reason for using at all

Zz

Zambezi is the common spelling today and the one to use; the Victorians preferred Zambesi

-ze in almost all cases use the -ise ending rather than the -ize. Two of the few exceptions are *capsize* and *synthesizer*. (If we were to adopt -ize, there would be far more exceptions to worry about, as there are quite a few words that have to end -ise)

zeitgeist (lower case, roman) means the spirit of the times

zeros prefer to zeroes as plural

Zimmer frame is a trade name, so cap

zodiac, zodiacal lower case, as in signs of the zodiac

zoo cap in full names: London Zoo, Edinburgh Zoo, Bristol Zoo etc